THE MOON'S NODES

Understanding the
Dynamic Ties that Bind

AGNETA BORSTEIN

IBIS PRESS
Lake Worth, FL

Published in 2012 by
IBIS PRESS
an imprint of Nicolas-Hays, Inc.
P. O. Box 540206 • Lake Worth, FL 33454-0206
www.nicolashays.com
Distributed to the trade by Red Wheel/Weiser, LLC
65 Parker St., Unit 7 • Newburyport, MA 01950-4600
www.redwheelweiser.com

Statues from the author's collection. Photo credit Lorraine Greenfield.
Images: Hindu Gods and Goddesses: Swami Harshananda, by kind permission.

Charts have been calculated by the author using
Placidus Houses and True Nodes.
Ephemeris of True Nodes and Eclipses generated by Astro Computing Services.
Times given are GMT

Library of Congress Cataloging-in-Publication data available on request.

ISBN: 978-0-89254-158-4

VG
Cover and text design by Kathryn Sky-Peck
Cover illustration adapted from "The Kiss," by Gustav Klimt

Printed in the United States of America

CONTENTS

PREFACE TO THE REVISED EDITION

In working with this new edition, my aim was to simplify and make the Moon's Nodes accessible to a wider audience. The first edition, subtitled, *A Churning Process of the Soul*, focused primarily on how a study of the nodes brings a deeper understanding of how the "Self" is manifest in the astrological chart. There is an endless, mysterious, and fascinating interaction of the Sun and Moon in the evolutionary progress of an individual's desire for growth—manifested through the Lunar Nodes.

I am both an astrologer and a student of Hindu Philosophy. In the Hindu philosophy, "Self" is defined as an image of the reflection of our own individual self. Thus Self (with the capital "S") is understanding that we merge with our own divinity—the God and Goddess contained within. My spiritual master, Swami Muktananda, taught that "God dwells with you as You." All I had to do was to look deep within. It is a timeless process; it can take a life-time or a split second. But once we desire to move further into that Self, then we truly begin to see the connectedness of all things, how what we consider to be our "parts" are truly tied together. This internal connection, this "tie that binds," is the dynamic that allows us to have a deeper relationship with ourselves as well as others.

In the years since the original edition was published, this concept of Self has become much more mainstream and widely understood by all who travel the spiritual path, both astrologers and non-astrologers. I felt it was time to revisit the Moon's Nodes so that an awareness of the duality that is contained within all of us can be more available to those who seek to add this level of interpretation to their astrological work. The Moon's Nodes add a level of depth to astrological interpretation, but they are often studied in astrology as "either/or." In other words, they can be understood too *simply* as *just* representing dark and light, past and present, good and bad. My emphasis in this edition, *Understanding the Dynamic Ties that Bind*, is to focus on the spiritual "wholeness" of the Nodes, how they work together as both body and soul combined—our complete Self.

Finally, it is with respect and a deep appreciation that I acknowledge Yvonne Paglia and Donald Weiser for taking on this project, allowing the depth of the Lunar Nodes to reach a wider audience.

Tusen Tack!

—AGNETA BORSTEIN
OCTOBER, 2012

INTRODUCTION

As a young girl growing up in Sweden, I frequently visited my grandparents' house in the country during the summer months. The summers in Sweden are lush with fresh, light green birch trees blooming. White daises, red poppies, and blue iris grow wild in the meadows. Those were happy summers in nature; I spoke to the animals as naturally as I spoke to my sister.

A very special time for me were the days spent taking long walks to a neighbor's farm. The farm had many dark red wooden buildings, and the farmer, with pride, would show me how to milk cows. One time, we went to one side of the farm where there was a woman sitting on a small chair with a wooden tool that she was pumping up and down. She was working hard, her face glistening in the shining sun. The woman was churning milk—the cow's gift. The wooden crate went up and down, up and down, over and over.

The churning of the milk was fascinating. Some of the cow's gift would become regular milk, and some would go through a complex process to become cheese. Cream was another gift from the cow, and butter would become an additional offering. I stood observing the process, and became mesmerized as curds from the heated milk were put into a large wooden bowl on the side of the churn. The stout woman looked at me, took the large wooden bowl with the curd, and told me that she had something special to show me.

She took me to cold cellar, which are still traditionally used during cold Swedish winters. I noticed, with awe, that on the left side of the cold cellar there were rows and rows of different sizes and shapes of cheese. The cellar had its own distinct aroma, strong yet sweet. I noticed the woman's hands; they were rough and dry, but also strong. She had endured hard work; you could feel her strong character and wisdom. I was handed a big round wheel of cheese wrapped in gauze. It had a pungent, almost foul smell to it. She asked me if I wanted to taste some. I hesitated because of the smell, but, since I was taught to be polite, I accepted her invitation. She cut off a chunk, and I tasted the pungent cheese. Its flavor was delightful.

While I tasted the cheese, she explained the enduring churning process that was necessary to make the cheese acquire this wonderful taste. The process itself is rigid; it is only through the years of ripening that the cheese eventually evolves its true quality. Some of the cheeses on the shelves had been there for only two years, others more than ten years.

I grew up with those memories from my summer months at my grandmother's house. There was something fundamental I had witnessed about the process of becoming; as I matured, the "churning process" would become a metaphor for the evolving Self.

In 1976, Swami Muktananda came into my life, allowing my meditation practice to move into a deeper level. I made attempts to understand myself and others through the rich diverse study of the Universe. Perhaps because my North Node is in Aries, my path allowed me to pursue rituals and healing in order to grow closer to my truest Self. As I started to consult others, I consistently took notes and kept records of their reactions, comments, and life stories, which allowed me to understand the depth of the Moon's Nodes. The blessings continue to show in my life every day, as I get closer to my Aries North Node. It hasn't been easy, but I humbly acknowledge and continue my journey every day on my quest to become my true Self.

In studying the Moon's Nodes we are looking at a "churning process" of the evolving Self. I am a practicing Western Astrologer with many years as a student of the Jyotish, or the Eastern, astrology system. At this point in time, the Eastern and Western astrology systems take each other's hand and learn from each other—growing closer to the truth that we all seek. The Nodal Axis in the natal chart indicates the important and powerful lessons we must learn in our lifetime. With the North Node and the South Node, each of us can be said to have an internal dynamic relationship that we must nurture and understand, a dynamic of past and future, attachment and liberation, excess and limitation. But the Moon's Nodes are also very significant in synastry—in understanding the relationships that we form with others, particularly in our love partnerships. It is perhaps no coincidence that the symbols for the Moon's Nodes are each one half of a knot. Nodal ties are powerful, and much can be learned by looking at the Nodal aspects, and house placements. How an individual's Nodal Axis falls on a partner's personal planets will reveal much not only about the dynamic magnetism that binds them together as a couple, but also much about what each individual will need to confront and overcome in order to grow and evolve personally.

Throughout the following pages, I will provide an overview of the Moon's Nodes, and put them in context of Hindu myth of the Moon's Nodes, which, through the gods and goddesses, brings to life the dynamic relationship that is found in the Nodal Axis. We will then look at the charts of Angelina Jolie and Brad Pitt—what better example of a dynamic bond!—in order to better understand the Moon's Nodes in natal, synastry, and composite astrological work. Finally, we will look at the North and South Nodes by house placement and aspect, illuminated by several well-known example birth charts, in order to fully appreciate the role the Nodes play in the churning process of the soul, as well as their role as the knots that bind us together in relationships.

The following chart, on page 6, will provide the reader a reference for the East/West symbolism that will be used throughout this book.

NORTH NODE −RAHU	SOUTH NODE−KETU
• Ascending North Node	• Descending South Node
• Caput Draconis	• Cauda Draconis
• New Moon	• Full Moon
• Muladhara: 1st Chakra	• Sushumna: 7th Chakra
• Attachment	• Liberation
• Born of a Lioness	• Born into Philosophy
• Dark Blue Color	• Golden Color
• Anabibazon	• Catabibazon
• Agate	• Cat's Eye
• Hessonite	• Turquoise
• Excess	• Limitation
• Power	• Intimidation
• Head−Mind	• Indicator of Enlightenment
• Materialistic side of life	• Meditation−Spirituality
• Outer world	• Inner world
• Saturn (Eastern system)	• Saturn (Western system)
• Jupiter	• Mars
• Future	• Past
• Head	• Tail−without any head!
• Exalted in Taurus	• Exalted in Scorpio
• Fallen in Scorpio	• Fallen in Taurus
• Rulership−Virgo	• Rulership−Pisces
• Masculine	• Feminine
• Wealth	• Poverty

Rahu (North Node) and Ketu (South Node)

ESSENTIAL FACTS
ABOUT THE MOON'S NODES

The word "Node" comes from the Latin word *nodum*, meaning "knot." Nodes are diametrically opposite points, which are created by intersections of the path of the Moon (or other planets) with the plane of the ecliptic. The Nodes are linked together with the path of the Moon to that of the Eclipses, and eventually the knotted Saros Series. All the knots are in a "churning process" at all times, affecting our birth charts continually. In this evolving churning process, the knots can be tied to relatives, friends, co-workers, and generally, to our world at large.

The ecliptic is the apparent path of the Sun across the permanent starry background as viewed from the Earth. The plane of the Earth's actual orbit around the Sun defines the ecliptic. We find the band of the twelve Zodiac signs centered here. The Moon's Nodes are 0° latitude on the ecliptic. The solar system could be said to be "flat." In other words, the planes of most of the planets' orbits coincide almost exactly with each other. The orbit of the Moon, too, nearly coincides with the others but is inclined about 5° to the plane of the Earth's orbit. Although the two planes do not coincide exactly, they do intersect. This means that twice a month, the Moon crosses the plane of the Earth's orbit at the predictable locations that we refer to as "nodes." The Moon crosses from south of the ecliptic to north of the ecliptic at its "ascending" path, or North Node, and it crosses from north to south at its "descending" path, or South Node.

We know that the Sun, as the central body in our star system, is a major source of life on Earth. The Sun is the focal point, with the Moon moving along its elliptical orbit around the Earth. Here we remind ourselves how the Moon always follows its path around the Earth. At the very same time, the Earth follows its elliptical orbit around the Sun. This journey takes a year to complete, and we can see here the dynamic "knotted" interaction that the Sun and the Moon—the Spirit and the Soul—have on our very existence, month after month, and year after year. Are we noticing the influence of this movement? What distraction comes our way when this path is eclipsed? Do we, as whole individuals understand our karmic connection to the Sun and the Moon and to our chart? Do we have a deeper sense of the "why" behind our lives? These are some of the questions we should ask when studying the Moon's Nodes.

The Moon follows the elliptical orbit around the Earth every moment, pursuing its path up toward the Spirit to the North celestial latitude. This movement allows the Soul to start to become aware of the potential for growth. As the Moon reaches the point of starting to travel down into the South celestial latitudes, having been exposed to the Spirit's potentials, the Soul matures with something familiar inside. The South Node is born. Experiencing the polarity of the "digestion" of the North Node with the "indigestion" of the old thought patterns of the South Node, the Soul becomes aware of a profound movement within. Dane Rudhyar employs this concept of digesting the North Node in his book The Astrology of Personality as a way to help us incorporate our lessons into our daily lives. The "indigestion" comes when we don't learn from our mistakes or are stuck in our process of individuation. (Hopefully, we do sometimes learn from our mistakes!) The South and the North Nodes are one and the same, only a little bit wiser every time that we allow them to be integrated and balanced into our daily life as a unified force that, though separate on the relative level, more ultimately forms an intimate and whole part of our psyche.

The Moon's Nodes are not bodies with substance, as are the other planets. They are, in a sense, a manifestation of "nothing" in the same sense that modern day physicist Fred Wolf describes Spirit as consisting of "a vibration of nothing." The "vibration" that Wolf is talking about is the motion of the Spirit coming into awareness through our Soul (the Moon). Mircea Eliade, author of Archaic Techniques of Ecstasy, says in a similar vein that, "temporal markers, even though they imply duration, are necessary for creating the immortal soul out of spirit." The temporal markers could be understood as a vibration or invitation to understand that even though we are immortal Souls, we now have clearly and decisively come into this lifetime. The Nodal Axis, the intersection of the paths of the Sun and the Moon, could also be understood as a "vibration of nothing." That "nothing" exists within us as a definite "something" that guides us to our fate, possibilities, and lessons in this lifetime.

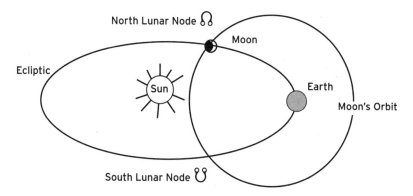

The Moon moves around the Earth in a counterclockwise motion as viewed from the North at a rate of about 13° per day. The revolution of the Earth revolves around the Sun at a rate of about 1.6 million miles per day. The Earth is moving counterclockwise, as viewed from North, around the Sun. The Moon's Nodes orbit the Earth in a clockwise motion around 3.18 minutes of arc per day. The Nodes are retrograde due to reasons we will expand upon further.

Eclipses and Their Association to the Moon's Nodes

The Moon's orbital plane, an inclination of about 5° to the Earth's plane, prevents eclipses from happening at every New and Full Moon. Eclipses can occur only when the Sun, the Moon, and the Earth are aligned within certain "ecliptic limits," which vary considerably but are always in close proximity to the Nodal Axis. A solar eclipse must occur when the New Moon is within 15° orb of a node, but it may occur when New Moon is within 15–18° orb of a node. A lunar eclipse must occur when the Full Moon occurs within a 9.5° orb of either node, but it may occur when Full Moon is within 9.5–12° orb of a node.

Any given solar or lunar eclipse may or may not transit over a planet. Any Moon's Node passing through a zodiacal house will make a contribution and make its presence known. An eclipse "season" moving through a significant house or planet will magnify the Moon's Node capability for significant changes.

A Solar Eclipse occurs at the time of the New Moon.

Solar Eclipses occur when the Moon comes directly between the Earth and the Sun. Thus, the Moon casts its shadow on the Earth.

Solar Eclipses relate to vitality and essential power on an external level.

The Moon's Nodes path, and a Solar Eclipse cycle, signifies new beginnings and major life changes.

A Lunar Eclipse happens at the time of a Full Moon.

Lunar Eclipses occur when the Moon passes through the Earth's shadow.

Lunar Eclipses affect the internal process of emotions.

The Moon's Nodes path and a Lunar Eclipse cycle, signify internal personal matters brought to the surface.

An Eclipse cycle is part of a Saros Series and will eventually return to almost the exact same position after 223 Synodic Months or 18.03 years, plus 10 or 11 days (depending on the number of leap years involved), plus 8 hours. The Saros cycle describes the cycle of solar eclipses with a periodicity of 18.03 years. Because the Saros itself does not contain a whole numbers of days, the visibility of eclipses changes throughout the geographical span of our Earth. After each gap of 18.03 years, there is a shift in the path of the eclipse series, westward by 115° and northward by 4°. The observed eclipse is part of a series of 74 or more Saroses, thus allowing individuals to become aware of the timing of the pearls threaded in our observation.

When we view the transiting Moon's Nodes (Nodical cycle of 18.6 years) and the 19 year cycles of the New and Full Moon eclipses (the Metonic cycle), we observe the deeper sense of the individual's involvement of their birth chart. We observe the correlation between the Moon's Nodes and an eclipse in question and embrace the houses and aspects to all planets affected by the transits.

Transits, Progressions, and Orbs

The Moon's Nodes in transit are used in the same method we work with the transits of the planets. The True Node, most of the time retrograde, moves around the chart in a clockwise motion from 29 to 0 degrees, and we observe the effect it has as it moves through a house. Because of the inclination of the Moon's orbit toward the ecliptic, the Moon spends half its time in North Celestial Latitude (North Node), and the other half in South Celestial Latitude (South Node).

Thus the North Node and South Node are always 180 degrees in opposition to each other. The invisible line between them is called the Nodal Axis.

The Nodal Axis transits through a zodiac sign in 1 year and 7 months.

The Nodes move through the entire twelve zodiac signs in 18 years and 6 months

A nodal return is a conjunction of the transiting North Node passing over the natal North Node. This occurs every 18.6 years. Half of a nodal return is about 9.3 years in duration. It occurs when either the transiting South Node conjuncts the natal North Node, or the transiting North Node conjuncts the natal South Node. As we have noted, the Nodes' orbit is retrograde, and thereby shifts the eclipse season earlier in successive years. No matter which system is used, there is the perfect union of eclipses manifesting at the same time, their distinctions manifesting themselves in the specific zodiac signs and in the particular language of the astrologer.

Mean Nodes versus True Nodes

The Moon's Mean Node is always retrograde. Its True Node moves retrograde most of the time but spends some days a month in a direct motion. Its speed varies a lot more than that of the Mean Node. The Nodes move clockwise around the Earth with a motion that averages about 3.2 minutes per day. So, why retrograde? A wobble of the Moon's obit causes the Nodes to regress.

The Moon's Nodes' retrograde motion offers the individual the opportunity to look at the past—to be able to live in the now

Natal Moon's Node Orbs

Sun and the Moon up to 10°
Mercury, Venus, Mars, Jupiter, Saturn, MC and DC—7°
Neptune, Uranus and Pluto, Chiron and Asteroids—5°

Moon's Nodes in Transits

Moon's Nodes, Sun and the Moon 3°

Mercury, Venus, Mars, Jupiter, Saturn, Chiron and Asteroids—2°
Neptune, Uranus and Pluto 1°

Moon's Node Solar Arc and Progression

Moon's Node, Sun and the Moon—2°
Mercury, Venus, Mars, Jupiter, Saturn, Neptune, Uranus, Pluto, Chiron and Asteroids—1°

Solar Arc and Secondary Progressions Methods

Solar Arc: Observe movement of the Moon's Nodes the same way as other planets. One degree for one year—moving counter clockwise. For example, a Natal North Node of 4° has moved to 14° within a person's first ten years. This is a crucial predictive tool in understanding childhood dramas or exploring various states of development in a lifetime. The Solar Arc Progression method allows us to observe the movement of three zodiac signs within a 90 year life.

Secondary Progression: The Nodes move approximately 4.8° in three months, in a clockwise motion. The method of noticing the Moon's Nodes with Secondary Progression is fine tuned with a tight degree if a natal planet is affected. Major challenges can occur when the natal Node is station R—or Direct.

• • •

Depending on the individual's nature and desire, recommending a mantra, a meditation, a visualization technique or other spiritual and practical methods to prepare the person for their Nodal transits can be extremely effective. The client's own response to, and understanding of, their choices during these times is a critical (and intimate) tool for personal empowerment.

Exaltation and Rulership

Unlike the planets and the Sun and Moon, the Nodes are not bodies with substance, hence there is much debates over their rulerships. There are a number of opinions that have grown out of endless studies in both Western and Jyotish astrology concerning the "correct" signs of the exaltation (a planet's highest position), debilitation (when a planet can't achieve positive effects), rulership (the lord, ruler of the planet's sign), and own sign (where it belongs). These inconsistencies in rulership of the Moon's North and South Nodes are due to the many different methods of the Indian Jyotish system (which are often handed down through oral tradition) as well as a Western blind-folded influence. Some sources claim that the Nodes have no rulership at all! From years of experience and contemplation, as well from many discussions with other astrologers, the following regarding rulership, exaltation, and debilitation are most commonly accepted:

The North Node (Rahu)

> *exalted in Taurus*
> *debilitated in Scorpio*
> *ruled by Virgo or Sagittarius*

To the extent that Rahu becomes exalted in Taurus, the North Node is allowed to achieve material gains, participate in the world, and lives fully content with the success that it naturally demands.

Rahu becomes debilitated in Scorpio, as the nature of Rahu is to shine. However, because Scorpio does not like to "shine," we are also humbly aware that all Scorpions are forced, through transformational circumstances, out of their shell, to show the world what has changed.

The most common rulership and own sign for Rahu is Virgo. In our exploration as of why, we might agree that Rahu, the North Node, as the ruler of Virgo, seeks methods to obtain a life of health. At times this might show in a compulsive manner, as Virgo's nature mirrors Rahu's intimate connection of its compulsive behavior.

The South Node (Ketu)

exalted in Scorpio
debilitated in Taurus
ruled by Pisces or Gemini

The South Node, exalted in Scorpio, allows shedding layers of wounds, revealing that healing can and does happen. The humility of Ketu, when it is not allowed to hide in the monastery to seek spiritual enlightenment, is a simple life lesson that shouldn't be ignored.

The debilitated Ketu in Taurus is just fine in the dungeon and actually prefers to sit and just wait for better times. Then again, we know that eventually the lazy and isolated Ketu will take the Taurus energy and pull itself out toward Rahu. The North and South Nodes are in actuality one and the same—only separated, decapitated, and humiliated if we don't continually, and mindfully, tie (knot) them together.

Ketu's rulership and own sign in such an approach is assigned to Pisces. We understand Ketu as the wounded soul hiding in the Piscean quality of escapism. Ketu and Pisces are fitted well together as they both might show us our possible spiritual enlightenment.

• • •

Note: There are differing interpretations over exaltation and debilitation. The North Node, Rahu, is at times assigned to Gemini as exalted and debilitated in Sagittarius. The South Node, or Ketu, is randomly given Sagittarius for exaltation status and Gemini for its debilitation. We also find other variations in the Jyotish Jaimini system where Aquarius becomes the rulership of Saturn and the North Node to Rahu. Common practice is that Scorpio rules Mars and the South Node ruled by Ketu. This observation has spilled over to the Western astrology system, with variations that are of confusion to many.

As a practicing Western astrologer, the exaltation and debilitation of Taurus and Scorpio application comes naturally, and will be used throughout this book. When the Eastern system comes into my practice, the exaltation, the rulership, and whole sign system becomes more important and prominent. The Eastern system relies more on the degree of exaltation and rulership than the Western system and thereby is in need of a more definite application. Thus, as far as exaltations, rulership, and own signs are concerned, there appears to be a process of evolution—not only in my own work, but also for many astrologers coming from a range of systems—toward a more complete understanding and agreement.

Application of the Moon's Nodes

When working with a birth chart, there are seven steps that I take to interpret the impact of the North and South Nodes for an individual.

Seven Steps to Interpret the Natal North and South Nodes

1. House of the North Node
    What does the house in question represent? The North Node house placement implies the area where an individual strives to mature, grow, and embrace.

2. House of the South Node
    What has the house in question brought forth in the individual's quest to let go of the past and integrate its house meaning? The South Node house placement indicates where an individual has come from (whether past life or this lifetime) and can heal without guilt of past issues, but rather understand its desire for conscious love for Self.

3. Signs of the Nodal Axis
    How has the individual understanding of the Zodiac sign and its implication of potential integration of past and future become conscious? By balancing the polarity of both signs of the Nodes, the awareness of the decapitation becomes the wholeness.

4. Planetary Lord of a House
    When necessary, in the case of no aspects to the Nodes, a desire for further investigation, the "Lord of a House; "Ruler of a Sign," or "has dominion over," can be used beneficially. Thus, the method becomes incorporated at times, making sure not to make the analysis

more complicated, too over analyzed but rather additional information is accessed.

5. Aspect between the Moon's Nodes, and any type of planetary energies.

6. A thorough observation between the Moon's Nodes, the Sun and Moon.

7. Interactions between any planets and the Moon's Nodes are incorporated with regular methods and orbs. Observe the North and South Nodal axis in interaction with the one or more planets; i.e. there is the past, present, and future to take into consideration. Has the individual understood the intimate, crucial, and karmic evolution of their Spirit and Soul connection to take their growth to a different level of healing?

Let's say a North Node is conjunct the MC and placed in the tenth house, in Capricorn. The South Node falls in the fourth house in Cancer. An individual with this placement is always looking for recognition for his or her success at work and general status in the world. If the South Node is not analyzed, the individual will not integrate his or her wound into a healing process throughout life. If the challenges of this house placement are left unexplored then success will not be achieved, and challenges will continue in the tenth house.

The next step is to find Saturn, ruler of the tenth house, and notice what type of aspect Saturn and the Nodal Axis form to each other. Let's assume that Saturn falls in the sixth house for work, health, and daily duties. If in orb, this creates a trine in relation to work ethics from the tenth house. Success should come easily, but not necessarily or automatically, as trines can have a lethargic quality to them. The same Saturn creates a sextile to the South Node in the fourth house. This sextile can be the promise and hope for rewards if this person analyzes old wounds and family dynamics. By reaching out to the sextile and the trine, the opportunity for that challenge will be enhanced.

Another factor to pay close attention to is when the Nodal Axis forms a square to a natal planet. Both the North and South Nodes will

Chart 2: Stages of the Moon's Nodes in Transit

Aspects	Age	Challenge
Square	4 years, 9 months	First Soul Awareness
Opposition	9 years, 3 months	Moving Out to the World
Square	14 years, 2 months	Critical, Formative
Conjunction	18 years, 6 months	Ritual Passage
Moon's Nodal Returns (conjunctions)		
	18 years, 6 months	Ritual Passage
	37 years, 3 months	Maturity
	55 years, 10 months	Re-group Mid-Life
	74 years, 5 months	Wise Man/Woman
	93 years, 1 month	Transition
	111 years, 8 months	Transformation
Moon's Half Nodal Returns (oppositions)		
	9 years, 3 months	Moving Out to the World
	27 years, 11 months	Preparation for Adulthood
	46 years, 6 months	Preparation for Mid-Life
	65 years, 2 months	Retreat
	83 years, 9 months	Initiation
	102 years, 4 months	Transformation

in practice be affected. Suppose the transiting North Node is on the MC, and both North and South Nodes form a Square to the natal Saturn. In this case, the analysis of the natal aspects between Saturn and the Nodal Axis becomes the first important point and step. Is there too much resistance or an awareness of necessary growth toward Saturn's strict persistency and timing?

The next step is to determine how you or another individual have responded to this natal placement, or transit, of the Moon's Node. With the awareness of difficulties from the family, the fourth house must—ideally be clarified. A more evolved Soul will declare clearly and decisively that the past is the past, and that their wounds are healed. When this healing of past wounds occurs, astrologers can focus on the deepest part of the client and give him or her a much-deserved and renewed inspirational goal for the future. The fourth house—the Soul—is, thankfully, endless!

Mars and Saturn correlate to the South Node in the Western system, and come into perspective as we observe the South Node in natal, progression, or transit work. Therefore, a close observation of the aspects between Mars and Saturn, and the South Node is necessary.

In the Eastern system, Mars becomes the planet related to the South Node and Saturn works well with the North Node.

When working with the North Node, Venus and Jupiter in the Western system are the corresponding relevant planets and should be examined closely according to the astrologer's method.

Chart 2 on page 20 shows the stages of the Moon's Nodes in transit. This chart will help deepen your experience and knowledge of planets in transits. By integrating the major planetary transits with the various stages of the Moon's Nodes in transit, you will gain valuable additional insight in astrological analysis.

Aspects to the Nodal Axis

There is a fundamental difference of a contact of the North Node versus the South Node. We know that the North Node represents what we are here to learn, understand, grow, and mature from; but it is also that which we respond to within our surroundings and environment, such as family, tribe, friends, business associates, and so on. Since we might not always be sure if the Moon's South Node presence in our lives actually comes from another lifetime, we should be in the good habit of knowing for sure that we have been together "before"; but how do we prove that? The South Node is asking for the great task of integrating the knowledge of past with the current person or situation as we face a difficult or beneficial solution and outcome.

The South Node is the impression of our conscious awareness of our subconscious. It takes us to the past, of being aware that one person might teach us lessons necessary to evolve. Taken for granted that the Moon's Nodes might be some kind of karmic attribution that we have to suffer from, then the North Node allows the results to be a decision based on facts or our awareness.

The True Master assures us that everything is Karma. Karma reflects fate and destiny and we are reminded that we are where we need to be at all times. Other planets or intersections are Karma as well, and in working with the nodes we respect them as their own true "personality," which concludes by the individual truly being aware of lessons learned. The Moon's Nodes are interaction of the Soul's (the Moon) desire for control (the Sun) of its own message and destiny. In that process the individual becomes free not to blame someone else for his or her "mistakes" (should there be such a condescending word).

North Node Conjunction

The conjunction shows the individual's personal evolution, understanding, growth, and surrendering to the planet in question. This aspect will always allow the individual's personal awareness to grow with consistent awareness of the South Node. Without a willingness to surrender to the South Node's clear intention, the conjunction to the North Node will hinder its potential opportunity for growth.

South Node Conjunction

South Node conjunction to a natal planet shows the individual's personal involvement from past lives, or subconscious memory, as well as conscious patterns from the past in this lifetime. Letting go of the past is imperative, or a stagnated residue lingers in the person's life and interaction of the planet in question. The work on issues from the past, and the awareness of those past issues, will be brought out as positive tools toward the North Node's zodiac sign or planet within aspects. The repeated pattern becomes understood when the individual becomes aware of his or her own pattern of denial and embraces the work and eventual healing. There is a tremendous inspiration for ultimate liberation and understanding of progress of our own evolution as involved human beings.

Opposition

We observe similarities to the conjunction when an opposition of the Nodal Axis occurs. For example: Venus conjunct Aries' North Node creates an opposition to the South Node in Libra. However, certain misinterpretation can arise if we assume, or pretend we know, that the individual involved in the analysis has a firm handle on the planet in observation. Therefore, has the individual in question worked out their South Node Libra challenge, making sure to not seek love in the other person, but rather in his or her own individuality—i.e. North Node in Aires—toward the Self? The eagerness of living in the "now" allows the integration of oppositions in natal and transit work to merge with that which is the "reflection" of the situations facing us. A mirror effect is created as the Self is observing her- or himself when surrendering to the opposition. The ouroboros, the snake that eats its own tail, is contained within our psyche.

Square

The square presents an interesting, and at times challenging aspect. Both the "past" (South Node) and the "future" (North Node) are in a process of evolution, awareness, and, eventually, understanding. But this process occurs on a different level with a square present. The work toward the planet in question will also be observed with other aspects toward that specific planet and its eagerness to heal and be understood.

The Nodal Axis is an opportunity to move toward wholeness when we have the awareness to integrate this aspect: a square brings the opportunity to balance the planet, or planets in question.

Trine

An often overlooked pattern is formed when the Nodal Axis, North or South Node, trines a planet. The trine of the Nodes becomes an awareness of ease, as it is considered with other planetary configurations. The pattern that forms to the "opposite" node creates a sextile to the planet in question. If that planet in question creating the sextile is otherwise overlooked or ignored it is an opportunity to work the trine in productive and beneficial manners is created.

Sextile

A sextile to a specific planet will form a trine to either the South or North Node. It is the same pattern as the above description of the often overlooked trine. North Node sextile a planet allows the individual to step out into the real world and enjoy life to its fullest. The planet forming the aspect will naturally trine the South Node, which allows the individual to understand that the past is part of our present to carry us into the future. South Node sextile a planet allows us to understand and learn from our beneficial situations.

• • •

Instead of using the specific aspect definition, the keywords on page 25 can be applied when the Nodes are in relation to each planet, and thus be applied to any astrological interpretive technique—natal chart, in a Dasa, or in transit.

Planet	North Node	South Node
Sun	*Strong career achievement; challenges with authorities, father figure, and partner*	*Modification of career path; exposure to personal secrets; vitality and power struggles*
Moon	*Personal wounds confronted; strong bond to mother and female friends; family complexity*	*Past issues to be confronted; creative forces from the past; strong bond to home surrounding*
Mercury	*Career in public image; strong bonds with siblings; desire for travel and writing*	*Confrontations; brilliant mind to be accessed; independent thinker*
Venus	*Overindulgence; weight concerns; personal charisma; success in the arts; financial gains*	*Self doubt; financial struggles or concerns; low metabolism; self-expression*
Mars	*Courageous; compulsive; adventurous; athletic*	*Accident prone; confrontational; release of anger; high blood pressure*
Jupiter	*Over enthusiasm; success gained; spiritual search; beneficial situations*	*Restlessness; wrong decisions; own philosophical path; karmic residue for stagnation*
Saturn	*Higher education; commitment to a cause; ambitious goals; restraint of achievements*	*Melancholy tendencies; challenges with parents, authority figures, and boundaries*
Uranus	*Freedom to choose; freedom, liberation; genius*	*Talent from the past; anxiety and nerves; radical thought patterns*
Neptune	*Intuitive, creative, and visionary; care takers; unconditional love*	*Illusion; deceptive; drugs and alcohol abuse; passion*
Pluto	*Compulsion; confrontation of death; personal growth; physical strength and power*	*Losses; power struggles; physical limitations; dissolving of matters*

In Part Three, "The Moon's Nodes: Synastry and Composite," we will bring this interpretation to life by examining the charts of a well-known and dynamic couple, Brad Pitt and Angelina Jolie. But before we put the method into practice, we will first explore deeper the Eastern symbolism in the myth of the Moon's Nodes.

In Hindu mythology, the gods and goddesses are in balance: the masculine always has a feminine counterpart, anima has animus, dark balances light, just as the North Node and the South Node are each a side of the same coin of Self awareness. Because the nodes are "bodiless," the following introduction to the myth of the nodes grounds them in personas, and will help us see how the nodes are the knots in the complex tapestry of human life.

Part One

≈≈≈≈≈

THE MYTH OF THE MOON'S NODES

A n understanding of the Moon's Nodes is one way of becoming aware of the true Inner Self. The Moon's Nodes and their impact on our psyche have to be experienced and integrated within that Self, rather than intellectualized, and one way we can do that is through myth. In the Jyotish system, the North Node and South Node—Rahu and Ketu— have been considered as planets for thousands of years. The myth of the Moon's Nodes has always existed in our subconscious mind. Throughout the ages, the correlation between the Sun and Moon has had an impact on our roles as male and female. The Moon's Nodes, as the interface of solar and lunar cycles, corresponds directly to our past memories and back to the creation of time.

The myth of the birth of Rahu and Ketu is a creation myth. At the beginning of all time, the gods and demons are purifying the Amrita, the immortal waters. The Amrita is our quest for eternal life; in the West, it is the same search that is contained in the myth of the Holy Grail. The symbol of the Holy Grail, as told in many stories from the Middle Ages, can be defined as the vessel of life as well as a means of restoring the dead to life itself. We seek to be safe and comfortable; some seek abundance, some seek simply to survive a life of suffering. The longing for the Holy Grail is similar to the function of the Moon's Nodes because through their agency we seek completeness within. Do we actually find it? Through the myth of the Moon's Nodes, we will see the abundance of wealth and wisdom that arise out of Amrita, the immortal waters, after the Churning Process.

As powerful as the gods are in their force, they are still humble, aware that they are in need of the Asuras in purifying the Amrita. The Asuras signify the demon consciousness within the human being. There is a fine line between the gods and the Asuras, as the contemplation of "evil" in man needs some clarification. In the Larousse *Encyclopedia of Mythology*, the following explanation is given for the Asuras:

> Generally, "devas" are translated as "gods," while Asuras are described as "demons," but in point of fact, both are essentially beings gifted with a remarkable and mysterious power which is manifested simultaneously by moral and physical attributes.

It cannot be overemphasized that without the knowledge of the Hindu Trilogy of gods—Brahma, Vishnu, and Shiva—the images and understanding of the Moon's Nodes would have a missing link. The missing link would be even larger if we didn't connect these gods to their complementary goddesses, Saraswati, Lakshmi, and Parvati.

Brahma

Although the three gods, Brahma, Vishnu, and Shiva, ultimately

 merge into one, they still express their relatively unique characteristics. The first image of the Hindu Trilogy is the god Brahma. He represents the Creator of the world and has an essential role in it. The law of creation is the eternal law of existence. In modern times, Vishnu and Shiva have overshadowed Brahma. However, each is ultimately as important as the other.

Through the Spanda energy—the motion of the beginning of anything and everything that exists—Brahma's manifesting energy comes
into existence. He creates over and over again. Brahma is there, and
the principle of the Spanda vibrating energy becomes that which we
create. The principle of the Golden Embryo, his breath, becomes that
which moves the stars, moon, earth, and each of us. In some writings,
it is said that Brahma created the Moon and the Sun and then placed
them in the sky.

Saraswati

Brahma created Saraswati, his consort, out of his own substance.
Saraswati, the river deity, also known
as the flowing one, is the patroness of
the arts, crafts, sciences, and other ar-
tistic and technical skills. She carries a
tremendous amount of knowledge and
wisdom within her. Her image is that
of a lovely young woman sitting on a
Swan and playing the Veena, or classi-
cal stringed instrument. She often holds
a lotus flower and a rosary in her other
hand. At times, she is depicted with five

faces and eight hands, the explanation being that she is busy in the fields
of creation. Because of her connection with the arts and sciences, Saraswati is the strongest goddess to invoke for creative endeavors.

As the goddess of the river, Saraswati is often said to be the river.
Using water for purification ceremonies is therefore necessary in invok-
ing her presence.

No matter where she is seated—on the swan, the peacock, or the
Lotus flower—she embodies the mother of creation. In the Hindu myth,
the swan (along with the goose) is linked to the universal mantra Ham
Sa, which allows us to experience the Self. When we integrate Saraswati
into our work with the Moon's Nodes, we allow our knowledge and
wisdom through education to become part of our wholeness.

Vishnu

Vishnu is the sustainer and maintainer of the universe, however, we should not doubt his ability to destroy! Vishnu is represented by twenty-two different images, or reincarnations. One of the most popular is Krishna, the eighth incarnation of Vishnu. In the myths, the milk maidens, or gopis, who become infatuated by the sound of his flute, adore Krishna. They dance around him, forgetting their own husbands and duties back home.

In the Southwestern Native American myth, Kokopelli has the same charm and mesmerizing effect on the women around him as Krishna has on the gopis. Kokopelli moves from pueblo to pueblo, and as he

approaches the villages, the memories of him make the women forget their daily obligations. Jupiter comes to mind with the association of Vishnu.

One debated aspect of Vishnu is the tenth reincarnation, which is Buddha. Buddha was born in India where he advanced his own interpretation of the Hindu traditions. For Buddhists, the Buddha and his teachings are separate from Hinduism, while, for Hinduism, he is regarded as a full incarnation of Vishnu.

Vishnu is the god who continually rules the Moon's Nodes. All cultures carry many variations of the Creation Myth. Thus, the involvement of Vishnu and the Moon's Nodes in natal work or transits becomes a tool to help us become our own gods, or divine forces, within the reality that we create.

Vishnu carries a club, which symbolizes authority. He also holds a conch. The conch sound is often heard in Hindu temples as a reminder of the origin of our existence. The primal conch also represents the six directions affecting us—North, South, East, West, above, and below. It's spiral form and the connection with water creates a resonance of universality.

Often, Vishnu (like other gods) holds his palm up and opened. This action represents reassurance and a form of protection. I suppose one could say the gods are telling us that one is in "good hands with us." Vishnu's fourth symbol is a wheel (Sanskrit: chakra). The wheel is represented as the weapon to cut through our ignorance and crush our ego. This weapon, the wheel, will become important to understand when Vishnu oversees the Churning Process of the Water—our impurities during transits.

Powerful as he is, Vishnu has had to step aside somewhat for his consort, Lakshmi, for centuries. We don't know for certain the reason for this. One speculation, the matriarchal society, has always been of importance. The woman's role in society, be it in a rural Indian village or a large modern city, needs to be in touch with the timeless quality of woman's wisdom. Vishnu as an abstract principle is still part of the trilogy of Brahma and Shiva, but seems never to have become one of the more popular, worshipped gods. Vishnu represents the force maintaining the world, and at times we require a support within rather than what we manifest in our outer world!

In contemplating Vishnu's importance in our lives, I am reminded of his ability to sleep for thousands of years. When he finally wakes up, he takes three big giant steps in the Universe and starts another creation. A lotus flower grows from Vishnu's navel, which symbolizes the beginning of every transit of the Moon's Nodes affecting our chart. The lotus flower has a tremendously independent way of growing: out of the mud while remaining sustained.

Lakshmi

Lakshmi is the most popular goddess in the Hindu mythology. She is part of many households in India. She is worshipped everywhere, as she is the embodiment of wealth and prosperity. The goddess Lakshmi rises up from the Churning of the Waters and brings the gifts that we might deserve. In the Roman myth, Venus also arose from the sea. For the Greeks, Venus was known as Aphrodite. The form of a goddess born from the water is universally embedded in our subconscious -desire for our own individual growth process, taking form already in the Mother's womb.

Lakshmi is the goddess of the harvest and is often pictured with elephants at her side. The elephant always represents the fertile soil around her. The harvest is abundant, and the water from the elephant's trunks will keep the soil moist and rich. In the fall, during the festival

Divali, she is brought out as the harvest goddess. In many households and temples, Lakshmi is prayed to for wealth, prosperity, fertility, and good fortune.

In various references to Lakshmi, she has a mysterious quality to her and often a great wisdom. Sometimes, Lakshmi is shown with an owl on her shoulder. The owl, in many cultures, represents a deep and caring wisdom. Death also comes into play when the owl shows up in meditation, visions, or in nature. The Greek goddess Athena carries the wisdom of the owl on her shoulder. We may note that to listen to the voice of death often allows us to accept death as transformational and not horrible and final. We see similarities to Lakshmi in many traditions around the world. In Roman mythology, Minerva is associated with serpents. Minerva carries the wisdom of the owl. The early Hebrew goddess Lilith is the goddess of abundance, fertility, and fecundity, and the feminine principle to invoke during the harvest. Lilith is associated with the owl as well and is also shown with the lotus flower.

If or when our dark shadows have been dealt with, transformation can take place. Snakes also surround Medusa, the Greek goddess. Snakes cover Kali as well, another manifestation of Lakshmi. These are consistent clues to the feminine power and the necessary acceptance of her role in all living forms. In the final analysis, the world is balanced in itself, and as such we are perfectly balanced human beings.

The Churning Process has to be clarified; the contaminated waters have to be cleansed. We must be patient, as this process is vast and ongoing.

Shiva

Shiva, the god of destruction, seems to have the most powerful impact on modern individuals and their awareness. Even though Vishnu becomes the main ruler of the Moon's Nodes, Shiva remains a prominent and important god to observe in our evolving society. He is the god of Kundalini. As Shiva destroys, he is also the one that shows us life through metamorphic experiences. He shows us that our destructive nature can also survive as a form of purging, healing, and change. As we have entered a new century,

we have noticed a broader awareness of Kundalini and Chakras, or contractions of psychophysical energy. The significance of such attributes is important in working with the Moon's Nodes. The Moon, depicted on Shiva's forehead, is the Soul's desire for new awareness.

There are mighty deeds that Shiva can perform. At one point, Daksha needed Shiva's help. Chandra, the Moon god, had married the entire twenty-seven daughters of Daksha. They represent the Nakshatras, the lunar mansions in Jyotish. Chandra preferred only one of them, the most beautiful and goddess-like, Rohini. Daksha was able to perform his own rituals, and thereby put a curse on Chandra, the Moon. The curse worked, and as each night passed, the Moon became more and more dim. Daksha then realized that he had asked for too much and didn't know how to reverse the curse. He was told to go and ask Shiva, who is the keeper of the sacred herb Soma, which could possibly reverse the curse and allow the Moon to shine again.

Parvati

Parvati is the goddess of power. She is primal energy. Without Parvati, there would be no life energy (Shakti), beings would be inert. Parvati lives in all individuals as the power that allows us to breath, to use our five senses, to think-—in other words, to be alive!

In the story of Parvati's marriage to Shiva, we see an allegory. Parvati represents the power of life energy. Shiva, the god of Kundalini and metamorphosis, symbolizes the soul's desire for new awareness. Their marriage represents the individual who wishes to reach nirvana— to achieve a state of liberation beyond human suffering.

Shiva would often be engulfed in deep meditation, and Parvati, his wife, would try to distract him to force him to pay more attention to her. One time she threw herself into the sacrificial fire (fire is represented by Kundalini), only to assure herself that she would be united with him in their next life. She survived the flames!

• • •

The images of the Gods and Goddesses discussed here are images; they are representations of the cosmic moments of transits in our lives. We have an ancient desire to balance our outer form as males or females, and become united with the greater completeness within our innermost, individual selves. This exploration of the Hindu Trilogy—Brahma/ Saraswati, Vishnu/Lakshmi, and Shiva/Parvati—should clarify our different layers of conscious desire for purification and growth as we each open ourselves to our individual Churning Process.

It is important to realize that the Nodes *embody* the qualities of the Hindu Trilogy, and as the Nodes transit the planets (which we will look at in depth in Part Four), they will bring those qualities to resonate with the qualities of the planet with which they form aspects. As astrologers, we have become used to the myths we've already learned: Mars as Aggression, Venus as Love, Mercury as Communication, and so forth. The Jyotish system introduces us to a new myth, that of Rahu and Ketu, and the symbolism they contain of the Hindu pantheon of gods. We must incorporate this new myth into our subconscious understanding of the Nodes; it will enrich and deepen our understanding of the Self.

And now to the myth of Rahu and Ketu!

The Churning of the Sea

This myth relates the story of how the Devas and the Asuras are Churning the Sea using the body of the snake, Vasuki. The snake is coiled around Mount Mandara and held up by Vishnu. The Churning of the Sea is to extract the Amrita. It is the birth of Rahu and Ketu.

Brahma, Vishnu, and Shiva accept the assistance from the Asuras—the demons. In actuality, the demons have the same strength as the gods. It is a profound and difficult task to create a whole world. This is not separate from our own experiences. Even if we don't desire immortality, we certainly have a quest, if not a responsibility, to live out our potentials in our life (mapped out in our birth chart) to the fullest and with joy.

The Refinement Process (which is the churning of the sea) with the gods and the demons occurs at the Mountain Mandara, which is equivalent to the houses in our astrological interpretation. In most myths, the snake Vasuki is being pulled between the gods and the demons. Vasuki will eventually become the North and South Nodes. The mountain Mandara is used as the stick to churn the sea that contains the Amrita. The snake Vasuki is tied around the stick to make the ocean move faster, thereby purifying and cleansing it. Vishnu has disguised himself as a Turtle who is supporting the stick upon which this process takes place. As the god in charge, he is omnipresent.

During this process, the waves of the sea become stronger and stronger until the sea starts to boil. The turbulence of the water creates the atmosphere of a powerful storm. At times, it looks like a hurricane is

engaged in a desperate attempt to devour certain aspects of the Churning Process. The gods work hard to push and maintain their balance as they can now see that their opponents, the demons, have tremendous strength in this purification ritual.

The actions of the demons, who can't control themselves anymore, show their true nature by drinking the Amrita. This is forbidden. "This can't be!" the gods exclaim. Lord Vishnu shows his utmost power by pulling the serpent Vasuki out of the boiling water, throwing him up into the air and then decapitating him with his spinning discus. The transformed cleansing process has now turned into a battlefield. This is the environment in which our individuation, the growth toward our true Self, must take place. At birth we were complete in our psyche, yet on earth we have become decapitated and humiliated. We were asked to help in the Churning Process, and our demanding nature seeks the same attributes as the gods. As we all come from the same god or Source, our purity, or our potential immortality and instinctive quest for wholeness, makes us walk the same path. Yet the same snake, our wounded, shredded body, often gets cut in half during our transits; we tend to wander around in confusion, seeing the Dark before we can understand the Light.

Vasuki, the snake, must now be totally confused! He not only has been decapitated, but has also been pushed and pulled from left and right, from the Shadow and then the Light, i.e., from the demons and the gods. As Vishnu throws Vasuki up into the air, the god takes his disk and cuts the snake in half, the head manifesting as the North Node (Rahu). The other half, decapitated, yet connected to the same Soul, takes the nature of the South Node (Ketu). They should be seen as one entity. Separated, yet still as one. The push and pull from society and all of our surroundings, including Karmic attributes, often forces our Moon's Nodes to work on the dynamic spanned by awareness versus non-awareness in our personal issues over and over again. The longing for the Amrita lingers within as a whole complete being, yet Lord Vishnu, the Maintainer, makes us humbly aware of our faults and vulnerability as we have been cut in half.

Like the Sea, our life in turmoil becomes more and more intense. We might then give up and surrender to our comfort zone, our familiar surroundings, represented by the South Node. Throughout our life lessons, as we start to become more whole, our lives become more purified and we start to see results in our lives. At first, the decapitation is devastating. We feel lost, separated, and confused, but we gradually find our way through this humbling process, understanding our dynamic North Node's desire for maturity!

There are writings of the Churning Process stating that the demons actually had poisoned the waters and were in need of purifying their own deeds, their own karma. In another version, it is stated that the snake pushed so hard that his venom escaped from him and spilled upon earth, as if he might destroy earth itself. Yet another version of the myth states that Rahu was thrown up into the air and caused the Full Moons to occur.

In his appearance, Ketu becomes the ugly and fearful looking "planet." His face is often somewhat comic looking with red dots. Chicken pox, pimples, scars, veins, and freckles are indications of various diseases manifested in a body. Ketu is often shown with a snake's head. However, more significantly, often with no head at all!

This is significant because it shows us the transformation that can occur if we pay attention to the ugly, or perhaps not-so-perfect, parts of ourselves. Metamorphic and euphoric transitional events in our life can and will change us. But we do have to pay respect to the message that Ketu gives. It is the planet showing us the deepest spiritual part of our chart. No, we will not be aware of Ketu's gift if we have not seen any darkness in our life—liberation or enlightenment does not come served on a silver tray.

Ketu's animal representation is the vulture, which we might not like at first. However, all animals are needed in nature. The vulture's job is to clean up what has already been killed. Cleaning up our "mess" from the past is an important aspect of the South Node's influence on our understanding of regeneration. A deeply embedded understanding of the past, i.e. Ketu, has to be brought forth and killed in order to be reborn into the understanding of the beneficial influence of Rahu's future.

The gods and goddesses will speak to us only when we learn how to listen to them. Our wisdom is contained in Ketu, our unconscious memories from our past. We have to judge for ourselves the importance that various events from our past hold. This is a tremendous hidden talent and a genius of evolutionary progress in our psyche: Individual conscious awareness, and the revolutionary natural cycles that alter mass consciousness, are contained within our South Node. It is the same Soul that becomes aware of one life time and yet another, supporting our inner Wise Woman or Wise Man who is whispering, supporting, and lovingly caring for our process of embracing our past.

We learn that Vishnu had eventually been told by the Sun and Moon about this intrusion. Thus, even the luminaries hold a high respect for the Moon's Nodes as they become shadowed and thereby eclipsed by the Nodal Axis. However, the promise from the Creator, Brahma, had to be kept, so Vishnu chopped off the head of the demon. Therefore, Rahu became the North Node. The same demon's tail thus became the South Node. Here lies some fundamental bitterness in the involvement of the Serpent's swallowing of the Sun and Moon at the New or the Full Moon eclipses. For some, an eclipse can have devastating and life changing results, but with preparation and awareness the Nodal Axis will bring illuminated results.

It is the Moon that pulls us back into our womb, back to where we come from, and it is the South Node that pulls us into our subconscious. Our wounded soul (the South Node), as it searches for identity, is looking for strength (the North Node). The soul often finds this strength in relating more openly to the Spirit. The Sun—Spirit—is leading the soul—Moon—forward in its search for identity.

• • •

As in creation, the Purification Process occurs at any given time in our birth charts, or during any transit we are experiencing. The Churning Process happened when the creator manifested this world. The ritual is still occurring even as the weather patterns change and as our ecological system is being destroyed. The process is occurring when horrendous events happen. These are the demons manifested in parts of us waiting to be purified.

Cause and Effects of the Moon's Nodes

As circumstances in our lives become more and more intense, we might give up and surrender to our South Node's tendency of retracting back to denial, abuse, depression, or being stuck in the past. As we transform throughout metamorphic life lessons and start to become more whole, our lives become purified, and we begin to see results in our lives. First the decapitation was devastating, and we felt lost, but as we slowly learned which side of the rope to pull, we became humbly aware of our right actions. Ashamed of our actions, we are naked and exposed to our family, the judge, to society, or our friends before we actually wake up to our fullest potentials.

The humiliation of transits of the Moon's Nodes can be just like this, but if we are courageous enough to allow the venom from the snake, Vasuki, to purify us, then we will grow more than we expected.

Here we will shed light on some imperative facts about the snake and its symbolism. Throughout many world religions and myths, we see dragons and snakes. However, the image of the dragon changes when our society changes. We will find that the dragon transformed into the snake and perhaps now moves into the images of monsters, Dracula, and the various horror images of the Halloween mask. The snake is still embedded in young people's minds, due to our collective unconscious.

In the Hindu myths, the snake is often depicted as a Naga; Nagas have many characteristics of the dragon. At times, they are considered half snake and half human due to their deep wisdom. In between incarnations, Vishnu sleeps on the snake, Shesha. Lying down, he prepares himself for another time (another transit) as he studies his inner state.

Snakes are often associated with the energy of Kundalini. Shakti, primal energy itself, is the latent, powerful force that is awakened through spiritual transformations in our life. The Shakti runs through the 15 million various Nadis (channels for prana or energy) in our bodies. The major nadis are the seven major chakras, which the holistic health field is working with today. Shiva and Shakti (Parvati) emerge over and over again as they cannot create or procreate without each other. In most cultures, however, the female tends to have a more influential aspect in snake symbolism and narratives. Often the symbol of the snake or serpent is polyvalent, universal energy, both male and female. It is Solar and Lunar.

This leads us to our continuing exploration of the rewards from the myth birthed from the Churning of the Sea. When the Ritual of the Creation of the world was finished, what was the result? Destruction, devastation, and despair? Or were there rewards? Wisdom, and material gain? The South Node is known for its spiritual gain, yet spiritual evolution is also measured in the worldly life. Through the process of growth toward the North Node, we experience the "Amrita." Our fulfillment comes from reflecting on our inner selves and starts to show externally in the specific unfolding of our lives. We might not attain eternal life, but we can learn about our destiny and karma as well as our duty or dharma.

From the ocean, Lakshmi emerges on a Lotus Flower. She will become the consort of Vishnu, but as previously noted, she represents much more than just a wife. She is born out of this "tug-of-war" ritual. Lakshmi is always the goddess of fertility, wealth, and prosperity. She is born out of the Ocean, out of chaos, and in the chaos there is order! Lakshmi embodies the same qualities as Venus.

Part Three

THE MOON'S NODES: SYNASTRY AND COMPOSITE

There is a certain mysterious, explorative, karmic, experimental, and fatalistic impression or understanding of the Moon's Nodes. One reason for this is that we pretend to be "the other" half of the North and/or the South Node. Hindu Philosophy would define this "other half" as the Higher Self—being present, aware, and observational. Acting out according to its own awareness.

There is the popular notion that the North and South Nodes bring people together as the possibilities of past life connections. But of course! And when the skeptic doubts the theory of coming together again in this lifetime, no one can argue the facts of the past from this life.

We are then embarking on meeting other people as a tool for self-awareness. Relationships are a personal quest to understand our Self before we truly embrace love in its totality.

We must remember that the Nodes are one and the same—decapitated—yet not able to separate. When we focus on two individuals we have to keep in mind that we have the decapitation's wounds and scars—yet with eagerness to heal in relationships. Ultimately, it is love for the Self, not others, that allows the North and South Node to grow together.

Seven Steps to Interpretation

In Part One, I introduced the seven steps to follow when working with a birth chart. This is the process I use to interpret the impact of the North and South Nodes for an individual. We will use the seven steps here as we consider synastry: understanding the relationships that we form with others. This is a system that will help you maintain humble awareness of integrating the facts observed in the chart, rather than speculating how someone else might feel about them!

1. House of the North Node

2. House of the South Node

3. Signs of the Nodal Axis

4. Planetary Lord of the House where the Node resides.

5. Aspect between planets and the Moon's Nodes

6. Composite Chart analysis—working with two or more charts

   A composite chart indicates the depth of the integration of two or more individual's path as one. The Nodes indicate the house, sign, and aspects' possibilities for further growth, and understanding past as well as future interactions.

7. Synastry—working with two charts side by side—or bi-wheel
   Through an analysis of a neutral observation by the astrologer, both individuals are allowed to be understood according to their natal chart interaction with each other.

An Example: Angelina Jolie and Brad Pitt

The natal charts of actors Angelina Jolie and Brad Pitt are dynamic examples of how two well known public figures can help us understand the Moon's Nodes in natal, transit, synastry, and composite astrological work. Certain natal charts do not have many aspects to the Moon's Node, which in itself does not matter when we use the above seven steps. We will work on Angelina's chart first with the first 5 steps, and then continue to focus on Brad Pitt's natal chart using the first 5 steps. We will then explore their composite chart (step 6), and conclude this chapter with their synastry (step 7 for each of them, Angelina to Brad, and Brad to Angelina).

Step 1: House of the North Node (Angelina Jolie)

Angelina Jolie's North Node in Sagittarius falls in the fifth house, indicating her commitment to her creative Self. She strove to become an actress at an early age. Her father is the famous actor Jon Voigt, and her parents divorced when she was two years old. The fifth house represents romance and children, and at the time of this writing, she has three adopted and three of her own biological children. Even though not officially married, a fifth house phenomenon, she is in a stormy yet committed relationship with the actor Brad Pitt since 2004.

Step 2: House of the South Node (Angelina)

Angelina's South Node falls in the eleventh house in Gemini, emphasizing her goals, desires, and hopes for the future. With the South Node in the eleventh house, her comfort with the public and with large groups in general seems natural for her. A South Node in Gemini brings memories from the past into the challenges to make decisions. Once they are made, changes will still occur.

Step 3. Signs of the Nodal Axis (Angelina)

The North Node in Sagittarius in the fifth house indicates Angelina's fate, destiny, and karmic path in dealing in a rational, idealistic, and op-

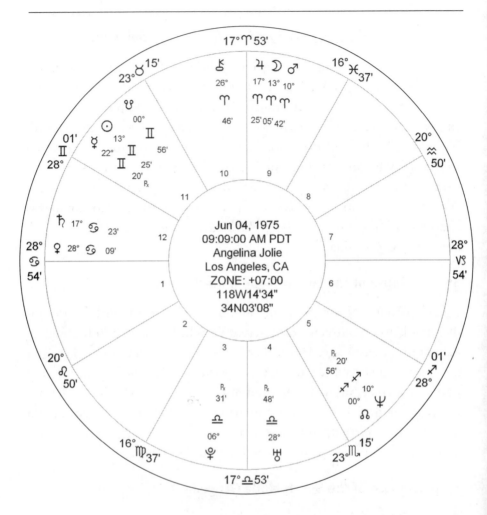

Jun 04, 1975
09:09:00 AM PDT
Angelina Jolie
Los Angeles, CA
ZONE: +07:00
118W14'34"
34N03'08"

timistic manner toward visions and decisions. Children play an important part in her life since her path toward fulfillment comes through her
creativity. Sagittarius is the ruler of "foreign" countries, which shows
her fascination with rescuing children from other countries as well being a Good Will Ambassador to the United Nations.

The South Node in Gemini throws her into stages of confusion,
unpredictable spirit, and unconventional lifestyle. This shows a changeable personality with a lifetime quest to become aware of this part of
herself. Her nerves will be shattered and unrealistic, and hasty, surpris-
ing decisions are habitually made. Angelina's Gemini South Node in the

eleventh house emphasizes her decision to have six children: adopting a boy in 2002 and a daughter in 2005, giving birth to a daughter in 2006, adopting another son in 2007, and finally giving birth to twins in 2008. We don't know for sure how Angelina's South Node extends to her conscious decisions, but knowing that the Nodal Axis is placed in the fifth/eleventh houses proves her Karmic residue of eventually giving in to her North Node in Sagittarius—commitment to children and creativity as well as what is in store for her future and goals in her life.

Step 4: Planetary Lord of the North Node (Angelina)

The Lord of the fifth house is Pluto. Pluto, placed in the third house is in Libra: a powerful and strong communicator, yet with a delicate balance of Libra's tendency to negotiate. Pluto also opposes Mars in the ninth house. Mars, the traditional ruler of Scorpio, falls in Aries and is placed in the ninth house. Angelina's Mars, Moon, and Jupiter in Aries can indicate a short temper when confronted with issues of deep concern. She travels fast, and is, at times, excessively irrational. The ninth house represents foreign countries, as well as the state of mind of an individual.

We connect her natal North Node fifth house to the ninth house and her eagerness for having many children. Her psychological reasons for this are her own and very private birth right. Angelina's natal Neptune in Sagittarius trine her stellium in Aries in the ninth house basically makes her a natural fighter for causes of injustice. It also indicates her eagerness to create a Tribe of International Children

We find the Sagittarius North Node in the fifth house, not making many aspects. Neptune is placed in the fifth house, allowing her to follow her intuition, but at certain times leaves her feeling confused about her future as well. She became an actress at an early age and insisted on attending an acting school. Neptune opposes her natal Gemini Sun. The fifth house represents "marriages" or long-term relationships, which could make her settle into relationships with a Neptune illusionary and hope for an ideal situation. By Angelina's first Saturn return at the age of thirty, she had already had a live-in boyfriend (at the age of fourteen) and been married twice.

Step 5: Planetary Aspects to the Moon's Nodes (Angelina)

Angelina's Venus in Cancer on her Ascendant trine the North Node attests to her unusual and sensual appearance. Natal Pluto in the third house sextile her fifth house North Node indicates her ease in the public and her success as an actress. She contributes her time and personal wealth as an Ambassador of the United Nations by saving and caring for children throughout the world. As natal Pluto sextiles natal North Node, the South Node creates an air trine to third house Pluto. This trine allows Angelina's opinion to be heard by a wider public audience. In her personal growth she might have the good fortune of doing just what she likes to do!

Her Gemini nature with a conjunction of South Node, Sun, and Mercury retrograde, makes Ms. Jolie changeable, at times irrational, and often unpredictable. The South Node in Gemini tends to have problems with the nerves—and with the important and strong ninth house impact, her mind will in various ways become challenged; perhaps when she doesn't get her way or when she gets another creative idea—or create another child?

The ninth house implies how our psychological, inquisitive, and expanding consciousness withstands everyday as well as life challenges. The South Node forming a trine to Pluto in the third house helps her out, since her opinion is what she believes in.

We will later observe how her natal North Node position becomes extremely activated and occupied as we work with the Synastry between Angelina Jolie and Brad Pitt. For example, she became pregnant with her first daughter as the North Node conjuncts her natal Jupiter, Moon, and Mars within 1° to 4° in 2005.

• • •

We will now analyze Brad Pitt's natal chart focusing on the Moon's Nodes and then conclude this observation with a Synastry and Composite exploration.

Step 1: House of the North Node (Brad Pitt)

Brad Pitt's North Node is in Cancer in the seventh house; his desire for caring, nurturing, and compassionate feelings becomes his quest and goal. A person with a North Node in Cancer is often forced into overwhelming situations; the most important characteristic of a North Node in Cancer is that it shows the individual's innermost fear of being left alone. Thus, when confronted to show their emotions, Cancer often either denies their true feelings or pretends they have none whatsoever. Cancer natives have the tendency to nurture everybody but themselves.

Step 2: House of the South Node (Brad)

Pitt's South Node falls in Capricorn in the first house. Through the first house we accomplish the task of knowing our true Self—but of course—through others! His subconscious—including that which he brings from other lifetimes—becomes imperative, which effects decisions that might hurt others. He falls back into the strong Mountain Goat that undoubtedly believes that strength and persistence will cover his pride within his Self, the first house.

Step 3: Zodiac Signs of the Nodal Axis (Brad)

Brad Pitt's North Node in Cancer and South Node in Capricorn might envision that the woman in his life would be like his biological mother—a caring, nurturing "home-maker." His Capricorn South Node brings him back to a subconscious memory of getting away from control (a Saturn issue). He reaches out to his Cancer North Node—nurturing, mothering, and kind—to learn how to deal with emotions. With his stellium of six significant planets in Capricorn, including his South Node, we might ask, "Who is controlling whom?"

We are reminded that we are becoming our birth chart through the development of the Self contained within the challenges of being true to that Self. Capricorn might indicate an individual that is cold, detached, and a selfish overachiever. Brad could have those qualities on some level, but as we observe him reaching out for causes in the world

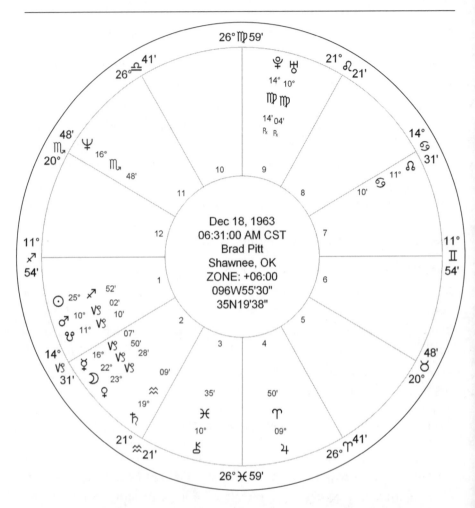

at large—especially the hurricane disaster left from New Orleans, Louisiana, in 2001—he continues to work on community issues; a Cancer caring for homes and those in need. As of this writing he is a father of six children. Capricorn often respects family traditions, rules and regulations, respect and discipline. His North Node in Cancer will strive to share his values in unconditional and loving ways.

Step 4: Planetary Lord of the Moon's Node (Brad)

Brad's fifth house cusp for children is Aries. The Planetary Lord of the fifth house is Mars (and Pluto), and falls in the first house in Capricorn, conjunct South Node. Thus we can understand the importance of Brad's involvement with a few marriages, observed by the media at every step that he takes, many children, and important romantic or unconventional non-marriage lifestyle. When the Nodal Axis falls in the first and seventh houses, an emphasis on multiple relationships or challenges in marriage often manifest; those individuals are in a constant challenge of staying focused on their own growth rather than the current partner. Capricorn seeks stability, traditional roles, and a responsible father figure.

Capricorn continues to play an important part in his life—the continuation of the Mountain Goat following his path from the past to establish security, success, and caring (North Node in Cancer) follows with his Saturn in Aquarius, the traditional ruler and the ruler of his second house, as a continuation of Brad's responsibilities.

Step 5: Planetary Aspect to the Moon's Node (Brad)

Brad Pitt's Nodal Axis creates a close conjunction (and opposition!) to Mars. A Mars/South Node conjunction indicates circumstances related to the physical condition, ability to work on anger, frustration as well as joy in sexuality, release of old stagnated resentments, and the ability to stand up for injustices. His South Node conjunct Mercury shows an innate and necessary call for taking charge of expressing both body and mind—and move toward the North Node—attempting to stand up for issues of concern for his personal as well as professional life.

Brad's North Node square natal Jupiter in Aries is in the fourth house; roots and respect from his family are important to him. How do his parents see his unconventional and demanding new role as a father? He might reach out for approval through others with his public views but never forgets where he came from.

The North Node in Cancer sextile is his Uranus—which also creates a trine from his Capricorn South Node. This indicates a beneficial aspect of growth and a certain guaranteed success. Cancer North Node creates a trine to Neptune in Scorpio sextile his Capricorn South Node; his path to his success as an actor seemed to be destined as he landed in Hollywood. Many say his good looks (and Mars body) gave him his first roles. The Nodal Axis creates a sextile to Pluto in the ninth house as well as a trine from Mars/South Node, Mercury conjunction (and Moon/Venus as well)—attesting to his ability to be firm—yet his North Node in Cancer strives to truly care—a balance and task of strength and sensitivity in dealing with others.

Step 6: The Dynamic of Relationships—Composite Charts

In addition to the above astrological observation and following techniques of synastry, the composite chart of two or more individuals can be used when observing the Moon's Nodes. The new identity is forming a continuing karmic link and growth—and we remember that we work with the Moon's Nodes to reach the deepest part of someone's psyche, Spirit (Sun) and Moon (Soul).

Angelina and Brad's composite chart (on page 53) has a 21° Virgo North Node conjunct Pluto in the twelfth house; changes and break-ups will be a common occurrence in their relationship. There is an intensity and control element of this aspect. Uranus in Libra is conjunct the Ascendant. The Ascendant in a composite chart shows what the individuals shows as a team—loving yet also not balanced at times. The composite Pisces Sun conjunct the South Node in Pisces indicates work and duties with challenges to continue their demanding public roles as a power couple throughout the world.

I have used a Composite Chart with Midpoint Cusps. A different type of chart, a Davison Relationship Chart, is one based on "Time/Space"—it would cast a new chart with the midpoints of times and the two locations of two individuals. The system of dividing their time and place would show the Libra Ascendant staying the same with unconventional Uranus conjunct. This chart creates a South Node conjunction to their Virgo Sun and falls in the twelfth house. Virgo, with its countless precise and detailed personas, would be a most suitable chart for their continuing growth as partners—and parents. Pluto conjuncts the South Node as well—their path of change continues. The Moon falls in Virgo and we will observe how their many roles as unconventional human beings add to their work in the twelfth house of unfolding karmic events.

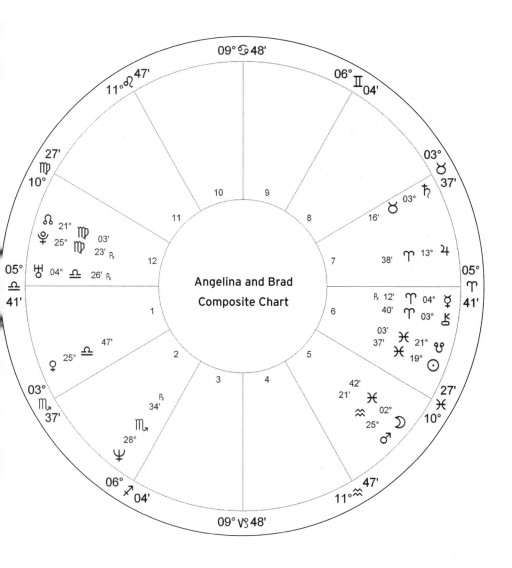

Angelina and Brad
Composite Chart

Step 7: Synastry—Angelina & Brad

The most accurate information will be established when the astrologer works with two natal charts and analyzes step by step how the planets are interacting within the individuals. A humble awareness should be established in that we are merely observing an arbitrary suggestion how a person in fact understands his/her own Self—and explore further with that understanding. We also have to consider who we are observing. A certain complexity grows—but our faith and desire for helping those that ask is established through the understanding of the birth chart and its Soul's essence! In the following paragraphs we will shapeshift into the body (and soul) of Angelina Jolie and Brad Pitt.

The following discussion looks at Angelina's natal Nodal aspects in relation to Brad Pitt's natal chart. Aspects between two individuals become more or less the same; but with keen observation, a fine-tuned method occurs when working with the Moon's Nodes and other planets. What creates the difference in aspects between two objects is the speed between them. It is by observing where and in which house the energy falls that we arrive at the understanding of the relationship.

Angelina's Sagittarius North Node falls in Brad's twelfth house; a house of service and karma—an unfolding unconscious event every day through conscious duties, and in his sixth house its connotation of taking care of one's own health in the process. The sixth house is a house of service and work ethics; Brad will often have his hands full when interacting with Angelina and their children.

Her Aries Mars, Moon, Jupiter, and Midheaven square his Nodal Axis. The Aries stellium falls in Brad's fourth house—root of importance, and his longing for a family. This can also indicate that she will force him through confrontation to "leave home." This also creates a conjunction to Brad's Jupiter, showing growth in their Soul and friendship, physical, and emotional attraction—her Pluto also opposes his Jupiter in Aries, constant eruptions in this favorable conjunction.

Angelina's Aries Moon squares his Nodal Axis; she is often in charge, a woman's touch and ability to conceive, in many ways, allows her to win through her femininity. On some levels, she might force him to become dependent on her; issues about Motherhood will surface

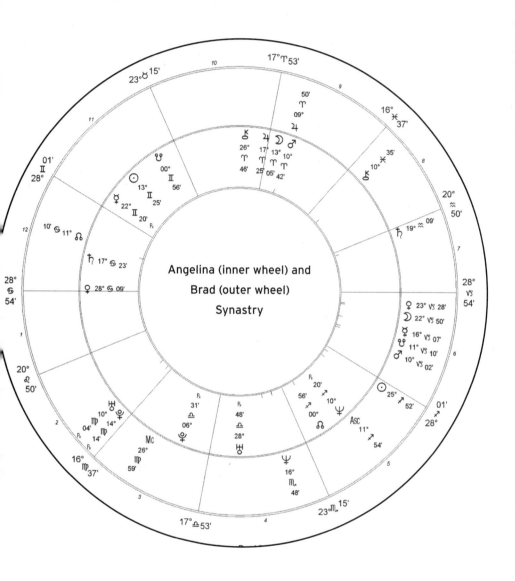

Angelina (inner wheel) and
Brad (outer wheel)
Synastry

and deep rooted connection from past lives; and this life's true meaning why they are together again. She also teaches him to go deep within his psyche and forces him to deal with his past issues of attachment to a traditional home and how to get in touch with a deeper sense of his Soul—and move away from traditions—perhaps in controversial ways unknown territory for Brad.

At the same time she forces him to discover how to grow toward the North Node in Cancer—endurance, confidence, family values, and his quest of caring for someone through his seventh house; a wife...

Angelina's Jupiter in Aries creates a square to his Nodal Axis as well—pulling in a natal Jupiter square to his natal Mercury in Capricorn; disagreements and explorative conversations will occur constantly. Her Jupiter square to his natal South Node forces him to get off the couch and not be lazy, accused of being manipulative, and forcing a certain pessimism away—moving toward the North Node in Cancer— and realize that he is forced to face his future growth.

Saturn in Ms. Jolie's natal chart conjunct Brad's natal North Node, in Cancer opposes the natal South Node in Capricorn. Her Saturn forces him—or allows him to face more discipline, Saturn; the ruler of Capricorn could consent him to become depressed; or melancholy for her constantly opposing his perhaps already disciplined nature. Also, her Cancer Ascendant opposes his Moon and Venus. Attraction; again!

Angelina's Pluto in Libra falls in Brad's ninth house of future visions and hopes create a square to Brad's natal Nodal Axis. As the South Node can force issues of trauma, destructive behavior and misuse of power in a relationship—the message of his North Node promises honesty, transitional stages of their relationship; and he often takes off on his motorcycle—to understand that the dynamics of their bond has created six children and charity work on many levels —so he has to stay!

Her natal Pluto in Libra opposes his natal Jupiter in Aries, which is a force of letting the traditions, habits, and connection to his family change on many levels.

Angelina's Midheaven in Aries along with the Aries stellium are placed in his fourth house; a house of roots, parental influence, and a necessary Soul search continues their challenges; yet dynamic, interesting, instant, and constant benefit of personal growth—they cannot hide their personal intimacy and love. Their synastry allows us to learn that what we see in the public through reputation and fame might be just that of a home of two individuals coming together because of their dynamic interaction.

At this point we are "reversing" the charts of Angelina and Brad. The shape-shifting takes place and we embark on looking at Brad's effect on Angelina's chart

Step 7—Synastry: Brad & Angelina

Brad's quest or desire to be born with a multiple energy of Capricorn—his predicament became clear with the interaction with Angelina to continue to be strong, focused, and successful; being elected as one of the sexiest and most prominent actors in the world. He has to prove his point as he embarks on the following interaction with a strong, successful, and beautiful, yet complex individual.

Brad's North Node in Cancer falls in Angelina's twelfth house (again, house of karmic links); South Node falls in her sixth house (work, duties, and health). Challenges and interaction with work and with six children within their Tribe—they will always have some type of connection. The South Node in Capricorn emphasizes his work and traditional role as an independent individual—he was married at the time they met—square her attractive personality and involvement with her ninth house.

His last marriage to the actress Jennifer Anniston seemed to have become "stale" and no children produced seemed to be a major part of them growing apart. His South Node/Mars conjunction in a square to Angelina's Mars (body) and Moon (mind) is instantly taken to another dimension; should it be a past life and his life's quest to release his stored up Martian ability to have children.

Brad's Nodal Axis: again twelfth and sixth house axis square Angelina's natal Aries Moon in her ninth house. The South Node in square to her Moon; both Cardinal signs allow their subconscious memories to surface with an eagerness to both be strong and courageous. The Nodes themselves are always in a process of bringing the subconscious (South Node) toward the conscious (North Node) and balance them with a new, intentional quest to bring that awareness into an individual's daily life. A female Aries Moon has a connotation of the Warrior and she challenges Brad's endurance of his Capricorn/Cancer nodal axis as a message for his "manhood" (strength), causing his traditional belief system to change and break down barriers within his psyche and daily life.

His action (Mars), his South Node (his past), and his Mercury (his communication skills) fall in her sixth house and so it becomes his duty to take care and nurture that which is created between the two of them. To be nurtured, maintained, and protected children need responsible parents. Brad's five planetary energies in Capricorn fall in her sixth house; work has to be performed in a disciplined manner. Both of them are in the tabloids juggling their children on their arms and hands—looking fabulous—yet he is also looking more tired... There is an enormous endurance in his natal Mars/South Node conjunction; but it is also the "past" catching up with him on many levels. Thus, he reaches out to his North Node, squaring her Mars in Aries, allowing him to be strong with his enduring personality.

Brad's Nodal Axis squares Angelina's natal Aries Jupiter, which allows or forces a therapeutic healing to occur. They will have tremendous upheavals as they embrace their differences and likeness! The ninth house is the natural house for foreign countries, the state of mind, psychology, and the house of in-laws. Jupiter travels to distant places and is often irrational in its planning of the future; yet Jupiter promises rewards to those who are conscious of its gifts. The involvement of the Nodes links their relationship and their need to communicate with honesty. This causes heated arguments as well as solutions that make either one of them the "winner."

An important aspect between their charts is Brad's Nodal Axis in conjunct and opposition to Angelina's natal Saturn in her twelfth house. Karmic residues persistently remind him about his responsibilities and love for the mother of his children. His Cancer North Node indicates his imbedded desire to nurture someone who might tell him what to do from time to time; Saturn will be pulled into his Mercury;

South Node and Mars in Capricorn and force him to stand up for issues of practical matters.

Brad's Nodal Axis—Cancer/Capricorn square Angelina's natal Pluto in the third house—promises tremendous change in their daily life as well as the reason why they came together in this lifetime. Pluto does not indicate an ending of a relationship but it does promise constant and recurring confrontations in communications, clarification, and transitional metamorphic understanding that they have to come to terms with. The Nodes creates a grand square that assures their personal, yet public, interactions of allowing Pluto to take them to yet another level of working their relationship out.

Brad's North and South Nodes square Angelina's Midheaven, pulling his Mars, South Node, and Mercury (and his Moon and Venus) into her public image. The Midheaven promotes not only our public image but also our social status, and our reputation. It has been noted that their appearance on the "red carpet"—the Aries energy color—has a direct competitive undertone to their looks and achievements. May we suggest to Brad? "Let the Lady go first!"

Through our astrological analysis of these two public figures we have found that aspects between two individuals are clearer as we systematically separate the aspects and focus on the House placement of the interaction. Their synastry is indeed a dynamic example of how two people come together to be together, and we have the opportunity to learn about the North and South Nodes placements and interactions of their goals to bring a tribe of international children together.

Part Four

NATAL AND TRANSITING NODES
THROUGH THE HOUSES:
THE DYNAMICS OF
THE SOUL'S DESIRE FOR GROWTH

Like any other planetary configuration, the Natal Moon's Nodes are used to support astrological interpretation. The "complexity" of a specific natal planet in aspect with the Nodes in the birth chart frankly depends on the context of the individual's dynamic desire to grow as a Soul. If the planet in question is not in aspect, or no planet is placed in the house in question, it does not mean that something is not occurring! Again, we apply the method of "Planetary Lord" to our work! Adding asteroids, the Part of Fortune, Chiron, and so on, allows the astrologer a superior picture that will enable the natal as well transiting North or South Nodes to make their presence known.

The Ascending Node—the North Node—has the tendency to endow the process of individuation with a certain forward-moving zeal or eagerness. The Descending Node—the South Node—regresses conversely to a source in the past. Through the South Node much can be revealed and integrated in positive, concrete, and practical experiences. Should we decide to recognize and draw on the tremendous wisdom acquired in past lives that dynamic realization can become a powerful tool for achievement in this lifetime. The pulsation and vibration of disintegrated issues, and their imprint on the psyche, allows the seeker to live in the moment. Individuals searching for wholeness through the Nodal Axis become more content, even if not fully liberated, by integrating the past with the present; and live in the now.

The ultimate inner search signified by the South Node ideally brings our psyche toward the North Node, our desire to grow through challenges rather than avoiding them. When we are in denial, and won't let go of our fears—when we constantly hold onto old wounds—then we are not permitting healing to take place, and the evidence is that we don't see changes in our external environment. However, every time that the North or South Node forms an aspect to the Natal Axis, we are presented with an opportunity to understand the Dynamic of the Soul's desire to be born and re-born. Our opportunity for growth begins every day that we to wake up!

Transiting North Node to the Natal North Node

Recognition of personal growth

As the North Node returns to its natal position every 18.6 years, we will experience out-of-the-ordinary events, unusual encounters with people from the past. These events will typically include encounters with people who with time become meaningful in our lives. It is not the person coming into our lives that are our final concern, but rather the lesson that we receive from that individual.

The North Node tends to indulge and overspend toward the goal of its fulfillment in the outer world. During the transit of the North Node, it is good to examine existing business plans and revise old ways of operating, but not take big new risks. Often the stock market is studied closely as it relates to the Moon's Nodes' cycles. Solid long-term investments, rather than short, risky ones, are better focal points.

The North Node and its natal house position, aspects, and most importantly, an appreciation for the dynamics of the Soul, are all always significant. When the North Node returns to its natal position through a transit, it is the most suitable time to seek out a spiritual or religious path or teacher, allowing a deeper sense of the inner quest for growth to be integrated on all levels in life.

The Nodes by their very nature can transform us. It is as if we have no choice to speak, yet that is somehow the only choice we have. To listen to and integrate our past experiences is to acknowledge the vivid present moment. We can in actuality participate in life as a whole, rather than subtly denying the possibility of living fully. We give permission to the transiting North Node to purify the Waters of Immortality to the exact degree we desire and need.

Transiting North Node to Natal South Node

Re-evaluation of individuation

This transit can cause us to be exposed to old issues that haven't been adequately addressed. The eye of the unknown is perpetually watching as the untold issues, karmic attributes, old debts or unfinished business gradually catch up with us. If we're working with a clean slate, we have the opportunity to understand the direction of our lives. To stop, contemplate, and accept our worthy accomplishments during this time will allow the path of the unresolved past to become integrated in a subtle, releasing, and fulfilling way. Until the South Node is fully understood, healed, and embraced will the North Node be allowed to move fully forward with the purpose of higher goals. The experience potentially benefitting all individuals who face the North Node transiting the South Node will be clear as we become wiser in the learning and growth process.

When the North Node transits—such as conjunct, square, or inconjunct to the South Node—there is the tendency for serious illnesses to manifest. Problems with the lymph nodes, any type of disorder of the reproductive organs, or at times other difficult diagnoses often emerge through this transit. During this time when the North Node aspects the South Node, situations relating to life purposes comes to the surface.

Circumstances beyond our control can happen, and we have to become humbly aware that nothing is truly strange. The word "out of the ordinary" or extraordinary could be more fitting, but synchronicity is more precisely what we are looking for as the North Node is in aspect to the South Node. Often circumstances such as running into people that we haven't seen for many years (an old friend calling who we haven't heard from since high school) will become catalysts during this transit. Our friends (or enemies) allow us to understand our potential for growth.

This is a time to focus on creative goals and write them down. Goals in life do not have to relate solely to work, family, or money, but can also tie into understanding our inner personal gain, and striving to be aware that our life is satisfying by relating to the Soul's purpose. Do we have the mate we truly desire to grow old with? Are we teaching our children to be honest and whole individuals? Have we understood that there is a voice within us that we can listen to?

As we respond to these questions with a sincere heart, we develop our sense of the impact of the North Node in aspect to the South Node, integrating our Soul's purpose into our life. Aware of its outcome, we make the Spirit content. This catalyst will change according to our understanding of the evolution of the clarified Soul purpose. Cataclysmic events are sometimes ways that our experiences become integrated into our true Essence and are thereby purified.

Joan of Arc—the Heroic Peasant

Of the little that we know about Joan of Arc, there is much evidence that she lived a short, unusual, and heroic life. Joan of Arc was born in a peasant family, and supposedly at an early age, Joan heard celestial voices and claimed to have had visions of saints. With her Sun, Venus, and Mercury in Capricorn, it might at first glance be difficult to understand such earthy planets as "celestial."

Neptune in Cancer is in opposition to her Mercury in Capricorn with a 2° orb which makes the Neptunian visions possible. Saturn, the ruler of Capricorn, is the "initiator" to our Earth plane. Joan of Arc's Saturn is trine the Sun and Venus is in Capricorn. Her Mars, conjunct her South Node in Virgo, forms a trine to Mercury as well. This indicates that nothing could stop Joan from her forceful, direct, and well-spoken opinions. The South Node and Mars conjunction shows a deep desire to fight for causes or release anger from the past.

Joan's Libra Moon conjunct Jupiter indicates her emotions were running too fast at times. She wanted to let humanity know her desire

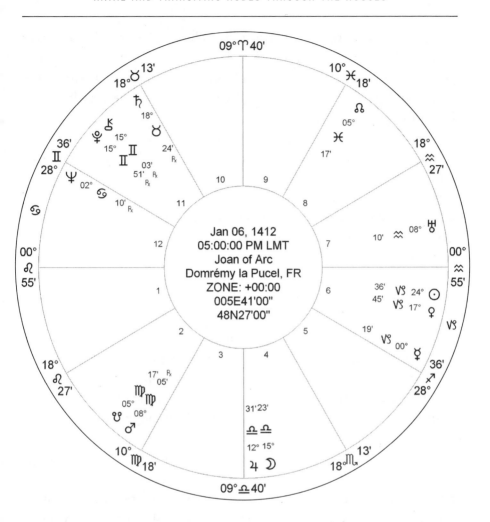

to help. The North Node in Pisces and her Moon/Jupiter conjunction makes her a determined martyr. This "martyr" aspect forms a grand trine to a Pluto-Chiron conjunction in Gemini and Uranus in Aquarius.

Years before her birth, there was much turmoil (Europe had been ravaged by the Black Death), and during her lifetime France was subject to constant invasion by the English. These long series of battles became known as the Hundred Year's War. Through her strong character—and the Mercury-Neptune opposition as well as the Venus-Sun trine to Saturn and her Moon/Jupiter trine to Pluto—she managed to convince Charles VII (whom she eventually helped become King of France) that her divine visions were an indicator that allowing her to fight for France was a holy mission. She dressed up in a warrior's full armor and was given her own troops to command. She fought and won battle after battle, and eventually she won a place of honor beside Charles VII at his coronation.

Charles VII, now the King of France, was opposed to any more fighting against the English, but not even a King could stop Joan of Arc's mission to continue to fight. In 1430 (the year of her Nodal Return) she embarked on her own military battle against the English at Compiègne, near Paris. She was captured, and her people sold her out to the English. Consequently, she was turned over to the French court system. Fully betrayed, she was accused of sorcery, witchcraft, and heresy. Her South Node/Mars conjunction turned out to be important again, because she was accused of wearing masculine clothing.

In November of 1430, the transiting North Node crossed her Natal North Node in Pisces and, thereby, her South Node/Mars conjunction in Virgo. Even though Joan confessed her errors and was condemned to life imprisonment, she would not allow the court to determine what she should wear. She kept her male clothing and therefore was burned at the stake on May 30, 1431. During a Full Moon in Aries, her South Node in Virgo ended her battle, proving that her life had not been in vain. During her last days, Mars was conjunct her Moon, square her Sun and Venus, and also conjunct her Jupiter and inconjunct to Saturn. Her North Node in Pisces formed a trine to Venus and Pluto, allowing her to die for her cause. We can only hope that she knew her own personal mission, being a unique young woman dressed in pants, would bring benefit, as she was canonized in 1920.

Natal Moon's Nodes, Mars and the First House

My True Guide is my Highest Self

The first house and its ruler, Mars, play an imperative role in our study of astrology. We show our personal image to the world through our first house. The planet occupying the first house becomes a significant factor in how we release our inner calmness or frustrations. We can't hide our body, so to speak. We often hear about the first house as "the doorway to the Soul." The vast Jyotish system information is based on the first house and its rulership. Where we "come from" is through the fourth house, that is to say through our parents. In itself it might not seem to be a "revelation," but the first house is in a square to the fourth, indicating the involvement of the Soul's desire for growth and separation.

Mars is not always the courageous planet we often make it out to be. All planets are in a state of development. We are in an evolutionary process of becoming. What Mars and the Moon's Nodes have in common is a process of recognizing one's courage and strengthening a healthy image of self within the social world. There is also often a surplus of energy in the North Node as its goal is to move forward, and often with blindfolds on. Just as Mars has the desire for achievement, the North Node has a desire to be noticed.

Individuals with the Moon's Nodal axis or numerous planets on the Ascendant can have an obvious lack of confidence. The people and the planets involved are too overcome by their own energy and tend to shy away from their own power. Within a tender and loving environment, the individual can overcome their frustration and deal in a constructive way rather than a destructive way. With the Nodal axis in the first and seventh houses, there are often multiple marriages. There is a need to work through the Self rather than through a partner or many individuals. In this process of realizing the North or South Node, individuals gain their own sense of value. As we mature, we learn that our own complexities are as extensive as those we notice in others.

North Node conjunct Mars challenges the process of learning how to deal with anger, frustration, or sexuality. South Node conjunct Mars has the tendency to hold onto frustration, irritability, intimacy issues, or anger from the past. When this combination occurs in analyzing two charts (synastry) it means that the two individuals have met in the past and are now working out their issues. The South Node person can hold on to the comfort and be too passive, and the partner may be too forceful. This relationship often signifies that this life or in another lifetime, both are involved with this dynamic.

Our society as a whole has had years of misunderstanding the effect of Mars. Frustrated serial killers have always existed, but how do they become this way? Perhaps a new awareness of our outer image, the first house, will soon start to reflect our inner consciousness? A healthy inner appearance can be encouraged with a positive self-image early in children's education. Yoga, breathing exercises and meditation has been used with healthy results in schools; these techniques allow Mars to act constructively.

Since Mars is the ruler of the first house, it is an indication of not only where the planetary ruler of the first house falls, but of Mars itself. Mars will show important connections to the individual's way of dealing with productive aspects in his or her life.

Wolfgang Mozart

Using the birth time reported by Wolfgang Mozart's own father, Mozart's North Node is in a close conjunction to his Virgo Ascendant. Mercury is the ruler of Virgo and falls together with a stellium of Mercury, Sun, and Saturn in Aquarius in the fifth house. The fifth house is our creative outlet and it shows Mozart's unusual way of expressing his thoughts and individuality as well as his discipline to create. Saturn is in a close inconjunct to retrograde Mars in Cancer in the tenth house. This indicates a strong drive to bring out the stellium of a unique individual.

Mozart was not a handsome young man, yet did not allow his physical appearance to get in the way of his creativity. By the age of six, he had composed four short piano pieces that are still played today. Uranus is in a 2° conjunction to the South Node, in Pisces. His genuine musical talents had a deep-rooted desire to be brought forth from prior lifetimes. His natal 17° Sagittarius Moon conjuncts Pluto in the

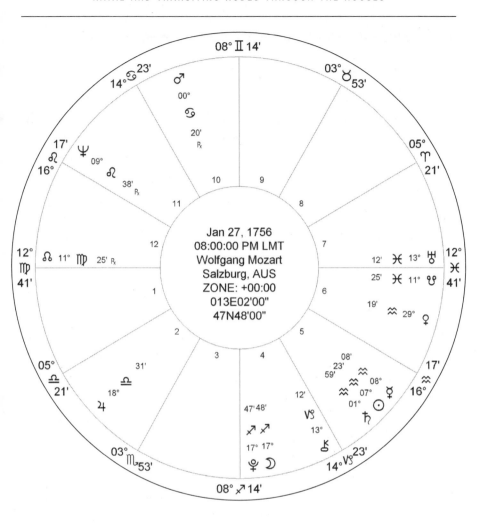

fourth house, indicating Mozart's deep desire in his Soul to explore his subconscious memories. This Pluto/Moon conjunction is in a square to his South Node, Uranus in Pisces, as well as his North Node in Virgo—exploring his imbedded talent to details and musical genius.

He had an unhappy marriage that lasted two years. Mozart had no children and died suddenly, supposedly of typhoid fever at the age of thirty-four. However, there has been speculation that a musical rival could have taken Mozart's life. Although that is possible, his Mars, retrograde in Cancer, is in a trine to his Venus in Aquarius, which may reflect the saying "only the good die young."

North Node Transiting the First House, or Mars

Productive activities

The transiting North Node has the ability to release hidden matters that Mars represents. A few months before the North Node approaches the first house (or Mars), it is advisable to start a self-defense class, join a gym (and go there!) or start a cleansing suitable for your body type. Any type of sexual frustration can show up in the body, such as impotence, lack of a confident self-image, or depression. This transit is also a good time to seek out healing through sexuality. Mars is the body, and our body will speak to us about what would be favorable to focus on in the months before the transit comes into an orb of 1–3°.

Aries is the sign of "me" which means this is a time to start a new venture with a goal in mind just for your own sense of achievements. The Moon's Nodes have the reputation, or tendency to become too comfortable, perhaps lazy and not moving forward. Now is a good time to take a year and a half to take a chance. A new business that you know intuitively can work is also worthwhile to explore. A strong self-confidence in success often matures and becomes beneficial.

Since the North Node indicates over-enthusiasm, cautiousness should be applied, but we shouldn't hinder our endeavors. Advice from others can be helpful, especially if we have doubts about our ideas. Your friends, a consultant, or even your parents might know that you are running a little too fast with your ideas, especially if your energy is running high at this point. Slow down, take a deep breath, re-focus and stay realistic.

Many individuals with a strong first house, and especially with the Moon's Nodes placed here, have a tendency for multiple marriages or many significant relationships. When the Moon's North Node is in transit in the first house, there is a strong possibility that the person will finally meet the right significant other. This is a time for romance and interaction with others. When we work with the North Node, a purification process will reveal layers of wounds can start to heal. In today's society, it is no longer unusual for a person to have two or three marriages behind them. This transit indicates that the individual has had enough lessons and longs to find her or himself.

The North Node in transit through the first house or to Mars can also indicate the person giving up on a relationship, and being comfortable with that decision! The Moon's North Node has the tendency to climb a ladder of understanding "Who am I?" The South Node pulls us down at times. We take our steps backward. No matter how many steps we might have to take, this transit reflects the potential to finally step out of the karmic journey and realize that "I" deserve to be in a good relationship.

South Node Transiting the First House, or Mars

Physical challenges

Many subconscious memories and release from old issues might arise at this point. Often conflict will occur as the South Node moves into the first house. Mars is a strong catalyst for old wounds. As the South Node approaches this house, it is worthwhile to seek out help. The South Node is a shadow planet, often hidden by Mars or in the first house as a mask. Observe the natal aspect between Mars and the Nodal Axis. A strong aspect connection often shows hidden, unconscious issues about depressed and repressed frustration. Of course, as always, it is good to "own" our anger. Ancient mythology tells us that Mars and Venus eventually got married.

This is a rewarding time to stay focused and stick to the long over-due diet for a year or more. This is also a fine time to continue to stay focused on issues that might have surfaced as the Moon's South Node starts to approach the first house. Issues emerging from the second house often show insecurity or financially difficult matters that can be released as the stagnation dissolves through Mars or the first house. (Reminder: the Nodes travel clockwise around the Zodiac Wheel). The integration of the Nodes from insecurity toward courage and letting go of old belief systems becomes prominent. Wearing red is encouraged! Do something that you never thought you could do before! Take the walk around the block; spend hours at the gym, and get your repressed energy out! It is about the body's desire for release.

People from the past may well contact you to clarify unresolved issues. Welcome them! You might want to express your own Mars feelings and thoughts . . . constructively, that is! Don't sabotage the opportunity for further growth with others by refusing the phone call. It is a great time to pick up the phone or arrange a meeting with an old friend or lover to release certain feelings that could not be expressed in the past. Speaking with firmness doesn't mean that the effect will be ruined!

The nervous system can be burdensome during this transit. Avoid anxieties by taking extra walks. Use the body in a most basic way by embracing intimacy. Old inhibiting and unresolved issues often surface at this point. It is good to stay focused and work on nervousness rather than letting the body run you down.

Poor blood circulation, headaches, and a general restlessness can occur. Stress comes into the picture. This is a time to watch out for reckless drivers, and be mindful of how you yourself are driving. If the signs of stress-related symptoms have occurred, and don't seem to go away with alternative methods, seek out conventional medical assistance. A sign of a healthy South Node transit in the first house is a healthy body and soul.

The Nodal Axis, Mars and Three of the Kennedys

At times, a family member is an outsider and connections can be harder to trace in relating to the Nodal Axis, however, it is overall quite uncommon that we cannot find clues as to a deeper sense of "who's who" when analyzing the Nodes. The Moon's Nodes signify tragic Mars's accident-prone indications between the former President Kennedy, whom I will refer to as JFK, Jacqueline Onassis-Kennedy, and John F. Kennedy, Jr., whom I will call John.

Jacqueline Kennedy's South Node is in exact conjunction to her Scorpio Ascendant. The South Node is fallen in Scorpio, which shows in her private nature, but she never managed to disappear from the public eye throughout her life. Her natal North Node is in Taurus, with a Chiron conjunction. The close orb allows the astrologer to determine her karmic link with many and important relationships in her life; as the Nodes on the Ascendant promises people to remember the personality. With the South Node in Scorpio and her discreet nature, Jackie often covers herself up with a scarf and dark sunglasses. The North

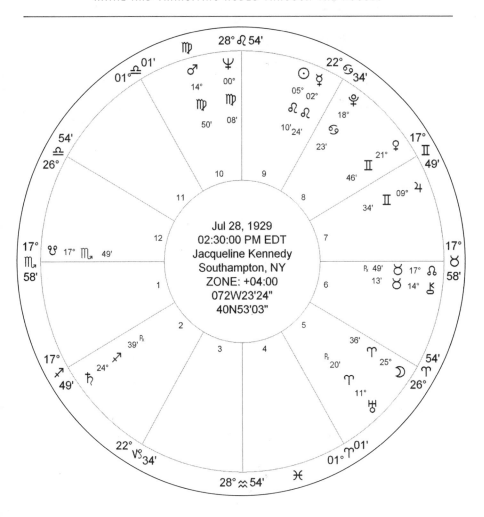

Node continually pulls her out into the public. Jackie is often not able to isolate herself at all. In her subconscious mind, she knows that she causes her feminine power to gain the security that her North Node in Taurus always pulls her toward. Her life itself is always moving toward the Taurus axis, which reflects the patience within her. Chiron conjunct the North Node also forces her to be humiliated in public, only to be able to heal her wounds in private. She has to endure her first husband's extramarital affairs, the death of a child, the death of two husbands, and later to fall in love with a man who is married. She has to be the "other" woman for many years.

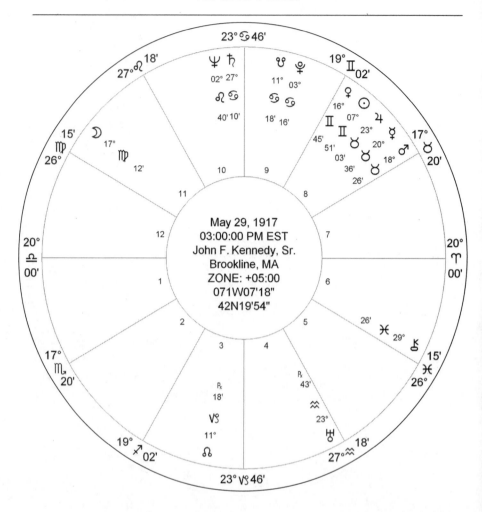

Her natal North Node trine Mars forms a sextile to the South Node in Scorpio. Perhaps the trine made her oblivious to the now well-known infidelity of her husband, or it may have helped her to be able to deal with this knowledge? Being a Leo, and with Mercury in close conjunction to her Sun, she could make her opinion heard. This conjunction also indicates an aspect of developing her sense of identity and ability to speak her own opinion. However, she sought comfort, security, and financial support through her North Node in Taurus.

President John F. Kennedy's natal Nodal Axis is placed in the third/ ninth house. The North Node is in 11° of Capricorn and the South Node falls in Cancer in the ninth house. His North Node forms a Grand Trine

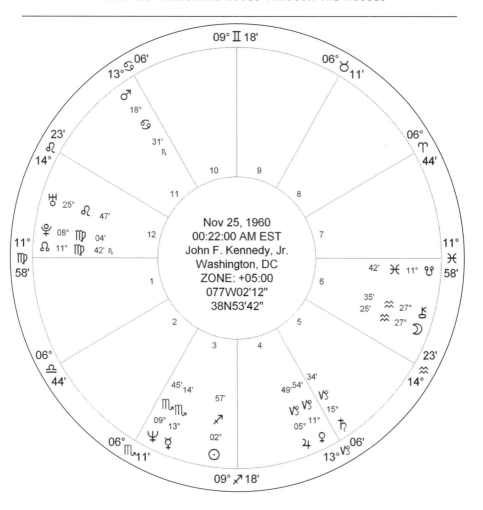

to his Virgo Moon and Mars in Taurus. Often this indicates a person who assumes his emotions are under control. This aspect often forms patterns of nonchalant behavior. A strong sense of sensuality is present with the Mars, Mercury, and Jupiter conjunction in trine to his Virgo Moon. The North Node in Capricorn; and South Node in Cancer, forming a sextile to the earth planets, allows him to reach out with his charm; people wait for him, often mesmerized by the charm of his Sun and Venus in Gemini. A wide conjunction of 8° should be observed as the South Node in Cancer conjunct natal Pluto. What type of communicator will this person become, will he travel often, how will his psychological mind work, and how will he meet his "death" in his life time?

Additional observations: The Planetary Lord of the third house is Sagittarius, and Jupiter falls in the eighth house. The eighth house consists of five planets, Venus and the Sun in Gemini, Jupiter, and Mercury and Mars in Taurus. JFK came from a family of wealth. He was the first President to bring Roman Catholic religion into the White House. Leadership and inspirational speeches gave people faith (an eighth house issue), but also his sexual liaisons outside his marriage became known, again an eighth house issue.

Let's take a look at the synastry between the famous couple. Jacqueline Kennedy's North Node in Taurus conjuncts JFK's Mars, Mercury, and Jupiter. The North Node shows a drive toward the security and comfort President Kennedy gave Jackie. Her love for him is unconditional. Her own life quest to understand her North Node (and Chiron) pulls her toward what he has in his body (Mars), mind (Mercury) and charisma/charm (Jupiter). He has what she is seeking to understand within herself. Her South Node in Scorpio might have offered a few teasing weapons of charm and strength that she used to beguile the President.

JFK's trine of his North Node in Capricorn connects to Jacqueline's natal Earth trine of Mars and her North Node in Taurus. Their physical attraction is strong and their love is destined to be. His Virgo Moon is conjunct her Mars in Virgo. Their appearance and physical attraction is very complimentary. The wife's 17° North Node in Taurus is in a perfect trine to her husband's 17° Virgo Moon. Trines are often "too good to be true" and we only know what we saw on the outside!

Between this dynamic couple there is also a perfect square between his 11° North Node and her 11° Uranus in the fifth house, the square is their unusual public influence and this "perfect" square also makes his South Node in Cancer semisextile to Jacqueline's Mars. Her feminine intuition and her role as the First Lady of the United States of America forced her into a role that she probably never imagined. The semi-square between the South Node and her Mars demanded that she display a faultless picture. Jacqueline did manage to establish a strong, popular image with thousands of women copying her fashionable, yet simple style.

The world will always remember the assassination of President Kennedy on November 22, 1963, 12:30 PM in Dallas, Texas. Shocking and devastating for many people, it was as if time stood still. The media coverage showed the President being shot in slow motion over and over again. At the time of the assassination, the transiting North Node was in a tight conjunction of 00°38" to his natal South Node in Cancer. (Another close aspect was transiting Mercury of 9° in Sagittarius in opposition to the JFK's 7° Gemini Sun.) On November 22nd, the Moon was in Aquarius—at 11°. The midpoint of JFK's Sun and Venus in the eight house is 11°.

Whatever happened that day in Dallas will unfortunately remain a mystery and the source of debate. Astrology and the impact of the Moon's Nodes show that JFK's life met his past and his South Node, as well as moving toward his North Node. The Churning Process was felt as a strong emotional wave throughout the entire world. The world still remembers "John John," the son of President Kennedy, saluting his own father at the funeral.

John F. Kennedy, Jr., has an 11° Virgo Ascendant. The North Node is also 11° conjunct his Ascendant and a Pluto conjunction. The attraction around him, as with his mother, is fundamental. His physical appearance is strong, always well dressed and handsome.

John's North Node is conjunct Pluto within 3° (As we noted, the father's conjunction of South Node/Pluto). This conjunction is in a square to his Gemini Midheaven. Mercury, ruler of both Gemini and Virgo, is involved with John's personal as well as public image. Mars is retrograde in Cancer. A retrograde Mars will often show in dynamic inner struggles for outer achievement and is always very personal. The forceful planet is in opposition to both Saturn and Venus in Capricorn. An opposition from the Capricorn planets to retrograde Mars indicates a person who has a tendency to have emotional flare-ups, which are hidden deep in the psyche of Cancer until they boil over.

The late JFK's North Node in Capricorn was conjunct his son's Venus. There must have been a tremendous impact on John's identity to become someone as great as his father. Needless to say, his father's North Node in Capricorn at 11° forms a trine to John's 11° North Node in Virgo. The tribe continues to connect!

Jacqueline Kennedy's South Node in Scorpio is conjunct John's Mercury/Neptune in Scorpio. He has an inability to make decisions, often requiring that he ask for help in organizing his thoughts. Her North Node/Chiron conjunction is in an opposition to her son's Mercury/ Neptune conjunction. This indicates that she often has to heal through constant confrontation with his confused stages in his pursuits and decisions. She has to be patient, learning ways of clarification as he goes through dilemmas of his life. He was not a great student and there has been speculation that dyslexia was a factor in this.

With a retrograde Mars in Cancer and a mother with Pluto conjunct his Mars, he is frustrated at times. It also indicates a certain control issue that they both have to learn how to work with. There is a significant Nodal trine from Jackie's Taurus North Node to John's Virgo North Node. This shows their karmic connection in a loving way. It proves that they have a mutual respect for one another. His North Node in Virgo conjuncts his mother's Mars. This aspect forces issues of Mars—frustration, anger, and assertiveness—to the front of his chart. Her South Node in Scorpio is in a trine to that position, again showing their karmic link of being honest with each other. Jacqueline's North Node in Taurus trines John's Jupiter, Venus, and Saturn in Capricorn, which reflects their tremendous love, friendship, and strong bond.

On June 19, 1999, John, Jr. was on his way to a wedding with his wife and sister-in-law, flying his own plane from New York City toward Martha's Vineyard, Massachusetts. Even with a recent injury to his foot, nothing would stop John Jr. from flying. He was not used to navigating the newly acquired plane over water at night, and it is thought that "spacial disorientation" resulted fatal pilot error. The plane was found three days later in the cold waters after all hope for survival had vanished.

The chart of the accident, June 19, 1999, 6:30 PM, is when the plane hit the water with a powerful, sudden impact. The Churning of the Ocean with difficult weather hindered the rescue team from recovering the plane quickly. The Moon is in 18° Virgo and conjunct the Midheaven; the emotions of individuals who are observing the search are intense. The transiting North Node is 13° of Leo; is conjunct 13° Venus; lessons of Love. Saturn, 13° in Taurus creates a strong square to the Nodal Axis and Venus; the world is watching as the structure of the plane disappeared. The Sun is placed in Gemini at 28°. Pluto is within 2° of the Ascendant which forms a trine to the North Node/Venus in the eighth house. Mars, the planet of accidents, is placed at 25° Libra.

The Moon was 18° in Virgo conjunct John, Jr's 11° Ascendant. As we know, the Moon moves quickly, but is a crucial clue to the Karmic implication that destiny brings us; the Moon is a perfect tool for timing of events! The Ascendant also ties into a trine to John's natal stellium of Jupiter, Venus\ and Saturn in Capricorn. Mars was 25° in Libra forming a square to Mercury within 4°.

Transiting Moon's Nodal Axis in Leo/Aquarius forms an exact square to John's natal 13° Mercury in Scorpio. More can be found at the time of this tragic accident, such as transiting Saturn in an opposition to the natal Mercury, but here we have observed the impact of the Moon's Nodes and Mars.

If it is true that our family members greet us as we pass through a tunnel and enter a magnificent light—moving on to the other side—can we study those phenomena in the charts of deceased family members? Let's see! Jacqueline Kennedy's chart shows the transiting Moon in Virgo conjunct her natal Mars in Virgo within a 4° orb at the time of her son's death. The Moon was in an exact sextile to her natal Pluto. The Moon in Virgo at the time of her son's death was also in a trine to her North Node in Taurus. It shows their fate of coming together again. However, the transiting Nodal Axis in Leo/Aquarius formed a grand square to Jacqueline's natal Nodal Axis. Their karmically "unexpected" event also linked transiting Jupiter with his mother's natal Moon in -Aries. The mother in the Spirit World greets her son.

Former President Kennedy's chart is also linked to the event of June 19th, 1999. The transiting Virgo Moon was conjunct to the father's Virgo Moon within 1° orb. The essential nature of the Moon coming together with this conjunction shows their bond of nurturing, support, and tribal connections. Transiting Saturn conjunct the father's natal Mars is within a 5° orb. A trine here indicates the unexpected call of the transiting Uranus to the father's Venus in Gemini in an exact 0° orb. The South Node follows within a 3° orb to this trine.

As we close the Kennedy file, we consider the chart of daughter and sister, Caroline Kennedy in relating to the Moon's Node. Caroline has a Mars/North Node conjunction in Scorpio. This indicates her ability to control her emotions (e.g., anger), yet she is continually teaching herself that control. Her Moon in Aquarius falls in the second house with Chiron conjunct the Moon in an opposition to an 11° Uranus in the eighth house. The Moon in Aquarius allows her to detach. Chiron makes her process her Moon and its deepest sense of her personal healing.

The comfort zone of the South Node in Taurus is what Caroline would like for herself and her family, but her North Node in Scorpio is teaching her that she has to heal and reach out for the legacy of the Kennedys to survive. The midpoint of her Mars/Node conjunction is 11° in Scorpio.

It is not my intention to present the Kennedy charts to show that Mars always has to have violence circulating. News anchor Barbara Walters has a South Node in Aries conjunct her Ascendant. She was driven to success at a time when few women entered the journalism field. Her dignity, balance, and manners have taught us how a person can be detached in their work. At times she let her tears show, yet, she has a smile that brings us back to reality.

Natal Moon's Node, Venus and the Second House

**Through understanding the value of money as energy,
I recognize my spiritual being – thus become secure within.**

The second house is most often associated with money. Our sense of value is important when working with the second house. Love for the true Self becomes transformative for individuals with a strong emphasis of one of the Moon's Nodes in the second house. It is rather dangerous to identify our entire existence in terms of the power of money. The impact of how we live and how life is lived to its fullest may comprise an important and a dynamic process. It is immediately useful to look at the Nodal Axis spanned by the second and the eighth houses. We are reminded that the Churning Process occurs within both Nodes being born again and again; hopefully always more wise, appreciative, and enthusiastic for lessons learned.

How can the second house be such an internal (not to mention spiritual) process, when the Moon's Nodes are placed here? It is basic karma that is played out here. Karma is a word that should be used with the utmost respect. Fate and destiny have the same meaning, but karma has a stronger and perhaps more mysterious ring to it. We know there is a certain fate involved in the destiny of being rich or being poor, where we are born, or what school our parents can afford to send us to. Needless to say, the list of conditions ultimately influenced by the financial situation into which we were born is endless.

Numerous charts in my client file have revealed again and again that no matter what the apparent destiny in a person's life may be in relating to money, their involvement and understanding can change it. A chart of a powerful woman indicated to me that she might lose most of her assets during one point of her life. For many years we worked on different cycles, and, at one point, as the economy got worse and her chart went through a Nodal return, she lost a major part of her business, investments, and her home.

When the North Node had completed a transit through the second house, she felt a transformation had occurred. She valued her self-imposed simplicity much more, and she gradually turned her business around. She re-focused her business on those who needed her as much as she needed them. She traded in her expensive car for a more economical one. However, her Karma, fate, and destiny—the Moon's Nodes in her second/eighth house—will always remain there. Now she deeply values that which she gained during the years of hardship—a greater sense of her Self.

With the Nodal Axis in the second and eighth houses, the individual's quest to gain a sense of value of life becomes a therapeutic journey. Life savings can be gone in an instant when a hurricane comes crashing through a home. A serious illness can take away the same security through failing insurance coverage. Millions of people around the world live without health insurance. These are typical second/eighth house issues.

The ability to value what we have created is the most important aspect of this placement. Money is necessary, no doubt about it. Nonetheless, often the individual with a Node placed in the second house is so busy making money they often don't take enough time to enjoy their lives.

The ruler of the second house in the natural zodiac is Venus. Lakshmi is the ruler of Venus in Jyotish. In our Western system, Venus is associated with the good things in life, such as gourmet foods, good clothing, and indulgence in love, but more importantly, it represents value. Having one of the Moon's Nodes falling in the second house contains a fundamental element of risk.

North Node Transiting the Second House or Venus

Self Worth and Financial Evaluation

When the transiting North Node moves into the second house, change in our social status often occurs. This is a time when, depending on the condition of the natal chart, one's life can turn around completely. This is a time when we can lose a partner and become financially insecure. We can also find a partner with whom we become more financially secure by sharing expenses. The condition and circumstances in the individual's life are in a state of new creation. The planetary ruler of the second house, Venus, along with its aspects in the chart as a whole, will show patterns based on the condition of the individual's karmic involvement with money and power.

It is an important time to be careful and not to be lured into emotional situations too hastily when the Nodes are involved. Too often, astrologers identify the Nodes with that "other person that I must have met in the past." Yes, we know that the Nodes can give us clues into past lives, but so do all the other planets. Venus, the planet of Love, can also hide another side of herself. Lakshmi, the goddess representing femininity, can also become obsessive in her desire for Love. A person who seems to move too fast or push too hard should be questioned during this transit.

Friends, especially female friends, play an important role during this time. They show you that they are actually your friends, and give you a sense of belonging. This is a good time to focus on real, valuable relationships. Additionally, when the North Node transits through the second house, it is a favorable time to seek some type of volunteer activity.

South Node Transiting the Second House or Venus

Inventory of achievements

When the South Node or Venus transits through the second house we need to be cautious about many aspects of our lives, especially old issues that re-surface again. In addition, unresolved, insecure emotions are brought out.

As the South Node moves through the second house, matters that have been hidden in our lives often surface unexpectedly. We might not feel rewarded at work. The loss of a parent can occur. This is an ideal time to re-evaluate goals. You might want to take this time to express yourself through an art class, a creative writing workshop, or perhaps even take up knitting. Something that enhances your self-worth and attitude is in order. A good solid financial plan for a year and a half will make the South Node release old, inhibiting patterns from the past.

For those who are more prepared to take calculated risks, observe your chart when the South Node is in transit through the second house, when considering financial moves and speculate perhaps more resolutely.

Your love life can be under pressure as the South Node moves through the second house. It is as if you can't quite understand or grasp it at first, but as you delve deeper and deeper into your inner being, you might find that you don't really understand yourself. "Love your Self" should be the mantra to repeat during the nineteen months when the South Node passes through the second house.

Take up singing lessons or start to chant. Regardless of the level of perfection, we were all born to sing! Singing or chanting is wonderful tools for releasing urges to have your voice heard with this transit.

The planetary ruler of the second house, and its impact on other planets placed in the second house, will indicate how strong the re-evaluation will become. There are many different opportunities for the South Node to truly explore the inner sanctum within our own divinity at this time. It does not cost anything to sit still and listen to our own inner voice.

Let's Rock and Roll!

Growing up I loved to watch Elvis Presley movies, but I hardly listened to his music. It was not until I had the opportunity to study his birth chart that I became fascinated with his life. When I continued this study with a close review of Michael Jackson and Lisa Marie Presley's charts, I became even more intrigued by the threads of connection between Jackson and Elvis. Graceland and Neverland have a lot in common.

Elvis's second house is strong with his Sun in 17° Capricorn. His Sun, Mercury, and Venus form a stellium in the second house. The Moon's North Node is at 1° Aquarius, which conjuncts his Mercury and Venus. His understanding and strong link to money followed him throughout his life. His destiny as a musician was already clear when he was in his early twenties. The lavish style of his home in Graceland can still be admired. Mars in Libra squares his Sun (and adds to the impact

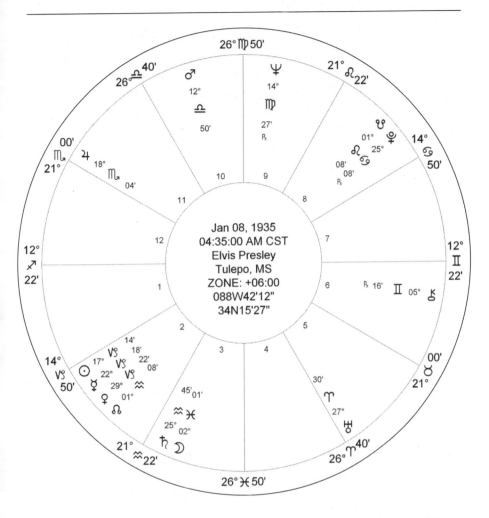

of the Mercury, Venus, North Node conjunction), revealing problems with his way of expressing his extreme paranoia about security and money—along with sexuality.

Elvis Presley had an impressive and exclusive collection of metaphysical books in his library. His glamorous outfits were emblazoned with many mystical symbols; for example, his capes were adorned with astrological glyphs, lightning bolts, the Cabalistic tree of life, ankhs, and images of the Buddha, the Star of David . . .

Toward the end of his life, his obsessive search for the truth made his existence miserable. The second house in Elvis's chart displays the magnitude of what the spiritual value of a life can bring. I was not surprised to know that at an early age he talked to angels. They sang for him. He told his mother about this, who at first spanked him for saying he saw them. Afterward, she regretfully started to cry. Elvis comforted his mother, as he understood that she didn't hear the angels. However, she told him not to tell anyone. They lived in Memphis, Tennessee; down in the fundamentalist South, it was not proper to hear the angels speak to you! But Elvis never forgot. At another point, two guardian angels came to him. Again, he got punished and was put in the closet, but he didn't stop singing.

Elvis has Saturn in Aquarius conjunct his Pisces Moon in the third house. He escaped into the world of music at an early age and later moved on to film. With Pisces being the ruler of the fourth house, and Neptune 2° away from the MC, his chart shows a profoundly Neptunian influence. I do believe that his mother was an alcoholic and that his attachment, his love, and his often over-extended generosity toward her were his ways of denying her substance abuse. He became addicted to prescription drugs. Elvis also developed phobias about people and the friends around him; in fact, he often was so paranoid that he carried a gun.

He married only once, and that was to Priscilla Preston. The marriage lasted five years. They first met when she was fourteen years old. In studying the charts of the connections between the Prestons (and later on Michael Jackson), Priscilla Preston seems to be the one on the outside looking in. Priscilla's birth chart does not have as many links and dynamic aspects as the charts of those around her. Lisa Marie Presley, Elvis's only daughter, was born as the North Node transited his fifth house, the house of children. With regard to her father, it has been noted through interviews with her that, "as she walked up toward him, she could feel an intensity around him and she saw him as a powerful spiritual person."

In 1972, as the North Node was conjunct Elvis's natal Venus, another woman apparently moved into Graceland. Elvis's marriage came to an end as the North Node was transiting his second house. However, if we analyze what has been written about Elvis, it becomes clear that he

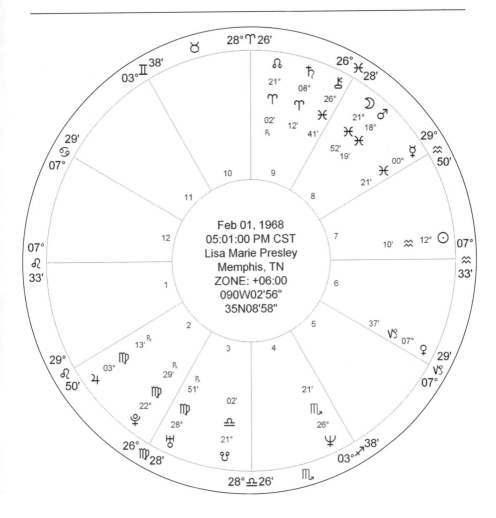

never seemed to embrace life after his divorce. He passed away in August, 1977, five years after being divorced. He was forty-two years old.

Daughter Lisa Marie Presley married the famous singer Michael Jackson, who has a Pisces Moon conjunct her own Pisces Moon. Her natal Moon conjuncts Jackson's Mars in the eighth house; this indicates difficulties with sexuality and power struggles with money. She has Mercury in Pisces as well, and, like her father, has a Neptunian influenced chart. As we recall, Elvis's Moon was in Pisces as well. There is a ten year age difference between Lisa Marie and Michael Jackson, just as there were ten years between her parents.

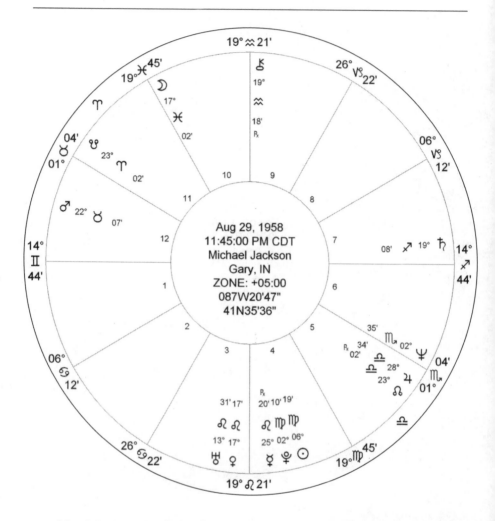

Lisa Marie's North Node is at 21° Aries in the ninth house. Saturn falls in Aries and forms a square to Venus, an aspect defining her difficulties with her relationships. Her Libra South Node pulls her into relationships in which she forgets who she is. However, she becomes aware of the message of the North Node when she is reminded that she has to come first, no matter what the challenge might be. This position often makes it difficult for an individual to be "alone" for too long. Her Piscean influenced chart makes her forget that she has to think about herself, which her guilt-complex personality shows. She is a kind person and gives a lot of herself. Her North Node will eventually prove her own sense of personality, individuality, and confidence, making her successful in her own right.

The daughter meets a man who makes her South Node shake as his North Node conjuncts her own Libra Node within 2°. Her subconscious mind set off a process that perhaps she could not avoid. Her hope that the God Musician (her father) has come back not only into her life, but also into her arms was true. Michael Jackson's North Node is in Libra, which would assure her that he is the one for her. It seems that they needed to explore their inner wounds and karmic links.

With the birth time 11:45 PM, Michael Jackson's Mars is placed in Taurus in the twelfth house. Sooner or later, his Mars square to his natal Venus had to surface in his life. He is a star, and a star can't hide in the closet too long.

Perhaps there are no mistakes in the universe? Perhaps these two famous, obviously wounded celebrities were in need of some healing. Why not from each other? Even if only for twenty months.

When the divorce was announced in January of 1996, the Moon's Nodes were in transit in both charts; a natural cycle with their Nodal axis close together… Public life might not be easy, but they clearly show us their short interaction on a metamorphic level. The transiting North Node was 22° in Libra. Ladies first: This is Lisa Marie's Half Nodal Return, i.e., transiting North Node conjunct natal South Node in Aries (and vice versa). She had made up her mind! And moved on.

Michael's chart, on the other hand, shows a more dynamic interaction in his life. The transiting North Node moved to a close 1° orb of his natal North Node in Libra during January of 1996. As the transiting North Node was conjunct his natal Jupiter as well, his process of purification became everything but that. His life seemed to be squarely in emotional turmoil on many levels. An image of the Churning Process with a divorce and accusations of child molestation (of younger boys visiting Neverland) had the media forcing Michael to face reality. An undisclosed settlement was made and Jackson left his home country for some time.

Did Michael wake up to face, as in his own lyrics, "The man in the mirror"? His Jupiter conjunct his Libra North Node in the fifth house should indicate favorable aspects in relating to creativity as well as children. Jupiter in the fifth house can hide many issues, but it also allows Michael Jackson to heal his own inner child as the North Node pushes his desire for completeness. He certainly proved to be an outstanding musician and a creator in the birth of his three children.

Michael Jackson died by an overdose of prescription drugs on June 23, 2009, 2:26 PM, in Los Angeles, CA. Mr. Jackson was preparing for his come-back after a long absence on live stage. His sold-out concert was to be a phenomenon. The strongest transit at the time of his death is his Chiron return, occurring approximately at 50 years of age. Only he knows how many different lives he touched, allowing creative urges to be explored throughout the world. Now his children will continue his fifth house quest of creativity. A transiting Saturn to natal Moon opposition, often indicating a tendency for a period of depression, was also present in his life during his last months of his life.

Natal Moon's Nodes, Mercury and the Third House

I am honest with the Fears in me as I strive to reach the Highest Confidence

To explore the third house with Mercury as its ruler, we embark on a journey of the mind. The mind is consciousness.

In Greco-Roman myth, Hermes is the Communicator between the unconscious and the conscious. He runs from one world to the other and delivers messages. In Hindu mythology, in the process of individuation of communicative skills, it is Vishnu who is the important communicator. Vishnu-granthi, the knot of Vishnu represents a knot in our throat, or the third Chakra. We communicate with Mercury, yet when the throat is blocked; it prevents a free flow of communication and creativity.

Mercury is the planet closest to the Sun. Therefore the aspects between the North Node and South Node axis and Mercury are important. If a natal chart consists of the hard aspects such as the squares, oppositions, or conjunctions, the individual will be forced to deal with challenging issues of the mind. Often an inhibiting feeling of inferiority needs to be overcome.

Hard aspects to the Nodal Axis indicate an individual who needs his or her challenges to be understood not only by society at large, but also within intimate family dynamics through sibling rivalry. With a strong emphasize of the Moon's Nodes in the third house one can find many clues from the past in relation to the mysterious, delicate, and often confusing aspects of brothers and sisters—and the phenomenon of the never-seen cousins.

Premonition, intuition, or simply being alert are the focal points when the Moon's Node is placed in the third house. If we listen to our inner voice, we can hear the warning signals. Perhaps a nasty argument with a friend (or enemy) gets out of hand. Or maybe we had a premonition the split second before a car accident? We didn't trust what our inner voice was trying to tell us. We might even have a near-death experience, which totally changes the way we see life and circumstances around and within us.. The mind, and indeed the whole body, can freeze when confronted with danger. Alternatively, we may enter a deep transcendental meditative state and get "blissed out, have indescribable visions, or simple enjoy our days in an Enlightened state.

We may go on a shamanic journey and encounter an animal guide and we must trust that the experience will be beneficial. The animal guide can be the same as a teacher or a spiritual master whom we also have to trust. This trust requires preparation. It is as if a voice takes over. We have to be aware of the force of our guides or guardian angels, yet the direction is not always clear. We cannot define where our mind is being taken. It is comparable to a dream state, yet we are not asleep. When the Moon's Nodes operate in the third house in a natal chart, there are many prominent opportunities to develop intuition. Writing, therapy, and/or extended reading usually take on a major role in the individual's life.

Some form of therapy, extended education or devotion to meditation or, on the physical side, forms of martial arts, become important for individuals with a strong Nodal connection in the third house. As frustrating as events can be, it sometimes becomes liberating to cry out in despair to get our true answer. More and more often, the vast ranging wilderness quest is being replaced by the single location vision quest in our apartment in a big city. However, we can still retreat to the forest and the parks. When we train our mind to listen, we can find a quiet, reflective place anywhere.

North Node Transiting the Third House or Mercury

Intellectual development

This is a beneficial period to overcome shyness. It is encouraged to take a communication skills program or class. Training the mind to stay focused through meditation, Hatha yoga, breathing exercise, and contemplation are positive strategies for this challenge.

The North Node in transit to the third house, or Mercury, is a favorable period during which to begin a writing course or a personal journal. Discipline is essential. Many revelations will occur during the

19 months that the North Node transits through the third house. The depth of the mind is tremendous, and this transit allows each individual to move toward his or her fullest potential. Opportunities can come your way without any effort. Someone close to you may become a catalyst for future planning in relating to your community or surroundings.

This is a time to seek out challenges that will benefit career, to forthrightly express personal opinions, and complete unfinished projects. Get back to the books and the knowledge that they contain. The journey of the third house is very enlightening and will clarify many hidden and deep issues. The more disciplined we keep our minds, the more answers we will be given. This is an excellent time to let old habits die, and to set new goals. The stronger, more clear, and more realistic we can be in setting our goals in preparation for the North Node transiting the third house, the more promising the outcome will be.

South Node Transiting the Third House or Mercury

Clarification of mental strength

When the South Node transits through the third house, it is a great time to seek out answers that haven't been clarified, especially when it comes to family secrets. You might seek out a sister or brother for a good talk or to listen to advice, allowing those secrets to surface. When there are no siblings, the journey is still taking place—cousins, therapists, or close friends often interact.

During this transit, it is helpful to start the rewarding study of your family's genealogy. As the South Node transits through the third house or forms an aspect to Mercury, our involvement with other members of our tribe and past lives shows important links to our subconscious desire to be born into our specific family. Individuals leave their subconscious thoughts behind and are able to start new ways of thinking about family members and the community around them.

Re-birthing, past life therapy, or exploration of the past are suggested as the South Node moves through the third house. The placement of the South Node reflects the inner place we don't release until the true feelings, always hiding in the North Node, are integrated. Eliminating and releasing old habits, negative thought-patterns, and those issues that still seem to linger is constructive when the South Node moves through the third house.

Emanuel Swedenborg

Emanuel Swedenborg, a Swedish scientist who was born into a family of Nobles and who held a position at the Royal College of Mines, is most widely known as a medium and mystic. He was born in Stockholm, Sweden, on January 29, 1688 (Old Style—Sweden did not use the Gregorian calendar until 1753). His father was a bishop, which showed Emanuel's Karmic-engineered connection with spirituality.

Philosophy was not accepted or understood, but it seems that with his South Node fallen in the ninth house in Scorpio, Swedenborg was predestined to search for the identity of God and the Soul contained within. Swedenborg would often travel abroad working at different positions within the Royal College, and he would always return to Sweden with new insights and new ideas. His writings seem to grow naturally into a search and understanding of the nature of humanity.

In the process of his writing and research, it seems that his thinking and understanding gradually transformed into mystical experience: "[A] Certain mysterious radiation—I know not whence it springs—that darts through some sacred temple of the brain."

He didn't know or understand his development, but he also did not resist it. The Scorpio South Node has an inherent desire for the transformation and death of old ways of thinking. The process of these metamorphic visions and insights all got written down in an earthly, persistent, and mathematical context through the placement of his exalted North Node in Taurus.

Emanuel had many experiences of Christ, who was the basis of the religion of Sweden. He fulfilled his duties at the College of Mines, but also developed a deep interest in studying the scriptures. The Churning Process in his mind, the third house, started and continued when the Moon's Nodes returned to its natal position during the years to follow.

After a Nodal return in 1744, the Nodes journeyed through his chart accordingly. He wrote many books during this time, too many to

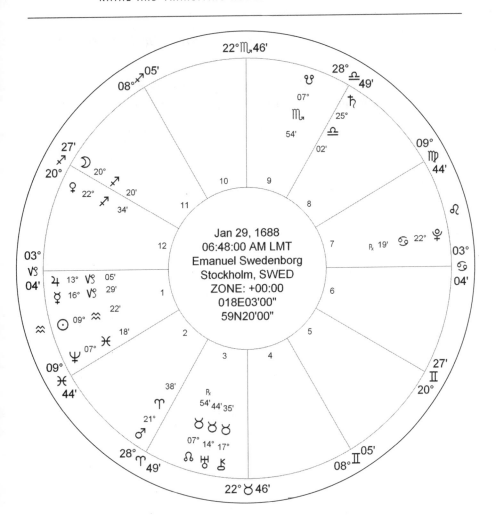

mention here, all reflecting his spiritual quest. He took on the monu-
mental task of re-interpreting the Bible.

At the age of eighty-four, Emanuel Swedenborg passed away when
the transiting South Node moved over his natal Saturn; together with
the liberating Uranus return. Swedenborg left numerous volumes of divine inspiration for our further understanding of his interpretation, of
his visions, and his quest for understanding God. He also extended a
comprehensive search for understanding angels and the subtle mineral
realm.

Natal Moon's Nodes, the Moon, and the Fourth House

In reaching to the deepest part of my Essence,
I merge with the Father, Mother, and the Inner Child

The Moon shows our deepest desires of belonging. This often occurs without our awareness on a daily level. As we start to work with the Moon and its energy, we dance and allow her to show us her movement. We can start to follow the cycles, and we use the New Moon's refreshing, creative, and innovative force to help ourselves blossom when she herself is full-grown in her maturity. In reality, the moon is actually full all of the time, but it is our responsibility to know her rhythm. It is we who go through periods of new, waxing, full, and waning phases, and she only lets us see one side of her fluid-like body from Earth.

The Moon signifies the Soul. The Soul is the desire to connect to the unspoken pulsation of life. It searches within our levels of unconsciousness, showing us the awareness of our mind and our desire for growth. The journey of this consciousness starts at the time of conception with the merging of two individuals.

We are at times unaware of a Soul's desire for growth on our earth level. The progressive shocks of the fact of the pregnancy, the waiting, the growth, the pain, and then the miracle of a child, are awesome. It is also painful to many individuals during this process.

Sometimes the nurturing is not there; the Mother's milk is dried up. She's nowhere to be found. The bundled-up consciousness might have been left on a doorstep and it cries out in despair. Someone finds the bundle and starts to nurture it, but a cruel awakening has already occurred. The Soul loss for such an abandoned child is tremendous; the psyche has lost a part of its essence.

We don't have an instrument (yet!) to determine the Soul loss that might occur within an individual. The impression, the power, of the fourth house has an imprinted cathartic impact on the Soul. The first factor of the Soul is that it is earthbound, here to survive—or not. The aspects between the Moon, the Sun, and the Moon's Nodes come into play as we search for our identity in our home. A home is a home, whether it is a mansion, a house in a suburb, a shed, a small apartment, or an orphanage.

The Soul is searching for the ultimate home within. C. G. Jung made the following statement: "Conscious and unconscious do not make a whole when one of them is suppressed and injured by the other. If they must contend, let it at least be a fair fight with equal rights on both sides. Both are aspects of life." It is our search for the balance within, our ego, and our conscious or unconscious desire for growth, that make us plunge into life.

We may trust what Jung declared about the conscious and unconscious actually being the same, but in the end, he also states, "out of this union emerges new situations and new conscious attitudes." It becomes, he states, "the union of opposites, the transcendent function." It is through healing, meditation, and the stages of a "transcendental" state, that we have the opportunity to become whole again in our Soul. Through the Moon, transits of one of the Moon's Nodes in the fourth house, and our Soul's desire for growth—we gradually remove the blindfold from our eyes, allowing the light of the Soul to become clear.

Yet there is a mysterious "yearning," sparked in the very act of being on this earth to experience wounds or disappointments one after another, and then one healing session after another. The journey of the fourth house becomes endless and timeless. The individual is finally throwing away the safety blanket. We have come to the place of final forgiveness with our parents, or caretakers, talking at the kitchen table freely, laughing about the past and our mistakes. Hopefully!

North Node Transiting the Fourth House, or the Moon

I seek her through my Soul;
I find myself moving with her Rhythm

When the North Node passes through the fourth house or creates an aspect to the Moon, it is rewarding to look at old pictures hidden deep down in the desk drawer. The memories brought up in our conscious mind allow the subconscious a chance to heal. As we bring the pictures out and look at them, a surge of the separation from the past occurs.

The wounds from our birth story and umbilical cord are washed away. Perhaps the cord should never be totally cut, so that we can make sure we connect to the deepest part of our desire to be born. Again and again!

The Hindu trinity of the three gods plays a major role in all houses but especially in the fourth house. Brahma, the creator, is in need of his consort Saraswati to keep educating us in our process of individuation. Vishnu, the Moon's Nodes close connection, shows us how to maintain what we create. He needs Lakshmi by his side for the good fortune we require in our society of constant change. Shiva is the destroyer of that which we create, which will be re-created during another time, another transit! And always by his side is Parvati—life energy and renewal.

Kundalini is the energy that lies latent within every physical body waiting to be purified in the ritual of birth and death. Shiva cannot be without the female energy, which is Shakti. The goddess Parvati represents Shakti, the creative female force. Both Shiva and Shakti are humbly aware of their need of each other. Shiva has no power to create without the female energy of Shakti merged into his total being. Shakti never becomes alive without Shiva. Individuals with a strong fourth house in their natal birth chart or any planet affecting the fourth house (or the Lord of the fourth house activated by a transit of the North Node) will experience significant events. They are often related to family dynamics, but more importantly, the search of the Soul is crucial.

The more pictures that we look at, the more powerful, purifying, lasting, clear, and integrated the healing becomes. Avoiding the power of a North Node transit in the fourth house can have results such as deep depression, isolation, and the inability to be able to live in the world fully. By confronting issues, whether right or wrong, we will move through distorted memories, memory loss, and confusion to a clearer whole person. It will benefit not only tribal members (as in close family relations), but also friends and acquaintances. Our understanding of, and respect for, other family members wounds can be clarified. Perhaps they will not be erased, but they can begin to be pointed out, their importance honored. Many clients of mine have moved back to their family home during this transit. Either coincidence or an illness has forced changes.

During the time when the North Node transits through the fourth house, or transits natal Moon, it is worthwhile to tie up loose business, real estate, and other speculative investments. It is not a favorable time to start expensive moves or projects, because it is uncertain where the journey will end. However, this is a beneficial time to plan a retirement home. It is also generally good to plan for your leisure time now and for the future. When this transit occurs, the reliable financial adviser is answering the person to aid in questions that you might have.

As the Moon's North Node passes through each house for one year and seven months, it is a potent and constructive time to seek out the past. It is a time not to dwell or be stuck in the past, but rather to seek to understand dysfunctional patterns. This is also a time to start to research one's deceased relatives. Many take up the study of their family tree. Their tribal impact unleashes many answers. There is an old saying that sums up the fourth house:

"We can choose our friends, but we can't choose our relatives."

South Node Transiting the Fourth House, or the Moon

Merging with my true Essence

This is the best time to seek out the methods of alternative healing; rebirthing, Soul Retrieval, hypnotherapy, or any method of psychotherapy that will allow bringing blockages from the past into our conscious awareness. The assistance of someone guiding us back into the South Node will be more than beneficial for further understanding and exploring old wounds, as we can't be partial ourselves. Clarification will start to occur as to why we even bother coming back to this earth plane again and again. It is the Soul's desire to eventually become a whole spirit and merge back into the genuine being, the Spirit, the Creator, the God, the Goddess, or the True Self who lives within our Soul. This desire is always there, ready to be re-awakened, to be reborn.

The South Node often lingers in the past, and since the fourth house is the past, it is essential to be aware of depression, gloominess, or melancholy. It is vital to be aware of individuals whom we recognize as putting us down. Keep your guard up and observe the inner Soul for answers.

When the South Node transits the fourth house or the Moon, it is encouraging, advisable, and rewarding to renovate your home. It is good to sort out old piles of papers and put them in order. Half of the piles will be in the trash bin, to be recycled.

During this transit, the opening of the hidden Kundalini, the serpent that lies dormant in the base of our spine, can naturally awaken itself. In the search for a master, a re-birther, a good therapist, or a Shamanic practitioner, we thrive in the surrounding of healing.

The North Node is truly not fully understood until the South Node has been met. That is true in any of the combinations of the Nodal Axis, but it is very true in the transits of the fourth house, a planet affecting the fourth house, or the Lord of the fourth house. The sharp piercing of the fire of Kundalini is a total purification, yet we have to kindle the fire in order to remember the healing that took place. The true master will assist us in this process since the true master lives within our heart. The natural awakening of the Soul's identity with the Self can only occur when the metamorphic experience has occurred.

The wounds from the South Node extend beyond this life. The wounds parents inflict on us can be physical, sexual, verbal, or pure neglect—yet we must not blame . . . . In the process of healing old wounds with our parents, we are forced to recognize our own master, in our own heart, and that is the Soul in its purest form. It is a notion that the Soul is endless from one lifetime to another! The possibility of the wounds starting to manifest again and again in future lives is superbly predictable unless we move away from the outer facts of the wounds, and dissolve them into the immediate process of this lifetime.

The South Node through the fourth house can be experienced as the purification allowing the elixir of life, the Amrita, to flow freely through every vein in us. We salute our own Self eventually!

O. J. Simpson

With a North Node in 0° Gemini, and the South Node in the fourth house, O. J. Simpson had the North transiting through his fourth house as he went through his famous highway car chase in 1994. The world stood still; his inner process did not. His mother was the only one he thought could save him, but I assume it was his money in the end that did. O. J.'s North Node is conjunct his Mars in Gemini, indicating unexpected rages, most likely physical abuse from his childhood.

During his world-famous trial, in which he was accused of murdering his wife, transiting North Node was in water trine to his natal Pisces Moon, as well as his Natal Sun and Mercury in Cancer: not a bad transit if you are trying to get out of a murder sentence. By August of 1994, the transiting North Node was conjunct his natal Jupiter, which enabled Simpson to be released on October 3, 1995. During that year, transiting Jupiter conjunct his South Node in that same fourth house, and the truth was covered up, disordered, manipulated, or paid for in front of the world.

As many people eagerly awaited the outcome of this trial, I was asked if I thought that he would go free. My answer was, "He could very well go free, but he might as well be in jail, because that is how his life will be." There are many morals to this case. If we don't heal that which we have in the fourth house, and/or when the North Node is in transit there, we may be jailed forever, never to explore life to its fullest.

Case closed? Not so! O. J. was acquitted of Nicole Simpson's murder in 1995, but would not go to jail until 2008, when he was convicted of a bribery charge. . . .

• • •

The following individual from my client file, Ted, exemplifies the growth of equality and merging with the Soul essence of the fourth house.

Ted started to dance when he was four years old and did not stop until AIDS struck down his strong and lean body. He knew that he was gay at an early age and never dated women. Born with the North Node in Libra in the fourth house and with the Sun and Venus conjunct the Node, Ted was a perfect example of the fourth house quest for total inner freedom. He and his partner, also a dancer, had a loving and respectful relationship for many years. Acting from an enduring force of commitment, they went to a Native American reservation

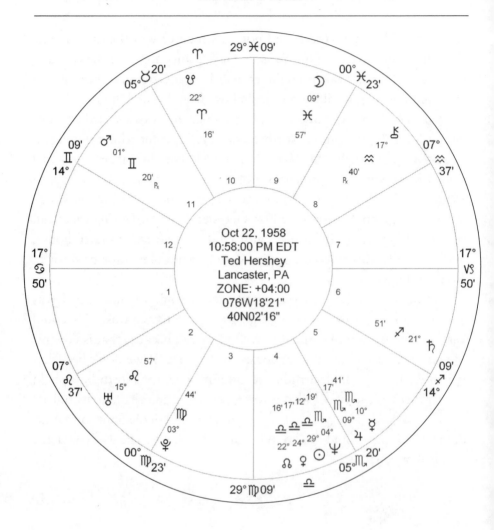

and exchanged rings. After fourteen years together, Ted's partner died of AIDS, and shortly after that, Ted showed signs of the same deadly illness.

During one of our sessions, I noticed that the North Node in Libra had returned to its original birthplace. A Nodal return, with its eighteen and a half year cycle, was a form of liberation for Ted. There had always been tensions between Ted and his father. It was hard for the father to accept Ted's unconventional lifestyle. Nothing stopped Ted from living life the way his fourth house expressed itself. His North

Node showed him that he always had more to learn from his home. Even though there was Love, represented by Venus, Ted's Sun and his identity for his own power and sense of Self is also conjunct the Libra North Node. This indicates a familiar feeling of deepening one's sense of the Soul's desire to be free from the boundaries of others.

On a sunny day, I met with Ted for lunch in a park. He was weak that day, but had his usual smile on his face. His blond hair was still beautiful and we sat down on my blanket. He told me that he was getting married and I said, "You never cease to amaze me. Who is the lucky one?"

Ted was to marry the first woman he had ever been involved with, and he knew he loved her unconditionally. Their commitment to each other was both intimate and spiritual. Ted continued to be free to explore his fourth house—again, another dance. The two married in their backyard with a few close friends present. They were married for three years before Ted left his body. I know that they lived a very full life. His wife protected him, nurtured him, laughed and cried with him.

On many levels, Ted conquered his fourth house and his Nodal Axis. He always showed in his way of living that he was aware of his free Spirit, and he loved everybody unconditionally. No boundaries or limitations!

Natal Moon's Nodes, the Fifth House, and the Sun

**By creating from my Spirit,
I form my goals with maturity,
and continue to play**

The Sun is a powerful influence in our lives and our astrological chart. Often we hear people say, "my energy is low today," or "the energy in the room is heavy," "the energy here is strange," "her energy is high." Energy is the essence of our inner connection to the life force, which is always pulsating within and outside us. It is activated consciousness.

This form of energy is not separate from our inner Being, which can be defined as the God or the Goddess. It is in a constant search to be understood. We have to look at the Sun to start to relate to this "energy." It is from the Sun, our Spirit, that our individuality starts to develop. We can read in many different sources how important it is to identify with the small dot in the circle, which is the astrologer's symbol for the Sun. This glyph usefully represents the energy field of the Spirit, both in unconscious states and conscious awareness. The Sun and its force both within and outside of us have indeed an undeniable power.

To identify the Spirit as it relates to the astrological symbol of the circle and the dot is a tremendous task. The Churning Process is a constant dance of our Universal Consciousness as well as our own process of developing Individual Consciousness. At the present time, the Collective unconscious is developing toward the feminine principles, sometimes addressed with the Western term as Sophia, or wisdom.

Shakti, the female universal energy, is coming to be understood in our conscious mind as the Universal Mother in all of us. We are being reminded of the female universal pulsation of God, which has been seen as a singularly male energy for too long. Our Spirit, represented by both male and female principles combining to make "One Whole Self," is represented by the Sun. When we are open to the enormous "energy" that the Sun infuses our lives with, we become humbly aware of the search for—and identification of—the Self.

North Node Transiting the Fifth House or the Sun

Self development

We associate the Sun and the fifth House with action, moving forward, impulse, power, and strength. When the North Node transits through the fifth house, we are in touch with hidden resources, and a desire to create or speculate on new endeavors. Not everyone will literally create an object such as a work of art, but the individual's subconscious desire to live more creatively and be more content with his or her surroundings will always be prominent. A purification process must be observed on an individual basis. Is the person in question in touch with any creativity? Has the person gotten in touch with his or her own individuality? Or power?

A North Node transit through the fifth house, or to the Sun resonates with the individual's search for the identity of the Spirit. How much self-examination of our power and understanding of our Spirit has been processed? Problems with any type of authority figure, father image, or simply someone who is not acknowledging our potential, causes difficulties during this time. If our resentment of becoming independent—our childlike state of resisting authority figures—becomes apparent, we are stuck with the South Node's willingness to stagnate. When the North Node transits through the fifth house or aspects the Sun, it symbolizes an individual's necessary time to recognize his or her own superior independence and strength. Results from past efforts will now be obvious, and work status and home life will be more complete.

During this transit individuals often speak up about rights and come to terms with their true calling. A true identity and personality will be noticeably more prominent during this transit. The North Node will challenge us to be more humble as well as more powerful in a positive sense.

With an overdeveloped urge for power, when the egoist comes out too strong, this is a time when the karmic pattern of "As ye sow, so shall ye reap" will be obvious and must be addressed. In the case of a person with an overdeveloped ego, those around him or her will hopefully clarify this aspect of the personality. The North Node tends to give us just what we deserve!

South Node Transiting the Fifth House or the Sun

Awareness through depletion of Ego

When the South Node moves through the fifth house or aspects the Sun, there will often be total humility in our life. We will have to confess our inability to access this power we so often want to reach. Laying claim to the power of the Source, god/goddess, or the Creator is a task that can only be achieved through awakening the subconscious memories of our Spirit within. Many people actually cry out loud in despair no matter how great their success has been at this point. A teacher, master, or friend can appear and give us support when the South Node is conjunct the natal Sun.

As the South Node conjuncts the Sun, individuals who have accessed a deeper level of understanding of their Spirit within move into different dimensions in order to clear old karmic debts. The debts will not go without a lesson. Vitality often diminishes during this transit; some individuals can feel totally disconnected from the body. This consciousness can be accessed more directly through meditation or therapy, as well as through any form of healing that the individual needs at the time. Some individuals will leave for meditation retreats or re-birthing seminars or other forms of healing opportunities to work out residual issues more consciously.

A new dimension of the Sun, the Spirit, can manifest depending on the individual's willingness to work on old patterns, no matter how much these might hurt. Letting go and allowing our potential to emerge from our inner source will lead to greater success. Failures in the past are worth looking at or contemplating. It helps to examine the deepest layer of our fears of failure when the South Node transits through the fifth house or transits the Sun.

The South Node in aspect to the Sun can at times be the very picture of the war between the gods and the demons during the Churning Process. Mandara, the primordial Mountain, will always be there, representing strength and our Sun Sign. Our Spirit Guide is watching over our shoulder. We have the ability to overcome and understand our mistakes. The dynamics between the Nodal Axis and other planets in our chart teach us ways to purify our own involvement as a process, rather than something final. The Churning of the Waters does not happen once; the cycles occur many, many times throughout our lives. Through the purification process, the water becomes clearer and the Sun's true identity is uncovered.

Chris: A Case Study – The Dynamic Ties that Bind

The Moon's Nodes do not fall in the fifth house in Chris's birth chart, but they have a direct link to a Sun/Saturn opposition, square the North Node in Libra, South Node in Aries. So the Nodes do not have to be in a house directly in order to have an important impact on that house. This case study is an example of observing the Nodal points during cataclysmic years in an individual's life. Chris is a client who has come to me for annual updates for many years, and in general has a positive outlook on life. Her primary question during her sessions has been, "What will I be when I grow up?" When I first started seeing Chris, she was already a married woman.

Her natal North Node, 8° Libra in the second house, indicates her desire to make her own living and to develop independent security. Her South Node in Aries in the eighth house indicates an inherent knowledge of how to become independent. However, the eighth house often benefits from other's resources. She doesn't understand it consciously, or perhaps she blocks her subconscious memories from past lives as well as her memories from this life. She is in need of her subconscious from the eighth house to acknowledge the Aries in her—i.e., her independent self-reliance—and move the clearing energy into the second house toward her North Node in Libra. Her Libra North Node seeks to be in a creative and harmonious profession, and has a need to be acknowledged. She very appropriately chose to become an art consultant in which she interacts with artists and makes arrangements for their art shows.

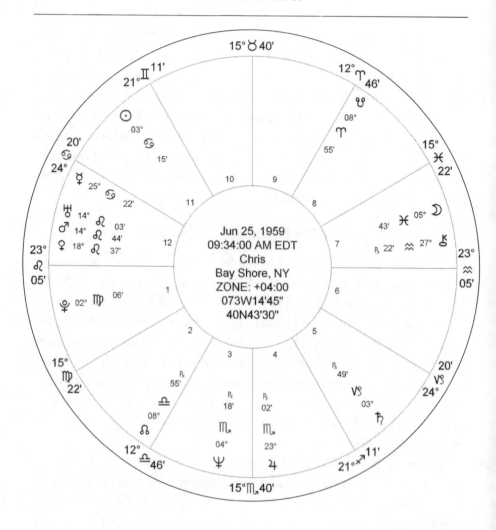

Her natal South Node in the eighth house is square to her Cancer Sun and Saturn in Capricorn. This sets the tone for her lifetime quest: to remember that she, somewhere in another life, "knew" how to be independent, self-assured, strong-willed, and courageous. She has to bring the independence from her subconscious mind into consciousness through her Libra North Node. Will she be able to become aware of her birthright to be independent?

She is surrounded by beautiful artwork and meets many interesting people. Her Cancer Sun in the eleventh house is in opposition to her Capricorn Saturn with a 0° orb. This natal opposition forces her into situations of challenge from her Sun, her own power, against the restricting Saturn which could eventually break barriers within her own structure. Using the Nodal Axis, we see the depth of her karmic attributes with a strong Sun/Saturn opposition enables Chris to fight for her rights, become outspoken but work for a minimal pay—she is an artist trying to make a living. The square gives her the opportunity to manifest the challenging issue of her karmic Nodal Axis: her independence in making it on her own. She manages to get promotions—resulting from the opposition from Saturn to her Sun—a clear statement that she does not give up easily.

Chris's Nodal Axis forms an inconjunct to her natal Pisces Moon; she deals with many people, often drawn to individuals in the arts or music. More intimate relationships causes conflicts at times, but she is aware of healing and growth through them—and perhaps astrology aid her in that quest! She keeps smiling!

Her retrograde Jupiter in Scorpio in the fourth house indicates a well-hidden pattern of control during her childhood. Jupiter in the fourth house can be a deceiving planet, often showing strong abusive tendencies from parents. Of course, no one in the outside world knows about it. The overextended, outward politeness hides deep wounds inside this placement of Jupiter.

In addition, Venus in Leo, squaring Jupiter, enhances her feelings of inferiority. The opposition of Saturn to her Sun is indicative of control issues from her parents; in this case her father drinks too much, and her mother does nothing about it. She comes from a home of poor communication, and her Pisces Moon has hidden her feelings of guilt and personal sadness. She says she feels like "Daddy's little girl."

In 1989, she went through her Saturn Return. Her Saturn in Capricorn is retrograde in the fifth house. She was in a creative field, but not an artist herself; however, the urge to create grew immensely. Even though her marriage was "just there," as she put it, she remained convinced she needed to bring a child into the world as an essential creative act.

I keep Chris aware of the challenges she is to encounter, explaining in lay terms the Saturn structure she will need to break to achieve her goal of becoming pregnant. When the final "no" for a pregnancy came, Chris took the news with a mature saturnine perspective. She didn't break down; instead she devoted herself to her work and began to see fine results in the art field.

Her life continues in this fashion. She continued to come for her yearly update, but early in 1992, I got a sudden phone call in which she told me she had an important matter to discuss. She had met another man and had fallen in love with him. The "good little girl" was upset and wanted to know what to do. Roy (not his real name) is an artist, an unusual individual with an unconventional and dynamic lifestyle. He has seven retrograde planets, which makes him inherently complex. His dynamic chart allows him to express the projection of his dynamic creative personality in unique, even revolutionary ways.

They met in October of 1991 at an art function. At that time, the transiting Capricorn/Cancer Nodal Axis began to square her natal North Node, but was still too great an orb for me to judge it a powerful effect (8°). During that time, transiting Jupiter in Virgo was in opposition to her natal Pisces Moon. This aspect alerted unconscious desires from the Moon to expand an understanding of her hidden feelings. This transit lasted until May of 1992. Jupiter then made a station at 5° of Virgo. During that time, Pluto moved to the conjunction of Chris' natal Jupiter in the fourth house, but was still 5° away from being exact. The Pluto conjunct Jupiter transit would take until October of 1993, when Pluto made a station directly on Jupiter. Many events came to pass around that time.

A transiting South Node in the eleventh house from November of 1990 through April 1992 allowed her subconscious instinct to break patterns from prior lives that had restricted her ability to set goals for herself and to see her full potential with her own resources. Chris remained married, but knew it would end up in a divorce. She got her own apartment as the transiting Capricorn 2° North Node formed a trine to her natal Pluto in Virgo in her first house. This move allowed her to heal the old limitations about her body image and her self-esteem as well.

I consider that Roy, the new love, stands in front of Chris like the image of Shiva. He destroys (Shiva's main function) all of her old feelings of "having to be good." She starts to look at her life and marriage, and feels she was too confined. With Roy, she starts to see much more potential in her life. She is radiant with new insights and power. Chris and Roy start to work on art projects together—he as the artist and she as the coordinator of his work. She also mentions that she feels her creativity blossoming very rapidly.

In another session, in which Chris was concerned about Roy "churning" her life, I mentioned that they would create something together during 1992—and Chris became pregnant! The transiting North Node was moving exactly on her fourth/fifth house cusp, and within 2° orb of her secondary progressed IC. In the next months, the North Node in Sagittarius approached a trine to her Leo conjunction of Uranus/Mars and Venus. She shined throughout her pregnancy, matured, and carried herself with both pride and astonishment.

Looking briefly at the solar arc connection to her natal chart at the time of this extraordinary conception, we find her solar arc Jupiter conjunct transiting North Node in Sagittarius, while the solar arc Aries Moon is in 0° orb to her South Node in the eighth house.

Her subconscious memories of limitation bring out her full potential as a woman, allowing her to be open and free with her feelings, as well as her sexuality (eighth house). This allows her to break the barrier of hidden blocks that not even her Saturn Return in 1989 was decisive enough to break. She devotes herself to life (again, an eighth house matter). She reaches out to the heavens and creates a baby, a fifth house activity, and she releases the issues of the eighth house.

A healthy baby girl was born in October of 1993. It was a natural process. Chris had been observed carefully during the pregnancy due to complications during the Saturn Return. Roy was present at the birth, though he never makes any definite personal commitment to Chris or the baby.

During a casual conversation by a kitchen table, Chris and her nurse friend talk about blood types. Chris realizes that her baby is not Roy's child, but that her estranged husband is the biological father.

Many statements have been made that the Moon's Nodes are mostly about interactions with other people. In principal that is true, but would also apply the symbolic links to our consciousness, since it is still the Self that interacts with others to learn our true identity. In all probability, we utilize our encounter with people as metamorphic experiences disguised as planets, such as Mercury, Mars, and so on, to get to know more about the endless individual we grow to become.

It was actually neither the hero—Roy—nor her husband who manifested her journey, but rather her own desire to overcome a deep quest for breaking barriers of control and becoming personally independent.

An unusual pregnancy gave birth to a baby girl with a strong emphasized eighth house. A recent update from Chris in 2011 finds the father dying suddenly by natural causes, leaving the now 18-year-old daughter a rather large inheritance. The nodal return shows its significant karmic power in the individual's life. The saga continues allowing the Nodal Axis to play its part of integration and understanding, the additional tribal connections becoming prominent and noticeable within family structures.

Natal Moon's Node, Mercury and the Sixth House

With an Open Heart to my Destiny,
My health and work merges as One

When the Moon's Nodes are emphasized in the sixth house, ruled by Mercury, a study of their interaction with other planets will help us understand their role in balancing good health. In the process of finding our Dharma and being content with work from "nine to five," we have to take especially good care of ourselves. If we don't love what we do, our health experience a setback. And at the same time, if we work too hard, it will take an even harder toll on our physical body.

Our blueprint is a constant throb of energy within and without and deeply embedded in our Soul's purpose for growth. The polarities of the sixth and the twelfth houses are always seeking solitude to actualize their healing qualities.

Virgo is the natural ruler of the sixth house, and Mercury is its planetary ruler. When we combine Virgo, with all its methodical preciseness and cleanliness, with Mercury, the planet of how we think, we would expect a "perfect picture." The methodical Virgo often forgets to take basic nutritional supplements. Or else too many! When we are working with the sixth house, we have to stay aware that our bodies are like machines that need constant maintenance. As our bodies grow older, they need different foods, supplements, and workouts. We constantly have to adjust to what Mercury is trying to tell us.

When the Moon's Nodes are placed in the sixth house and are in a strong aspect to Mercury, or the planetary ruler of the sixth house is emphasized, there is a need to evaluate how the individual is living. A weakness becomes strength when we use astrology as a tool for preventing possible illnesses. A high-powered lawyer with four planets in Aquarius (including the Moon's Nodes), and placed in the sixth/twelfth houses, sighed with relief when I explained why he had to have a room of his own to be able to deal with his demanding work, family, and children. The special room he had created was painted bright green, and he kept it locked. It was his room! It was his natural way of re-charging his Aquarian way of being by him Self.

Through the study of the sixth house, the planets there, and the planetary Ruler of the sixth house, we can start to determine a preventive gap or weakness in an individual's constitution. Weakness occurring with the Moon's Nodes placed in this house can often be challenging to diagnose. The following are typical problems when hard aspects are formed to the Nodes—thyroid issues, Multiple Sclerosis, rheumatism, and a weak digestive system are prominent. Unfortunately, insanity and nervous breakdowns are also common. The immune system can be weak.

As the Moon's Nodes can manifest in unusual ways during transits, any individual with either Node in the natal sixth house should make it a lifetime focus to pay attention to their health. The sixth house emphasis, and the Ascendant play an important role in determining health issues; thus, the same rules apply to the Ascendant when one of the Moon's Nodes is placed there. The energy of Virgo, Mercury, and the Moon's Nodes play an interactive role with each other through the sixth house.

North Node Transiting Mercury or the Sixth House

Daily attributes to work and health

When the North Node transits through the sixth house, new opportunities to seek another, or better, position at work can occur. You can receive recognition when you understand your small, yet important role in society at large. For people who have no pressing need to work for financial security, this is the time to seek out an organization that is looking for volunteer help. This transit will also allow us to reach out to help those less fortunate than ourselves.

This period has the ability to integrate our true Dharma, or path, with the regular task at hand of raising a family, being a volunteer, caring for an elder; but most importantly, it can help us become involved with our Whole being. At this time, Seva, or selfless service, can become a catalyst for personal achievements. During the months the North Node moves through the sixth house or aspects Mercury, there is the tendency to be able to fully welcome and embrace life on many levels.

If we meditate, if even only for ten minutes a day, our awareness of the Moon's Nodes and its benefits become more focused.

The purification process is as powerful as it can be painful at times. We will wake up old wounds, because addressing them is necessary for wholeness. With the North Node in transit, we seek to understand what harm we do to ourselves, rather than just remaining in ignorance. We allow the surrounding cataclysmic forces in to our daily lives to effect change.

South Node Transiting the Sixth House, or Mercury

Immortality and wisdom of the ages

Medical astrology is a methodology of analyzing the natal chart for indications of possible illness, and thereby helping to prevent those illnesses from manifesting. With the complementary aids of homeopathy, herbs, medicine, meditation, and any other treatments which might be appropriate, it is up to the expert in the healing field to write the prescription; but with an integrated 21st century approach, the astrologer can aid the client to a healthier existence. When the South Node approaches the sixth house, or a transit to Mercury, it is good to observe and to discuss the individual's awareness of the family medical history as well as their own medical background.

Negative or doubtful individuals tend to focus on bitterness, pettiness, and self-deprecation during this transit. A chant, a self-esteem seminar and/or a visit to a nutritionist are recommended. This can be a time of purging the body through fasting and becoming aware of what might not be good for the digestive system. A nutritionist may be able to help with weight/food issues that the person really knows exists but may not have been able to face. The South Node allows people concretely and constructively to use their mind to set goals. The South Node transit through the sixth house can be the time to reap excellent benefits of improved health in general.

Many health experts say that stress is the most common cause of illness. The South Node is about looking at both the spiritual side of our lives and the many aspects of our daily practical routines. Discipline of the mind improves health and work conditions. As the South Node indicates issues not dealt with in the past, this transit can sometimes bring serious terminal illnesses. With more pervasive illnesses such as Lyme disease, fibroid problems, and the increasing prevalence of cancer, many individuals can become overwhelmed with the forms of treatment available. The South Node can bring unusual diseases to an individual; the nervous system in particular is the most vulnerable when dealing with the transit of the South Node.

Vincent Van Gogh

A powerful example of the catalyst of an individual sharing his creative evolution is found in the life of Vincent Van Gogh. He created nearly 1,000 paintings during his short life of 37 years, and they show his intense quest for expressing who he was.. We will focus our analysis of Van Gogh's chart with attention to the Nodal Axis. The Moon, the South Node, and Jupiter in Sagittarius are within 4° in the sixth house. He brings with him the Soul's purpose of finding some vehicle with which to unleash his deep-rooted desire, passion, and fire.

We often read that Van Gogh suffered from mental illness. Jupiter, the South Node, and the Moon indicate that he became obsessed with whatever he took on. The North Node falls in Gemini in the twelfth house, the house of insanity, asylums' seclusion, and hospitals. The Midheaven of 22° Pisces forms an exact square to the Nodal Axis. Vincent's Mars and Venus in Pisces are significant since they are in square to the North Node in Gemini, as well as to the conjunction in the sixth house of Jupiter, the South Node, and the Moon.

Van Gogh's intense style showed in the violence that erupted among his friends and family. Some speculate that he cut off part of his ear as a sign of remorse resulting from one of his many arguments. Another speculation is that it was somehow intended to mitigate his schizo-phrenic-like symptoms. The cry of the past, evident in the configuration of the South Node, Jupiter, and the Moon, displays the madness that forced him into an asylum.

On July 27th, 1890, only after two days out of the hospital, Van Gogh was fatally shot. Whether accident or suicide, the incident was

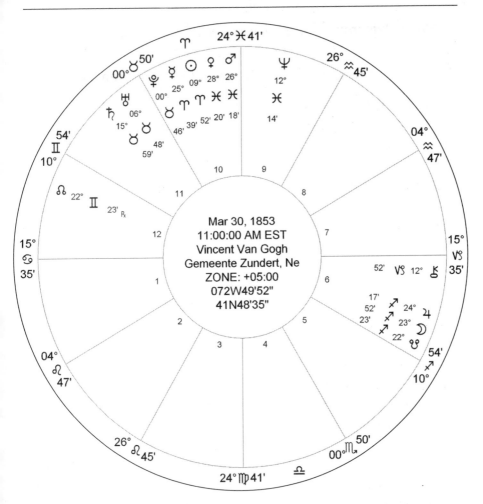

an inner call to end his misery, and occurred during a Nodal return. It was a Soul in despair—deep within him—and always present. Perhaps as it was the appropriate outcome and legacy of his life to have it end just this way; regardless, it was the right path for him. His career as a painter had already produced what he came to show the world. His many self-portraits reveal his desperate eyes, which show us the despair of what his inner being was constantly trying to express on canvas. Van Gogh's brother Theo, who had supported Vincent's intense career, couldn't seem to bear his death and died only six months after Vincent.

Natal Moon's Nodes, Venus and the Seventh House

All Others are but an Instrument to know who I am

In the process of individuation, we come to understand that we are truly on our own during this lifetime. We do have mothers and fathers, brothers and sisters, children, friends, enemies, husbands and wives. However, when one disappoints us, or another one hurts us, we may respond by not speaking or by getting stuck in our feelings. The necessary interactions are often the catalysts that allow us to look at our own issues. Family and friends do care, yet we are still uniquely, individually responsible to become our own true healer. And sometimes not!

A common statement and misconception concerning the Moon's Nodes is that they represent "significant others." This may be! However, a problem occurs when the Moon's Nodes become the scapegoat for our dilemmas of our social involvements. Also, often the Moon's Nodes carry with them the connotation of Karma. This may also be! In a more positive and healthy fashion, we might agree that we actually are using others in order to know who we truly are. In the process of becoming, many individuals are eventually forcing us to confront our own unresolved issues in relating to deceased parents, old friends, and siblings who don't speak to us; as well as all of our ex-husbands, ex-wives and all the other "ex's" in our lives. Again, we are on our own.

In working with the Moon's Nodes in relation to Venus as the planetary ruler of the seventh house, we can truly see how our interaction with people brings out our inner, vulnerable, wounded child. It will continue to be this way until we have learned how to embrace our wounds. We truly have grown mature when we allow our own life to take center stage, and we take responsibility for our own interactions—understanding them to be the "play" of our own consciousness.

Venus, the planet of unconditional love, is often benefic and promising. Represented by Lakshmi, Venus is born out of the Churning of the Waters. She is commonly depicted as beautiful, but through life's hardships, she also represents the "bitch" in us. She can show inhibition and self-doubt as well as a greedy nature. According to ancient myth, Venus courted Mars, the god of War. Venus as the Morning Star was honored as a Goddess of War. Why would she pursue someone with the tendency to fight her? Is it so she can learn the lesson of -unconditional love? On the highest level, Venus represents the ultimate compassion in us.

The Moon's Nodes, Venus, and the seventh house show how we carry unresolved wounds out into the world when interacting with people. Venus, queen of the seventh house, can be the mirror of the first house, Mars or the king. Again, Venus and Mars ultimately married each other. The Male-Mars and the Female-Venus essence in their union will relate intimately through their aspects in our charts. We discover that "Loving Thyself" is ultimate liberation; we find that those around us will accept us just the way we are, unconditionally.

North Node Transiting the Seventh House or Venus

Encounters of Other; versus Self

When we process the transits of the Moon's Node through the seventh house, or its transit to Venus, we often find what we truly deserve. With that in mind, we all have to embark on the knowledge of what the North Node has given us previously. Perhaps it is okay to get married more than once in this fast-paced society that we have created. If we don't learn from the past (i.e., the South Node) we will not realize that we have to work through various relationships to know what we truly want, attract, and can handle. Further, it is not only intimate relationships that can provide the knowledge of the seventh house. More generally, many interactions, with a great variety of people during the time that the North Node transits through the seventh house, can help us recover our knowledge of who we truly are.

Often during this time, we may enter into relationships that are not right. We are hopelessly drawn to a person, even as those close to us are telling us that something isn't right. Often this pull is a resistance in our psyche (the South Node), and we should allow time to be the wise omen during this transit. During the nineteen months that the Moon's North Node passes through the seventh house, gifts of patience and observation we have gained in the past will benefit the future.

This transit can come in the form of a business partnership. In that case, an in-depth analysis of the natal dynamics between the partners involved is important. The Moon's North Node in transit here often gives the lesson about how to adjust to another person. It typically comes with a challenge, but not necessarily a detrimental outcome. Therapy might be the answer and at certain times, especially if challenges occur during a 19-year relationship, a most common cycle in the observation of the Moon's Nodes.

Thus, given the time it takes—when North Node transits through the seventh house, or the North Node to natal Venus—this phase can be the indicator of when the person is ready for a commitment. For example, if the North Node is in a hard aspect to Neptune, this is the right opportunity to listen to the inner voice and allow it to be heard. If the North Node is in a hard aspect to Mars, this is a rewarding time to bring out unresolved issues and clear the air.

South Node Transiting the Seventh House, or Venus

Changes in "karmic" relationships

During the phase of the South Node in transit through the seventh house or to Venus, we have the sense that a separation has occurred inside. We are forced to face the challenge of more deeply love and appreciate our own Self. A different layer of the subconscious memory embedded in our psyche is now released and surges through our entire being. Some might not understand that an individual can actually be content living on his or her own.

We are on our own individualized and often lonely journey, whether we share it with a partner or not. With the transit of the South Node, it is common to be forced by circumstances beyond our control to face the rich immediacy of our own personality. Another person is often the catalyst that pushes us to face the past and our own mythical story. All of us are writing our myth as we live each day. It is thus invariably helpful to keep a journal, not just as an aid in the present but also a record to reflect back on in the future. It is not always an intimate encounter; it is often a friend, co-worker, or family member who spurs us to change.

Often enough, this transit also brings forth a situation that forces us to look at how people see us. A friend can point out to us what needs to be purified or honored in our way of relating. When the South Node transits through the seventh house, there is a natural tendency to blame others. This time is an opportunity for deep growth and maturity through honesty to those around us. Our self-indulgence or self-doubts are forced to be challenged. Thus, with time and honesty, it is an excellent period to grow in a marriage, or close relationship—or get ready for one.

Carl Jung and Sigmund Freud

There are interesting correlations between the charts of C. G. Jung and Sigmund Freud in relation to the seventh house and the Moon's Nodes. Jung began his relationship with Freud as his student; their first meeting was a conversation that lasted thirteen hours. Their friendship is reflected in a South Node and Jupiter conjunction in Libra. They came together because they have been friends in a past life. Their difference of opinion about sexuality and its complexity was eventually what broke them apart.

In the many writings of psychologist C. G. Jung's on the search of the Self, he reveals his discovery of "consciousness." Jung's natal North Node is in Aries, which means that in his lifetime, he sought to find his true Self. He had to reach back to the Libra point of the South Node—others. He would often get stuck in his relationship with his partners; remaining stuck in his South Node rather than moving toward his own Self—the North Node. However, he stayed married for 52 years—with numerous women outside his marriage.

Let us look at Jung's search for spirituality for a moment. It is very clear that Jung had to stay with his clinical research, but as his effort was undertaken, his spiritual search continued. We see his true Spirit in his autobiography, *Memories, Dreams, Reflections*, edited by Aniela Jaffe. It was only with strong resistance, at the ripe age of eighty-one, that he agreed to be honest with himself and wrote, "India affected me like a dream, for I was and remained in search of myself, of the truth peculiar to myself." He avoided all so-called holy men. About this Jung

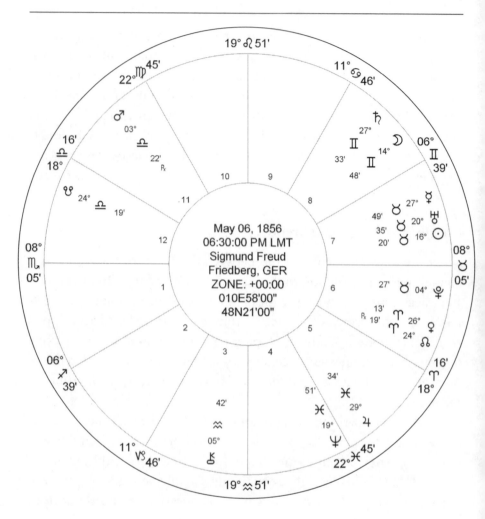

19° ♌ 51'

22° ♍ 45'

11° ♋ 46'

♂ 03°

♎ 22' ℞

16'
♎ 18°

☊ 24° ♎ 19'

10   9

8

11

12

May 06, 1856
06:30:00 PM LMT
Sigmund Freud
Friedberg, GER
ZONE: +00:00
010E58'00"
48N21'00"

7

6

1

2

3   4

5

08°
♏
05'

♃ 27°

♊ 33'

♊ 48'

☽ 14°
♊

06°
♊
39'

49' ♉ 27° ☿
35' ♉ 20° ♅
20' ♉ 16° ☉

27' ♉ 04° ♇

08°
♉
05'

℞ 13°
19' ♈

♈ 26° ♀
24° ☊

16'
♈
18°

06°
♐
39'

42'

♒
05'
⚷

34'

51' ♓
19° ♓ 29°

♃

11° ♑ 46'

♆
22° ♓ 45'

19° ♒ 51'

wrote, "I did so because I had to make do with my own truth, not accept from others what I could not attain on my own."

Jung had to become ill to realize one part of his search for the Self
in a dream, or a vision as he himself calls it. His natal South Node in
the eighth house consists of a natal square to his Venus and Mercury.
Jung has a personal quest to release his understanding of separation and
growth. The eighth house represents many different matters in life—
transformation and death, regeneration, dreams, metamorphic experiences, sex, power, and philosophy. With the South Node placed here,
Jung had a deep desire to bring forth his "past." After a heart attack in

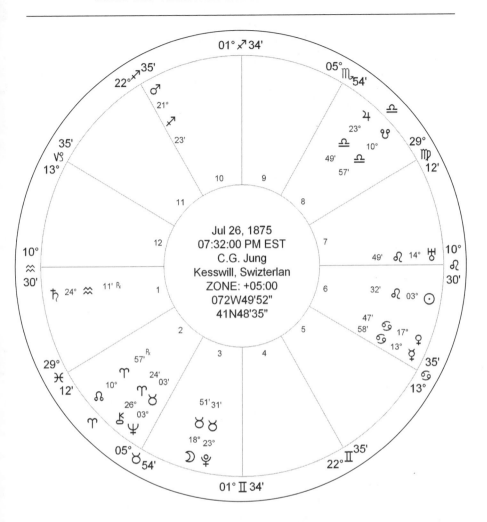

1944, his three-week stay in the hospital forced him into a tremendous period of "purest bliss." Jung claims he was "thronged round with images of all creation." He later said, "It was not a product of imagination. The visions and experiences were utterly real; there was nothing subjective about them. They all had a quality of absolute objectivity."

Jung had an experience of the Self; i.e., he experienced his Moon's Node's true quest. The quest is anchored in the Libra South Node, forcing him to remember his passionate need for people, yet his need to understand his Aries point of his total being, his Whole Self, is equally important. He continued to separate the scientific from the spiritual after his illness. Jung seemed to have connected to a "void" that is often understood as self-realization and an experience of the Self as one.

The images from this life and other lives are all interwoven in the totality of the Self. However, this Self is a Void (as Buddhism defines it)—there is not an Ego to analyze and question. When the Self has been experienced, there is no need to define what it is. It simply is. Buddhism provides the concept that understanding the ultimate of Nirvana is to simply exist without any attempt to harm anyone in our surroundings.

The Spirit in us is always alive. It is a powerful agent of a distant observation throughout our different lives. There is a saying that states:

When the Spirit is ready to take a rest,
It lies down
And the Soul begins its Journey.

The connection between the Sun (Spirit) and the Moon (Soul) is essential for the Ego (the bridge between the two) to manifest its important relative purpose—to bring out the fullest potential in each individual.

Freud has a conjunction of the Sun, Uranus, and Mercury in the seventh house in Taurus. He is a determined individual on many levels. The Planetary ruler of the seventh house is Venus. Venus conjuncts his North Node in Aries and falls in the sixth house; indicates a strong urge to know him thoroughly as he relates to his path of work and duties. The North Node in Aries forms a sextile to Saturn in Gemini, forming a trine to natal South Node in Libra. This allows Freud to grow on many levels. His Saturn in Gemini square natal Jupiter which shows his necessary confrontation with his own student. Neptune in Pisces square Freud's natal Gemini Moon with links to his subconscious. This aspect also signifies illusion about women, thus sexuality. Both Freud and Jung analyze patient's dreams in detail; dreams are an eighth house issue. They are both involved in exploring their own dreams as well.

C.G. Jung's Sun in Leo falls in the sixth house, with Uranus in the seventh house; this indicates a combination that makes him dynamic and important, as it represents his individuality, and Uranus indicates his unique character. The Leo Sun/Uranus trine his Aries North Node—assuring his independent thinking. The South Node forms a sextile to the Leo energy—his many interactions with women were public knowledge.

The Nodal Axis, Aries/Libra, forms a square to a Mercury/Venus conjunction in Cancer. This aspect indicates challenges in the development of personal security and being able to communicate what one truly wants to express. He became a writer, astrologer, and professor but he is most famous for his contribution in the development of analytical psychiatry and the link of personal to collective unconsciousness. Jung's natal Mars in Sagittarius is trine his natal Chiron in Aries—a sign of the continuing healing of analytical psychiatry through his famous work.

And now to the Synastry of the two charts!

This is where the Nodes and the seventh house influence come into play. Both men have North Node in Aries, and South Node in Libra. This is a first house/seventh house Nodal Axis. So in this example we are not looking at a transit through the seventh house, bur rather how the nodal placement in the seventh house "flavors" the relationship between these two men, the issues of "Other" vs "Self."

A South Node conjunct Jupiter indicates a friendship from the past. Jung and Freud have an exact 1° Jupiter and South Node conjunction in Libra. Freud's Sun conjunct his Taurus Moon controls the student, Carl. Clearly, Jung's honest Soul will also teach the stubborn Freud a few lessons. The teacher's Moon in Gemini is in an opposition to the challenging student's Mars in Sagittarius. Jung probably made Freud nervous at times because the Moon in Gemini is often changeable and mentally challenging in nature.

With Jung's Mars in Sagittarius, trine Freud's North Node, debates and aggressive opinions would be the norm. In addition, Freud's North Node-Venus conjunction with Jung's Mars in Sagittarius indicates that Jung forces Freud, on some level, to trust his process of believing in himself.

Jung found himself utterly surprised about the "prudish" sexual opinions expressed by Freud. These personal, intimate planets—Venus and Mars—are important in the comparison of these two brilliant psychiatrists. Does it mean that they had some sexual or intimate relationship from a past life? No writing has indicated that... What we do know from this conjunction is that they had issues to work out in relating to sexuality, anger, and frustration. And their results are still carried out in many therapist offices

There was also love and healing involved in this relationship. Freud's North Node conjuncts Jung's Chiron exactly within a 0° orb, an aspect showing the deep healing that occurs. In addition, Freud's Aries North Node is in a 2° orb to that same Chiron; thus, there must have transpired tremendous healing for Jung in this relationship. Jung was taught how to trust himself, as well as in his spirit guide, Daimon—as he described this support. He broke away from a friend who in fact taught him to take responsibility for his own actions. This shows in Jung's Saturn in Aquarius in a trine to Freud's Saturn in Gemini, which connects to the South Node in Libra.

Even though not a conjunction of Jung's and Freud's North Node in Aries and South Node in Libra, the foundation of the Zodiac signs are imperative to consider. Jyotish does not incorporate degrees but rather incorporates whole sign Zodiac system.

The North Nodes simple, yet magnificent, purpose is to aid the individual in finding his or her true Self. The South Node implies that the only way that one can even attempt to find that true Self is through interactions with others. Even though not in a tight orb, Freud's and Jung's Soul Essence and purpose become the same. Other points between their charts—especially our focus here, the Nodes—indicate many personal issues that became public. And in that, they both taught thousands of people to listen to their dreams and look at synchronicity in their lives.

And who was it that said, "As the Teacher teaches the Student, the Student becomes the Teacher"?

Natal Moon's Node, Pluto and the Eighth House

I allow my Life to be lived Unconditionally to the Fullest

In studying the eighth house, we will see many of the innermost layers of life and their accompanying challenges. Traditionally, the eighth house represents practical phenomena such as other people's money, inheritances, escrows, insurance, pension funds, and retirement funds.

The eighth house rules abortion, vasectomies, and prostitution as well as birth control. The impact that sex, the domain of the eighth house, has in our society today is unquestionable. The powerful impact that the life force itself has on our subconscious is revealed as direct and prominent when we observe the eighth house. This house also rules our dreams—we are just as alive when we are asleep.

The power of how we live life fully should be understood when working with the eighth house and the connection between Pluto and the Moon's Nodes. The fourth, eighth, and twelfth houses reflect the Spirit's growth at different stages. The eighth house is a yearning for a metamorphic challenge of "birth" and "death."

As astrologers have worked with this dynamic "planet" for over seventy years now, we have come to understand its dark side as well as its forceful capacity to help us see the light at the end of the tunnel. In its evolutionary and transformative structure, one hopeful message for the North Node placed in the eight house, and its Plutonic influence is to remember that we are alive every day that we wake up.

A typical scenario of the Plutonic manifestation is to hide wounds, pain, and secrets. The polarity between Taurus, security, and Scorpio, losses validates the transitional stages of the eighth house. Large bank accounts that hide one's sense of loss have often come to individuals through manipulation, corruption, and lies. However, there always exists the possibility for an abrupt, spiritual break from such patterns: also an eighth house issue.

Rahu, the North Node, is fallen, or debilitated in the eighth house with its corrupted connotation of manipulation. Ketu, the South Node, is exalted in the eighth house, and we understand its rulership when the eighth house is fully manifested in life and its beauty contained within the challenges people take while living on earth.

With a strong emphasis of the eighth house or with the placement of the Nodal Axis here, any type of a separation, especially divorce, sexual abuse, or the early death of a parent, is similar to a physical death. They may have lost their feeling of belonging as the parents went through the divorce; or such a sense of loss can even be a loss of faith in life and its challenges.

The eighth house rules the sensitive and exploited part of lovemaking: often referred to as "sex." Love making is part of life, but sex is necessary for procreation. It is a most fundamental matter of Life and Death. Many ages, not only in the society we live now, have had complex issues with sexuality. The concern of sexual abuse is also an eighth house issue, and examining this house can often be a fine-tuning tool to determine if in fact there has been sexual abuse. An abandonment issue (loss of a parent) often leads to various emotional problems. Regardless of whether it manifests as a sexual issue, a soul loss has occurred. The Soul has been raped and deprived of its security to live. In working with a client or studying the impact of this powerful house, it is important to follow the rule of being the astrologer and not the therapist.

Edgar Cayce

Mr. Cayce, a trance medium who recorded 14,000 "reading sessions," has Venus, Saturn, Mercury, and the North Node in Pisces in the eighth house. His Pisces Sun is placed in the ninth house.

With the stellium of these three planets and the North Node, his true calling was placed in the eighth house, the exalted house for the North Node. The planets here allowed him to move on to the realms of the "other side." At the age of six, he had displayed his psychic abilities—to his parent's dismay. Later he became a devoted father, yet often failed to provide financially for his children. At one point in his life, his family had to ask other relatives to help them due to Mr. Cayce's inability to support them financially.

Cayce's North Node in Pisces with the other planets in the same sign indicates an unusual desire for the ultimate religious experience to

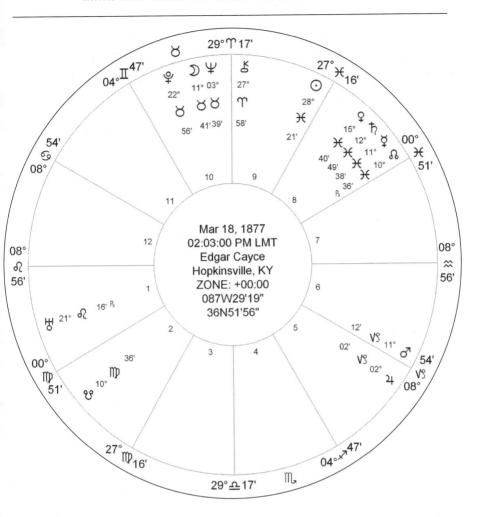

be realized through helping others. At his death on January 3, 1945, transiting Saturn and the North Node were both in a trine to the natal Pisces planets. This allowed his Soul to be free again.

North Node Transiting the Eighth House or Pluto

Separation of life's process

The North Node transiting through the eighth house or in aspect to Pluto is one of the dynamic moments in life that we don't forget. A 5° orb as the Moon's Nodes approach Pluto is one way to fully be prepared, but as the transit closes in, the 1° orb is noticed in force.

Just as Pluto is a planet of transformation, the Moon's North Node embodies the stability that we might seek within us. This period allows us to see what we have accomplished, as that stability can crumble in front of our eyes. Securing our future for unexpected events, which indeed always seem to happen, makes us feel that we reach out to the possibility of manifesting through the North Node. This is fine time to apply for a loan or rearrange insurance policies for the future.

As the North Node is transiting the eighth house, there is a subtle—if desired—time of healing the deepest wounds. When we work with the eighth house, we should respectfully keep Mars—the traditional ruler of the eight house—in the back of our minds. No matter what system we apply, or what works in natal and transit work, we can't ignore the release of energy from the body. If we consider the traditional interpretation of Mars as a planet of anger, we are now allowed to follow the awareness of that dynamic energy even further to Pluto, to fully embrace life and not just be angry. With Pluto, we have the responsibility to ourselves to move beyond the anger and feel the very essence of our anger transformed into love and zeal for life.

The potential healing that the North Node brings as it transits through the eighth house can be an important time for many individuals. One example is a client who sought out relationships in dangerous ways by going to bars that she otherwise wouldn't patronize. She allowed herself to dance all night long without inhibition or any forethought about who she might sleep with during the night. The client had become weary of being in therapy for incest survival issues, and began a release of revenge as she became aware of a dark side within her being. Thus, her dance became her own metaphor for the North Node transit. The final healing was when she met a man at a work-related conference, with whom she felt nurtured and safe enough to date on a regular basis.

South Node Transiting the Eighth House or Pluto

Metamorphic confrontations and release of past

As the South Node is transiting through the eighth house, or is in aspect to Pluto, we have to approach the transit with an aura of protection.

This is a time to be careful with unresolved legal matters, from being audited by the I.R.S., to standing up for our own right in the court-room. During the nineteen months that this transit takes, make sure to keep good records of accounting matters. This is not a good time to overspend. There is a possibility of bankruptcy. The South Node seems to catch up to those who have not been cautious in the past. If you owe money to any of your friends or enemies, make sure to pay off the debt before this transit comes into orb.

During this transit, the world of dreams can naturally become more prominent and understood on a different level than before. It is valu-able to keep a journal and observe the changes and transitional stages that the eighth house brings. We become our own therapist. A major rebirth in life—one that can only be determined by our eagerness or willingness to participate in life and accept its many challenges—may genuinely waiting to take place.

Sometimes we have to lose initially in order to gain a tangible un-derstanding of our purpose in life. By losing someone close to us, we might gain an inheritance (an eighth house issue), yet the loss of the loved one will always, should always, stay with us on some level. What we gain in this process will be measured by our understanding of our birth and death process that occurs every day. If we don't integrate it thoroughly, our regular births and dependable death (the "final" death this time around) become devastating facts. We have to embrace life every day, and in doing so prepare for our own death every day.

Recently, I had to put my understanding of Pluto in the eighth house into practice when my friend Phil passed away suddenly. We were friends through our astrology group and meditation practice. We had a lot in common, and the richness of Phil's horoscope could inspire me to write many pages, but for the sake of focusing on the Moon's Nodes and the eighth house with its Plutonic influence, I will keep this as con-cise as I can.

His deeply Scorpion qualities influenced his strongly occupied fifth house, which made him deeply responsible toward his only son. Phil did not like his own chart. He especially disliked his stellium of Venus, Sun, Mercury, and Mars in Scorpio in the fifth house. His Taurus Moon in

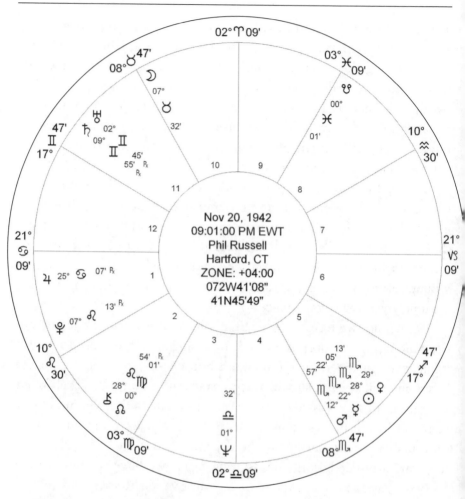

Nov 20, 1942
09:01:00 PM EWT
Phil Russell
Hartford, CT
ZONE: +04:00
072W41'08"
41N45'49"

opposition to his Mars made him stubborn, and he was aware of it. He was handsome, and a warm person to be around. His Cancer Ascendant with Jupiter conjunct within 4° made him well liked, especially by women. Jupiter is in a good trine to his Scorpio planets, and, as he once said, "that is the only good thing going for me."

With his South Node in the eighth house, he often complained he never had money to do what he wanted. His North Node and Chiron conjunct in the second house in Virgo reflected his ongoing discontent with his finances.

In late summer of 2000, Phil called me and we talked about why he hadn't felt good the last few years. There was a slow-growing tumor on the left side of his brain. It was not cancerous, and his physician gave him great hope that all would be well. The operation went well. After the operation, an X-ray was done, showing no evidence of the tumor remaining. However, Phil, who had laughed and spoken just after the operation, fell into a coma half an hour after an X-ray had been performed. For a month, his best friend, his son, and his sisters came and went.

I became an instrument of healing for his family and friends. He had a lot of support from others as well. As I studied his chart, sat by his side, journeyed, meditated, chanted, and cried for him, I also processed a lot of despair about the remarkable accuracy of astrology. As Jupiter and Saturn approached his natal Uranus/Saturn conjunction, preparing Phil for a second Saturn return, Pluto opposed Saturn; a three year duration. I knew his chances of a full recovery were very slim. The Leo/Aquarius New Moon eclipse on July 31, 2000 was conjunct Phil's natal Jupiter and squared his natal Scorpio planets. The Leo Sun was conjunct natal Pluto. Some prepare for Saturn to return to its original birthplace and are known to "take" people to the other side, some don't make it—many do!

His body was too weak to fight it, and his family decided to help Phil cross over to the other side. One hospital staff member praised the family for their right decision. Phil would have said—as he would often state in his blunt Scorpion fashion—"life stinks."

In sharing a personal experience, I hope that the Moon's Nodes' involvement in Phil's last month will clarify the work in Nodal transits. The presence of the Moon's Nodes with other planets can, over time, be clearly noticed. What are we looking for? We are looking for signs that will enable us to connect to sources of positive and healthy ways of understanding both birth and death as a process of embracing life.

Natal Moon's Nodes, Jupiter and the Ninth House

I pay attention to my Guides,
and Teachers, As we merge as One

There are two sides to every planet; they could be defined as male/female, positive/negative, hot/cold, or beneficial/detrimental. Through observation, Jupiter is often found to hide many unspoken wounds, surprises, and family secrets. Many individuals are able to hide the wounds connected with Jupiter even as they present a perfect appearance to the outside world. When we work with the Moon's Nodes and Jupiter, we have another tool in supporting our astrological knowledge—the Moon's Nodes help to clarify Jupiter's role as a positive model for future growth. As the layers of Jupiter are uncovered, clients are able to share their deep-seated hidden inner pain and story.

Jupiter is the planet that represents the Guru in the Hindu religion and philosophy. According to George Feuerstein's Encyclopedic Dictionary of Yoga, Guru's core meaning is as follows: "The syllable *gu* [signifies] darkness; the syllable *ru* [signifies] the destroyer of that [darkness]. By reason of [his power] to destroy darkness, he is called guru." Since ancient times, the disciple sat by the teacher's feet and listened. So it is that today, we need a teacher in order to learn how to drive a car as well as to learn astrology, how to meditate and become conscious on levels that benefit us.

Sagittarius, the Archer, which Jupiter rules, is not shooting anybody, but rather simply looking for more knowledge. Individuals who have the Nodes placed in the ninth house have a prominent desire for knowledge. The Archer with his bow and arrow has the ability to reach unlimited heights of growth. The ninth house represents higher education, philosophy, psychology, metaphysics, astral travel, and foreign countries. Clairvoyants and mediums often have a strong ninth house influence.

With the influence of Jupiter and the Moon's Nodes in the ninth house, we also seek religion, rabbis or preachers, religious ceremonies, and visions. We also find that this house rules chapels, churches, and synagogues as well as temples of all kinds. Indeed, there is a lot to worship and celebrate in life. No matter where we turn our attention, there is a time when we have to allow the higher mind to lead us out of the therapy room to create a sacred event rather than one marked by problems.

Jupiter, the planet and symbol of consciousness, brings us to new heights of awareness. When we study our basic information on the houses, we find numerous clues as to the importance of the Moon's Nodes in a natal chart, or in transits that are significant. The Nodal Axis in the ninth house—or in relation to a powerful Jupiter via strong aspects—shows us new directions and how to move forward in life. (It is a rather short one, after all!) With the trilogy of the three gods, Brahma, Vishnu, and Shiva, we understand that Brahma creates our thought patterns, Vishnu shows us how to maintain our dignity, and Shiva forces us to change our path of accepted wisdom through new adventures.

North Node Transiting the Ninth House, or Jupiter

Breakthrough in consciousness; new levels of awareness

When the Moon's North Node is in transit through the ninth house or in aspect to Jupiter, there is a breakthrough in awareness. Clients who have been in therapy for a lengthy time will find their own answers. It is a time when the therapy room can become stagnant, and other healing modalities are possible. It is an opportunity to ask the therapist for other ways of breaking through old issues.

The year and seven months that the North Node is passing through the ninth house presents us with an excellent opportunity to take up personal writing and explore our own awareness. A need to explore other parts of our psyche becomes prominent. If you have had a longing to make a pilgrimage, this is a beneficial time to finally undertake that journey. It can be a life-altering event. Observe all living things around you. Many answers will be found in the wisdom contained in the North Node. As is often the case, you just have to ask.

This is a beneficial time to start a committed meditation practice. If that is a bit challenging at first, begin with a creative visualization tape, join a meditation group, or simply sit in a quiet space and observe your own thought processes. This is a time when a new teacher might come into your life. It can also be a time during which you find a new life path that you are comfortable with. Prayers just might be heard.

Jupiter can overextend its growth toward the potential for fanaticism. For individuals who have come to a point in their lives where they have been overwhelmed in their search for the Ultimate, this is a time to become grounded and walk in nature. The North Node is, among other things, the future. Jupiter will show many signs for the next phase of evolution in the soul of the wise woman or man. An old wise man said, "We are not supposed to know it all." This is a good time to simplify, look firmly, and clarify the Shakti, chi, life force, or presence of nature around and within us.

For people with a strong natal ninth house, the North Node in transit here will inspire an academic degree. Often there is no end to the quest for learning in the ninth house. This transit can also aid in making the decision to go back to school or to finish up what hasn't been completed earlier. Often laying a good solid foundation for a new expression of identity can lead to great success as the North Node moves into the ninth house or in transit to Jupiter. The completion of projects, beginning of new endeavors, starting your personal biography, and the sorting out of thoughts in your mind will lead to productive results during this transit.

Long-standing, unresolved issues involving lawsuits can have beneficial results during this transit. During this transit of the North Node through the ninth house, you may specifically want to pursue your own necessary lawsuit, if it is justified and you are in need of it. Divorce cases are often prominent during this time.

South Node Transiting the Ninth house or Jupiter

Trusting the Higher Self

The South Node represents that which we like to hold onto, or never totally give up because of the reassurance it gives us. However, the maturity and surrendering toward the North Node is necessary. Through the transit of the South Node we can be forced—at times clearly confronted—by a friend or a family member to face consequences of the past. It can be a word, a statement, or a long overdue argument that will force that which has been hidden out into the open. And that can hurt!

It can also be the time where we find tremendous hidden talents, and also understand why we might have been drawn to a certain culture, era, race or religion. We might draw from our own talent, and Jupiter allows us to explore, search, and grow with territories that are new, yet still familiar within our subconscious.

When the South Node moves through the ninth house or creates a hard aspect to Jupiter, the possibility of a lawsuit or legal matters from the past may surface.

During this time it is important to be aware of our general mental health. The process built into the South Node can readily sneak into the mind and body. Jupiter can make us optimistic, but Jupiter's – and the North Node's pull can be excessive in nature, and cloud our vision.

When the South Node moves into the ninth house, it is a powerful and rewarding time to seek out a counselor for unresolved issues. Understandings or separations occur with siblings, or close friends; misunderstandings in family dynamics occur. A shamanic practitioner, an alternative therapist who works with past lives, or someone in general who can assist in breaking old barriers can be helpful. A loyal friend can also be the right person to confide in at this point. The South Node represents not only issues from our past in this life, but our past in other lives. With attention and focus, we will be able to access subconscious layers in significant and dynamic ways.

Aleister Crowley

Pisces rules the ninth house of the famous writer and occultist Aleister Crowley, and his Moon in Pisces is located there. His North Node in 8° Aries falls in the ninth house as well. Crowley traveled on many different levels. He wrote, traveled extensively, and became dependent on cocaine in his search to understand his dynamic, and rather complex, mind. His North Node in Aries is within a 1° orb inconjunct (quincunx) to Jupiter and Mercury in Scorpio in the fourth house. This inconjunction from the ninth to the fourth houses indicates constant psychological adjustments to major issues in his family. The fourth house has the Sun and Venus in Libra—signifying a Spirit's desire for wholeness and perfect condition. The inconjunct of the North Node in Aries from the ninth house also affected his Mercury in Scorpio within a 6° orb. Extreme manipulation and control during his childhood are issues Crowley had to work through.

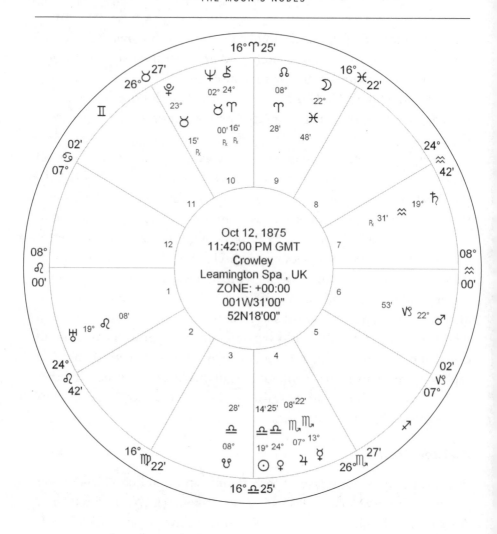

Because he inherited a large sum of money, he did what people did in those times—he traveled. His ninth house and his quest for something more became obvious during his lifetime. Crowley became further involved with black magic and was also accused of using his power to attract young boys into his study. The ninth house rules "astral travel." The complex link between the ninth house and the fourth house shows his perverted personality, yet simultaneously, the brilliant conquest of his work through Alchemy, and his still popular Thoth Tarot deck.

Natal Moon's Nodes, Saturn and the Tenth House

My Spirit is the force of my success

As we experience life and make progress on the path toward individuation, we need to break free from old patterns of control and intimidation. The Nodal Axis, when placed in the tenth house, gives us the opportunity to break through stagnation, resistance, and dependence on others. Our birthright and desire to live on this earth plane in a new century is to capture Saturn and incorporate its dynamic force into our whole life, down to our bones—our structure. The ultimate therapeutic process is not to blame anybody. Not even ourselves. And "that ain't easy"...

We will not have the success in life that we all so well deserve until the South Node, with its tendency to hold us back, reaches out to the North Node. The feeling of being stuck in Saturn, even when we try our hardest, connects with the Nodal Axis' of taking steps backwards – as we are teaching the forward steps. Observing! However, it takes a mature individual to confess the value of Saturn, the ruler of the tenth house, as a true teacher.

When the Nodal Axis, with Saturn as the foundation, is placed in the tenth house, our ability to stay focused on goals, success, and self-respect becomes extremely important, if not crucial. We have to assure our parents or those who took care of us that they did the best they could. In a society focused on self-help, we are coming to terms with new methods of healing.

The Moon's Node placed in the tenth house or in transit to the tenth house becomes free as a liberated Soul. And what does it mean to be a liberated Soul? It means that in all circumstances, the individual has reached a state of equilibrium and will allow challenges, as well as rewards, to be integrated into his or her life rather than become separated from the Self and merely observe external events. Looking within gives us many answers!

The Moon's Node in the tenth house may represent a good marriage or relationship, and a solid social status in general. The Moon's Nodal Axis placed here gives any person who feels marginalized by society—

whether through race, class, gender, disability, or religion—the possibility to be accepted in society for what we truly can accomplish in this new century.

The Moon's Nodes are not planets of substance, but rather important points that are crossing the plane of the ecliptic. The Midheaven, the southern highest point of our chart, versus the Nadir, the lowest point below the earth, along with the Ascendant/Descendant, is vulnerable points in relating to the Moon's Nodal Axis.

The Nadir, the fourth house axis, is the innermost cry of the Soul reaching out toward the tenth house. The tenth house represents our personal reputation and our social status—how the world views us. Our physical mask, behind which we hide what is hidden in our birth chart, is the Ascendant. This imperative axis becomes integrated with our Moon's Nodes as they are processed in our Soul's desire to be born.

Through the Soma, the elixir of immortality, we are only here for a split second of eternity. We might as well enjoy it! In many tribal societies, the Ayahuasca plant is used by the Shaman to enter an altered state of consciousness during rituals. The purpose of this ritual is for a healing to occur. The Shaman has to experience "death" before being able to access the many levels of consciousness. He or she has to become initiated, often alone in the wilderness. However, the modern integrated alternative Meditation Retreats are also beneficial in achieving this initiation. The Soma that many people seek may also be accessed through the workings of the Moon's Nodes and the growth they bring naturally. Our growth consists of dying as we become more alive. Our quest is to move beyond our limited understanding of the true healing within us. Knowing Soma, neither by means of substance nor in the form of an addiction, ultimately requires us to become practical in pursuit of both material and spiritual success initiated in Life.

North Node Transiting the Tenth House or Saturn

Social achievements

The North Node can cause us to become shy and to doubt our ability for necessary growth. The self-doubt and control from others is prominent when the North Node moves through the tenth house; but this can assure more concrete accomplishment in the years ahead. Soul searching and a breaking through of a new identity prior to the transits are beneficial. What is not working in your life? Do you feel deprived in your work? If you have been out of the workforce, could this be a time of acquiring a new job or career. How aware are you at this point of your life of your own self-worth? Have you been able to let go of stagnated issues from the past? Now is the time to stand up for your rights!

A sense of humility needs to be balanced with what has been achieved already. If you have any type of workaholic syndrome, this will become prominent as people comment, "you work too hard." You might have to realize that over-achievement is not always the best solution.

When the North Node transits through the tenth house, there is the tendency to feel unappreciated. There is a need for you to clarify whether you should stay at the current situation. Look to see if your future, the North Node, will benefit both you and your superior. If another planet is placed in the natal tenth house, the influence and impact of that planet should also be noted.

This is a time when a person can come together with someone who they truly deserve and who deserves them. Many places in a chart can determine when we meet the right person in our life. During the transit of the North Node in the tenth, there is a certain aura of maturity that makes Saturn work beneficially. Often the North Node in transit to Saturn or to the tenth house allows the person to explore a new side of her or himself: a new social status and image often manifests.

Through the year and seven months of the transiting North Node in the tenth house, or to Saturn, a form of helpful self-discipline is to engage in some area of serious study. It is advisable first to adjust to a lower position and then work up to a place of comfort and stability. The rewards for discipline—a common word associated with Saturn—will not be reaped unless the work of the North Node and its relation to our Dharma is met. To know the potential in our own life and to actually set limitations will lead to rewards.

To determine an individual's Dharma or what the person's tenth house represents, especially in relating to the Moon's Nodes and their integration into society at large, the following points should be reviewed:

The planetary Lord of the tenth house, its aspect to Saturn and the Moon's Nodal axis.

An observation of other planets in the tenth house, their rulerships and their aspect in relation to the Moon's Nodes.

The planetary Lord of the sixth house and its aspect to the Moon's Nodes.

An observation of the Ascendant with its planetary Lord, and its relation to the Moon's Nodes.

South Node Transiting the Tenth House, or Saturn

Endurance as the teacher

South Node's movement through the tenth house is a vulnerable time frame of our life. Being aware of the self-inflicted denial that the South Node brings can force us to deal with old fears and denials of the past. Old parental control issues are brought out into the open. A parent's living situation can change during this time.

This transit can also bring the vulnerable experience of a parent passing away. If they have already passed, this is an exceptional time to look at unresolved issues in your own life. Their presence and their Spirit tend to visit through reminders of small, yet subtle whispering through a photograph, another member passing, or our own search for another level of our Essence. This is a good time to visit their place of rest, perform a ritual, or contemplate parental influence. If your childhood was a difficult or devastating time, the South Node in transit through the tenth house or to Saturn has the force necessary to set us free.

The South Node transit through the tenth house indicates control issues from various sources. An unexpected challenge at the workplace or the sense that our life is not working properly often brings out problems at work. You finally realize how inhibited you can act and feel when you are around people. It is advisable not to make drastic changes during this time of discomfort, but rather work on the issues that are coming up right in front of you.

People from the past will remind you what you need to learn and grow with. This is a good time to ask the teacher, "What else can you show me?" When we know how to surrender, we can teach from a steadfast position. We learn from the South Node how to control our own sense of who we are and what we desire to acknowledge from previous wisdom.

Celine Dion

The Canadian female singer Celine Dion was born into a family of four-teen children. Both of her parents were musicians, and Celine grew up with music around her. When she was five years old, she sang on stage for the first time, and knew that her calling was to be a singer. School was not of interest to her. By the time she was twelve years old, she had recorded music that brought the attention of Rene Angelil, who would become her manager and eventually her husband. There is an age differ-ence of twenty-six years between them.. Since Celine is disciplined and extremely Saturnine, there is the strong possibility of Saturn controlling her image in public, and influencing her decision-making.

Saturn conjunct Celine's 14° Aries MC is prominent with the North Node in close conjunction to the Sun in Aries; a New Moon Eclipse. Mars in Taurus falls close to this stellium, magnifying her success and strong personality. Her Sun and Moon in Aries indicates a person with the Spirit and Soul destined to show the world who she is. Celine has an aura of self-confidence and with a Leo Ascendant, she has a long, beautiful, and slender appearance.

The planetary Lord of the tenth house, Mars, conjuncts her Moon, indicating a scenario of her developing sense of motherhood, security, and her body image. At the age of thirty, she started to show signs that she wanted to slow down and establish a family. Scorpio is in her fifth house—children—and Pluto conjunct Uranus is in the third, which is in opposition to her Venus and Mars in Pisces. In combination with her natal Neptune in fifth house, this all indicates challenges with pregnancy.

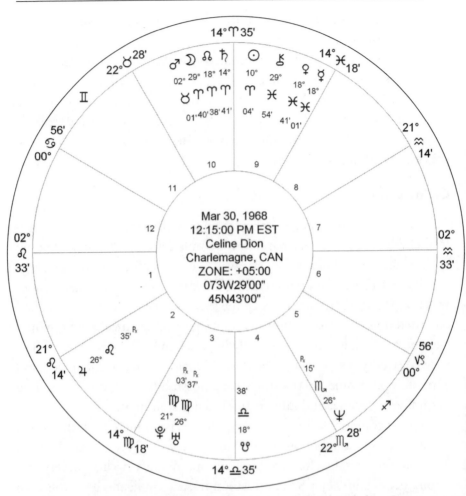

The ninth house often represents state of the mind; her Saturn return in 1997 indicated that her life would take a difficult direction. It
became public knowledge that it was hard for her to conceive a child.
However, when she did become pregnant in May of 2000, this also immediately became public knowledge. Celine's pregnancy and the birth
of their first child in 2001 became a healing point in their life. On October 23, 2010, she gave birth to a set of twins, and Celine has continued
to perform ever since.

Natal Moon's Nodes, Uranus and the Eleventh House

My Intentions are my Goals in Life

Uranus shows our true identity because it allows us to recognize that which we already are. Basically, when we come to terms with our individual ability to be free to explore the creative process of life, we appreciate where we are maturing.

With Uranus or the influence of the Moon's Node in the eleventh house, the individuation process is extremely personal. We set our goals according to our understanding of what we want to achieve on this earth. As we become familiar with our uniqueness, we can accept how perfectly normal we really are. During a visit to my homeland, Sweden, I had an opportunity to attend a lecture by His Holiness the 14th Dalai Lama. During his speech, he said, "I recently found out that I am just an ordinary human being." And then he laughed wholeheartedly.

The polarity of the Nodal Axis in the eleventh house indicates an embedded desire to achieve goals that will bring about a societal change. With the Nodes in the eleventh house there is the potential for a successful career that brings large crowds. The creative outlet that we manifest in the fifth house is as strong in the opposing eleventh house.

The eleventh house brings the karmic attributes of fulfillment, because there is a strong urge for the Soul to reach its fullest creative potential. Obstacles and interruptions can challenge this process. For example, a woman gives birth to children and puts her own career or education on hold until the children are grown. There is a drive toward wholeness and comfort, dealing with the future and a desire for success—no matter what it takes.

Our many support groups for people with addictive behaviors reflect the modern Uranus mode of expression. Before Uranus was discovered in 1781, people were put away in asylums for any type of "Uranian" behavior. When those with addictive personalities meet their challenges by confronting their egos, they are encouraged to bring issues to the forefront by becoming honest in front of the group such as AA or NAA. When we are in a group, something dissolves within us and we merge with no-ego; or the Self has been accepted.

Another type of support group is an astrology group in which the study of natal and transit charts allow many personal issues to be discussed. The eleventh house challenges us to become conscious of how we are experienced by others. We are accustomed to relate Astrology to Uranus and the 11th house.

There is a certain tension or challenge in finding and refining the qualities of what makes us unique individuals. With strong, or many, natal aspects influencing one of the Moon's Nodes, an individual's tendency toward a desire for wholeness becomes prominent. A person with less challenging natal influence of the Nodal Axis will have less dynamic interaction between natal planets and the Nodes.

North Node Transiting the Eleventh House or Uranus

Humanitarian growth opportunities

The North Node transiting through the eleventh house or to Uranus brings a time in search for another project, education, or retirement plan, or even a new reality. An effort to become more disciplined about achievements occurs when the North Node transits the eleventh house. This is a time when many individuals have become closer to understanding their own self-worth, as well as their own limitations.

Individuals will leave old limited feelings behind and become freer in their expression of their goals and purpose in life. A sense of appreciation of our personality becomes normal, and we begin to accept those around us as equally unique. It's all about letting go of old limitations, perhaps by piercing an ear or getting that tattoo. Some individuals don't bother with such outside demonstrations of originality. Regardless of its specific form of expression, our true individuality comes from within, not without.

A transit of the Moon's North Node to Uranus, or to the eleventh house, can promote a prime opportunity for individuation. For example, if the Lord of the natal eleventh cusp is Capricorn and Saturn falls in the second house, this is a time when the Moon's North Node in transit will benefit financial stability. When the Moon's North Node passes through the eleventh, the planetary ruler is a strong clue as to where we choose to change our direction in life. The impact that the Moon's Node has in this house is showing us what our healing process in life has been. We feel free and without limitations to explore even further.

South Node Transiting the Eleventh House or Uranus

Surrendering to Ego

No matter what our ego may show to the world, it is still the individual Self that knows in our heart what the Spirit wants to accomplish in a lifetime. The South Node brings out hidden knowledge from previous influences. Prior times are reflected in our birth chart, along with our reaction to transits in this life and previous lifetimes. The substance of assimilation and its content is residing within our own memory bank. Our conscious desire to move forward and create accordingly becomes more prominent when the South Node is in transit in the eleventh house.

If we linger, feeling that everything is just fine, we are often re-minded of our limitations—the South Node is the energy of that re-sisting change! Often, we hear that the South Node doesn't even have the potential to overcome its comfort zone. However, if we buy into that thought process, we might as well not bother to understand the Moon's Nodes to begin with. Fortunately, we are not meant to linger in the unknown, but to move forward to that place that is forbidden, but changeable. The true fear is that what is now comfortable will eventu-ally become potentially stagnant and boring.

We break old habits and become actively involved with new goals and achievements. It is important to study the natal aspects as they relate to the Lord of the eleventh house, especially the squares, opposi-tions, and conjunctions. The polarity of the Moon's Nodes is habitually complex, yet when worked as one, they encompass our true Spirit and Soul. The planetary Lord of the eleventh house often shows the way to freedom. Through this, the potential for success is much greater.

The possibilities of the South Node in the eleventh house in transit can become life changing. For example, we can be happy to have fin-ished the degree that we have worked on for many years. This transit can also mean accepting our goals of simply going to work every day and earning a stable income with which to retire. The South Node in transit brings out this acceptance. Many times our natural instinct is to change, but we may have to accept instead.

People in general and friends from the past will often contact you to check into how your life is transpiring when the South Node passes through the eleventh house. We will be reminded about what we have accomplished. We may also realize that we haven't been in touch with old friends, and now understand how much they mean to us.

This transit is beneficial for starting to become more aware of our own surroundings and of the mythologies and stories we have created about our Self. We may look around and notice what we have accomplished. A desire for simplicity might very well seem appealing. If you don't recognize this feeling of stability, you have to reach out to the message of your North Node. This is the wonder of working with the dichotomy of the Moon's Nodes! Through our life's decisions, we can continue to balance and reunite what was "decapitated" along the way. Accepting the "decapitated" parts of our existence is the acceptance of the unique healer inside of our true essence. Shedding that which has to be cleansed...

Oprah Winfrey

Oprah Winfrey's success as one of the world's richest women shows in her eleventh house. She puts children, marriage, and often her own private life aside for the success of the eleventh house and its endless future possibilities for further successes.

Uranus is placed in its own house, the eleventh, in Cancer and conjunct the South Node within a 4° orb. Her past (whether it is this life or another life) shows the unique path of someone with her own exceptional personality. The emotions sometimes covered up, but often expressed through the Sagittarius Moon in the fourth house, provide an understanding of how the South Node works in Oprah's life. She has a message to relay from the past. Her North Node in 23° Capricorn conjunct her 23° Chiron in the fifth house; her willingness to bring out

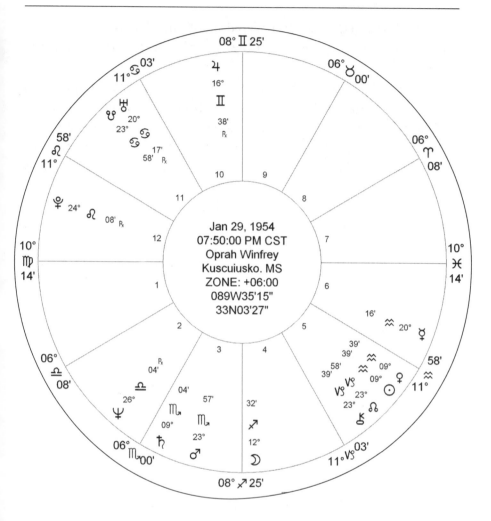

wounds through her creative self is powerful and direct. Chiron is the
wounded part of her that has the mission to bring out her specific and
personal wounds from the past through her own expression.

The planetary Lord of Winfrey's eleventh house cusp is Cancer,
and we find the Moon in Sagittarius in the fourth house. The fourth
house correlates to the Soul's desire to be born into this world. Many
know her childhood trauma, and she openly talks about the rape
that occurred early in her life. Her mother, represented by the Moon
in the fourth house, obviously becomes a catalyst for Oprah's own

feminine but often logically ordered emotions. The Moon is in op-position to Jupiter in Gemini in the "open" house of the public and communication.

In the fifth house, we find the Sun and Venus in a 0° conjunction. Her Aquarius Sun shows the ability to bring Venus out as a secure woman on a road to continuing success. Yet Venus also shows the struggle of the Sun, the identity of her spirit forcing a re-evaluation of her self-worth and personal image every day as she continually displays her wounds to the world.

The potential and obvious step toward healing and wholeness are supported by strong sextile from the Sagittarius Moon to the Sun and Venus. In general, her mission to help herself through healing others is the first thing we notice about her. Oprah's South Node and Uranus in the eleventh house allow her personality to shine through in dynamic ways—allowing millions of individuals to have hope in their own personal healing.

Natal Moon's Nodes, Neptune and the Twelfth House

By Listening to my Inner Voice,
I receive the Wisdom contained within...

A fine line can often be noticed between the fool and the genius. In this process of losing the parts of our self from the past, people often have had metamorphic experiences when they think that they have "lost it," that is, they feel their minds and identities are in chaos. Clients of mine have described either their own belief that they had "lost it" or that they perhaps wish to. However, since they are still sane enough to talk about it, they really didn't lose "it" at all. They were, though, aware of a change within them. They were lost in a mist of illusion. The illusion is that they might experience themselves as crazy. Such endless internal battle is often catalytically necessary for healing.

The twelfth house, with its ruler Neptune, often indicates matters of madness, seclusion, meditation, hospitals and jails, as well as monasteries and places of retreat. Stage and screen acting, and also drug and alcohol abuse, comprise an additional aspect of the twelfth house. No matter how we define this house, whether Neptune or the Moon's Nodes are placed there, we have to accept how real Neptune is. Neptune is the fourth largest planet in our solar system. Though watery in its interior, we have to respect its presence as a body of substance influencing our life here on earth.

The Sanskrit word Maya comes into play in relating to the Moon's Nodes in the twelfth house and Neptune's influence. Maya is often defined as an illusion. According to many, this earth plane is an illusion. However, as we dwell deeper into its more true fundamental nature, Maya is as real as Neptune. Neptune can manifest in an individual's desire to escape from reality. Escapism can also entail prescription drugs, alcohol, obsessions, and spiritual fanaticism. In reading scriptures and metaphysical books, we often come across the term Maya. But it is also true that Maya was an earth goddess, and in Greek and Roman mythology, she was the mother of Hermes/Mercury.

The philosopher Plato referred to Maya as a "changing physical world that is not real, but shadows of a distant fire." Maya is as real as this physical reality in front of us, but a universal consciousness of other lives, past lives, and future lives imparts to present physical reality a relative importance. When we know the reality of living here as we experience the essence of the Universe, all "worlds" are truly one and the same. Neptune and the influence of the Nodal Axis in the twelfth house are understood as something real and alive within us when we are sleeping, eating, dreaming, working, or meditating. Illusion and reality are then not so far apart. We have to agree to live a little on both sides of Neptune.

When the Moon's Nodal Axis is placed in the twelfth house, there is a deep desire from early childhood for the individual to seek out some form of spiritual path. The search is often hindered by situations beyond the person's control. Those situations can entail separations from parents, a sense of loss, and/or a feeling that one does not belong to one's family of origin. A feeling of abandonment is repeatedly felt when either of the Moon's Nodes, Neptune, and a strongly influenced twelfth house is in question. The tendency for Soul Loss, depression, and a deep desire not to be in the physical body are often present. "Soul Loss" is a term common among shamanistic traditions, used to describe what occurs when a person has been in a serious accident, experienced rape, fought a war, or undergone other traumas that have been repressed. Neptune acts like a catalyst, savior, and healer, allowing the wounded individual to delve into deep-rooted, forgotten issues.

As the twelfth house is the house of the subconscious, this also permits the subconscious to become more present and conscious. We allow the old myth of the twelfth house—with all its traditional connotations of "bad" karma, the house of issues related to self-undoing challenges and matters from the past—to be integrated into our daily life; we commune sacredly with this house and allow the true beauty of Neptune to influence our practical daily life.

North Node Transiting the Twelve House or Neptune

Retreat to Inner Peace

The potential for true healing occurs when the North Node transits through the twelfth house or conjuncts Neptune. The effects of the healing become clear when the individual is transformed through daily grateful observations, or an auspicious miracle. What is a miracle? A miracle can be defined as an event that transcends both human powers and the laws of nature.

The twelfth house is often associated with yoga and meditation. We are seeing the rising popularity of meditation and yoga in the twenty-first century, as well as alternative healing modalities being sought out and accepted. When we know that the North Node will transit the twelfth house for one year and seven months, we know this will be a valuable time to seek out the silence within and listen to our inner voice. The voice of silence in our heart is the strongest, most valuable, and familiar voice we can listen to. This is a time to seek out meditation re-treats or continue to engage in deeper spiritual practice on a daily basis. Meditation can also found while walking in the woods, or even while cleaning house—as long as it is practiced with an aware mind. Walking meditation is a beneficial alternative for those who can't sit still!

As the North Node transits through the twelfth house, it is essential to pay attention to dreams. The subconscious desire to remember every detail of them might at times be confusing. Using a notebook, or a recorder, and keeping an open mind that does not analyze the images from the dream world intellectually, but rather allows the images be incorporated throughout the days close to the dream. And then the "aha" moment..What we reap during the dream stage, this deep subconscious, aids in the process of healing.

The transit provides a play of our own subconscious memory, and it's a play of our own myth. This is a beneficial time to participate in activities out of the ordinary that allow us to move internal progression out into the world. An acting class, a dance routine, the magnificent tango, or a yoga class will benefit the movement of the North Node or Neptune to act out its strong influence from the subconscious. Creative movement, especially dances like samba or salsa, allows us to move closer to the inhibited feelings that we hide in this house. Imaginative play is also an important part of the North Node through the twelfth house. Who said that we have to grow up? We have to mature, but never forget to play.

As the North Node transits through the twelfth house, family secrets often come to the forefront and what has been hidden behind the scenes, or in the proverbial closet, is often revealed. This is a promising time to solve the mysterious link of "forgotten" relatives or siblings. Distant relatives knock on the door and are able to untie many knots from the unbroken link between the past and the future. The tribal connections become stronger as we welcome the healing from the past to come forth.

We allow the play of the Purification Process to take on another role as Neptune plays the part of Shiva, the god who loves to meditate. Shiva kills our ignorance as we face reality. Shiva Nataraja (Lord of the Dance), the most popular form of Shiva, dances the dance of life, stepping with his foot on the goblin of the Ego and thereby forcing the nature of our innermost humble ignorance to a different understanding of our personal growth.

South Node Transiting the Twelfth House or Neptune

Signification of Enlightenment

As our subconscious mind allows us to understand hidden, often secretive and shameful memories from our past, we have the ability to let go by allowing our South Node to work with new healing modalities. The South Node, Neptune, and twelfth house resonate with many modern, alternative healing therapies. Re-birthing, cranial sacral work, primal, and movement therapy, regression, or any type of experimental therapy is rewarding during the transit of the South Node through the twelfth house. We must allow deep images, rather than just the stereotypical therapy, to lead us from the subconscious to our consciousness. The twelfth house, with its many, often hidden layers of the past, has the blessed tendency to give us only what we can deal with.

A client related during this transit that he was in a deep state of regression moving toward the answer to a difficult situation he was in. A black-hooded image came and cut off his head, and my client woke up from his deep regression with a terrible feeling that he himself was a murderer or executioner in another lifetime. After a long discussion and examination of the chart, we resolved he was not yet ready to know the answer to his question—the time was not yet right. A few years later, the client was able to sort out the question in talking about his recently deceased wife and their relationship. But he was indeed not initially ready to know the answer, i.e., at the time of his self-imposed regression session. We have to be careful what we ask for. Often we get it—but only when we are ready to know the answer!

When the South Node transits through the twelfth house, or Neptune, we have to be able to take time for ourselves. We have a tendency during this time to want to isolate ourselves from society or friends. Thus, it is important to separate the two. It is important to be aware of this transit so that it doesn't "sneak" up on us. With concrete and aware planning, this is a beneficial time to seek seclusion. However, when taken by surprise, the South Node in the twelfth house, or in transit to Neptune, can make a person mentally unstable. Layers related to unresolved issues can surface and have to be dealt with on an individual level.

The South Node is the indicator of enlightenment, and the twelfth house represents monasteries and meditation. Spiritual liberation can occur at any given time, but if there is a specific period during which one can spend time in a monastery, an ashram, or to start a meditation practice at home, this is the most favorable time. The commitment to a spiritual journey or retreat is rewarding on many levels. Through various retreats, many unresolved issues can surface in a natural, safer way as the South Node—with it's infinitely embedded layers of desire for the Soul to heal—transforms the individual.

One of my clients, Colleen, is an interesting example of how the Moon's Nodes unfolded during one point of her life. The North Node is placed in her twelfth house, an aspiration for spirituality, with challenges nonetheless from the subconscious. With a natal Virgo Moon in the sixth house conjunct her South Node in Virgo, her karmic attributes

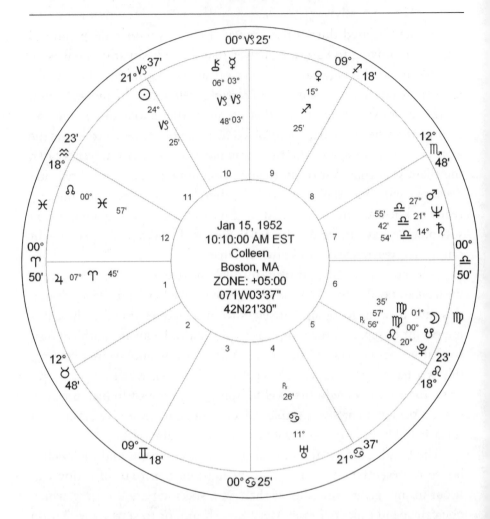

from the past are important. Her relationship with her mother was difficult. The mother often criticized Colleen, and at one point refused to let her daughter interact with others.

She became an independent, strong, and professional woman. She is not married nor does she have any children. However, she is a warm, positive, caring, and spiritual individual who cares for her friends and family. Her North Node is accustomed to being by her and she seems to thrive on it. She meditates on a regular basis.

As a Nodal Return approached her chart, she needed some new inspiration for her existing business and in her life. I suggested that she engage in spiritual chanting before the exact conjunction of the return. To make sure she would notice the effect, I timed her chanting schedule before the exact degree of her natal North Node of 0°57' in Pisces. She asked me what she would get out of it, as she hoped to change her business location or expand the existing business. I answered: "Whatever the universe wants to give you." In a disciplined fashion, she chanted as the transiting North Node approached her Pisces/Virgo Nodes (with her 0° Virgo Moon involved as well) through the fall of 1988.

During a meditation retreat, Colleen met a person who was to become essential in this transit of her Nodal Axis. They became intimate, yet with a distant, mutually non-committed understanding between them. Through an unusual circumstance, her friend gave her a large sum of money to invest further in her business. He gave her the money without signing any papers or arranging for a return of the investment. At the time of the transaction itself, the transiting North Node is in a large orb, 8°, which is a rather wide orb to work with. However, at the time, the transiting North Node was in a 6° sextile, and the South Node in a trine to her natal Mercury on her Capricorn Midheaven. Colleen's natal Chiron was in a trine to the natal North Node at this time as well.

By the spring of 1989, her plan to move her successful existing business to a larger and better location came about accordingly. A Nodal Return occurred in May of 1989. During those months, Colleen worked very hard on this move, eager to hear from her friend and show him the new establishment.

All is well—until one day in early summer of 1998 when Colleen received a letter indicating that she owed all the money that had been given to her (plus interest) and is to pay it back within a month. The situation that had occurred in 1988 of her North Node Return started all over again. Except this time, her friend, now represented by the court system, insists on taking back what was originally given to her (and which she had completely spent on her new business). The original business had been dissolved.

Through the vehicle of a registered letter, the Churning Purification process started accordingly as the transiting South Node conjuncts her natal Pisces North Node in the twelfth house. Of course, the reverse was taking place within the Nodes in the sixth house, with the addition of the Virgo Moon, indicating a half-nodal return. During the court hearing, it became clear that the business had dissolved with neither of the sides (the god/goddess or the demons) winning. The half Nodal Return, the South Node transiting over the North Node, has in this case two morals to it. Moral number one is that Colleen learned about a depth within herself connected with the sincere, spiritual intention which she had stated during her meditation. And moral number two for this case is that you should never give away or accept a gift without signing papers.

≋≋≋

MEDITATIONS AND CONTEMPLATIONS
ON THE MOON'S NODES

The following exercises can be beneficial during various transits in your life. It is helpful to schedule time before, during, or after a specific transit of the Moon's Nodes to a planetary configuration, a New or Full Moon, or an Eclipse, thus allowing the merging, understanding, and surrendering to take place.

Select a quiet place. Sit comfortably in a chair or on the floor. Relax with a few deep breaths. Take a deep breath in and count to three. Hold your breath. Release your breath with the count of three.

Relax your body and mind. Take deep natural breaths! Relax! Bring the image of your Nodes to your senses, or see them; visualize them. They might talk to you! Listen and Observe...

Rahu seed mantra:

Aum bhram bhrim bhraum sah rahave namah

Ketu seed mantra:

Aum sram srim sraum sah ketave namah

Phase One: Clarify your personal impressions from the Myth of the Moon's Nodes—Purification of the Soul.

Phase Two: Refer to the twelve Affirmations related to your Natal Nodal Axis, (in the beginning of each chapter), or create your own words, your personal affirmations, or mantra of your Natal North and South Nodal position in your Birth Chart – during a Transit, Dasa period, or research.

Phase Three: The following suggested Meditations, Contemplations, Journeying or Visualizations are merely suggestions for personal growth. As always before one embarks on an encounter with the Spirit World, one should be in the good habit of number one, ask for protection, number two, ask permission for guidance, and three, thank the divine with respect, honor and love for the understood outcome.

Suggested Focal Points:

- Observe the two opposite sides of the Gods and the Demons—or Rahu and Ketu. Decide what side of this exercise you will emphasize at this time.

- At another time, or transit, change the side of the Gods or the Demons – Rahu and Ketu.

- Focus on a situation in which you felt "decapitated." What was your involvement in the Churning Process? Which side of the Purification process were you on? What did you gain? Is this situation still upsetting or lost in the battle of the purification process? Understand the rewards of merging with the divine – showing your strength of growth through surrendering to the South Node – moving with unconditional love toward the North Node.

- Contemplate the outcome and understanding of a rewarding and beneficial situation that transpired in relation to Rahu: North Node and Ketu: South Node. Did a person or a group allow you to observe and transform your involvement in the cleansing process? You might have confronted a person or situation, the contemplation benefiting the push and pull from the gods and the demons within. The awareness of your Self involved allowed all to heal.

• Allow your Self to be quiet until you are clear about your personal Churning Process.

• Write down your impressions!

Birth Data Sources

Cayce, Edgar, March 18, 1877, 2:03 PM, Hopkinsville, KY, USA. Source: family records from the library at Case Foundation and his own statement.

Colleen, January 15, 1952, 10:10 AM, Boston, MA, USA. Source: B.C. (permission to use).

Chris, June 25, 1959, 9:34 AM, Bay Shore, NY. Source: B.C. (permission to use).

Crowley, Aleister, October 12, 1875, 11:42 PM, Leamington Spa, England. Source: Equinox of the Gods.

Dion, Celine, March 30, 1968, 12:15 PM, Charlemagne, Ontario, Canada. Source: B.C. Astro Data Bank.

Freud, Sigmund, May 6, 1856, 6:30 PM, Friedberg, Germany. Source: Photo of father's diary, written in Hebrew.

Hershey, Ted, October 22, 1958, 10:58 PM, Lancaster, PA, USA. Source: B.C. (permission to use).

Jackson, Michael, August 29, 1958, 11:45 PM, Gary, IN, USA. Source: DD, from Tabloid magazine.

Joan of Arc, January 6, 1412, 5:00 PM. Source: Profiles of Woman and Astro Data Bank.

Jolie, Angelina, June 4, 1975, 9:09 AM Los Angeles, CA. Source: B.C. Astro Data Bank

Jung, C.G., July 26, 1975, 7:32 PM, Kesswill, Swizterland. Source: given by daughter.

Kennedy, Jacqueline, July 28, 1929, 2:30 PM, Southampton, NY, USA. Source: Frances McEvoy quotes her to mutual friends, data not released until after her death.

Kennedy, John F., Jr. November 25, 1960, 12:22 AM. Washington, DC, USA. Source: From news.

Kennedy, John, F., Sr. May 29, 1917, 3:00 PM, Brookline, MA, USA. Source: Lois Rodden.

Mozart, Wolfgang, January 27, 1756, 8:00 PM Salzburg, Austria. Source: Authentic data recorded by his father.

Pitt, Brad, December 18, 1963, 6:31 AM Shawnee, OK. Source: Astro Data Bank.

Presley, Elvis, January 8, 1935, 4:35 AM, Tupelo, MS, USA. Source: B.C. in hand.

Presley, Lisa Marie February 1, 1968, 5:01 PM, Memphis, TN, USA. Source: news report.

Russell, Phil, November 20, 1942, 9:01 PM, Hartford, CT, USA. Source: B.C. (Permission to use).

Simpson, O.J., July 9, 1947, 8:08 AM, San Francisco, CA, USA. Source: Contemporary Sidereal Horoscopes, Gauquelin Book of American Charts.

Swedenborg, Emanuel, January 29, 1688, (OS) 6:48 AM, Stockholm, Sweden. Source: Introduction to the Swedish Noble, 8th volume, page 56, by Gustaf Elgenstierna.

Van Gogh, Vincent, March 30, 1853, 11:00 AM, Gemeente Zundert, Netherlands. Source: B.D. in hand from Steinbrecher.

Winfrey, Oprah, January 29, 1954, 7:50 PM, Kosciusko. MS, USA. Source: from her TV show, DD.

Authors note: although the above data has been carefully researched, there is always the possibility of errors. I have obtained most data from The Astro Data Bank *by Lois Rodden. I wish to thank her for the superb Virgo work that she did for all astrologers.*

Ephemeris

TABLE OF MOON'S NODES AND ECLIPSES
1938–2050

1938

Jan	1	North 5 Sa 51	South 5 Ge 51
Feb	1	North 3 Sa 37	South 3 Ge 37
Mar	1	North 0 Sa 38	South 0 Ge 38
Apr	1	North 27 Sc 44	South 27 Ta 44
May	1	North 26 Sc 53	South 26 Ta 53
May	14	*Lunar Eclipse*	8:44 22 Sc 56
May	29	*Solar Eclipse*	13:50 7 Ge 31
Jun	1	North 26 Sc 52	South 26 Ta 52
Jul	1	North 26 Sc 05	South 26 Ta 05
Aug	1	North 23 Sc 43	South 23 Ta 43
Sep	1	North 20 Sc 45	South 20 Ta 45
Oct	1	North 18 Sc 36	South 18 Ta 36
Nov	1	North 17 Sc 51	South 17 Ta 51
Nov	7	*Lunar Eclipse*	22:26 14 Ta 53
Nov	21	*Solar Eclipse*	23:52 29 Sc 01
Dec	1	North 17 Sc 36	South 17 Ta 36

1939

Jan	1	North 16 Sc 21	South 16 Ta 21
Feb	1	North 13 Sc 26	South 13 Ta 26
Mar	1	North 10 Sc 28	South 10 Ta 28
Apr	1	North 8 Sc 41	South 8 Ta 41
Apr	19	*Solar Eclipse*	16:45 28 Ar 44
May	1	North 8 Sc 25	South 8 Ta 25
May	3	*Lunar Eclipse*	15:11 12 Sc 15
Jun	1	North 8 Sc 14	South 8 Ta 14
Jul	1	North 6 Sc 38	South 6 Ta 38
Aug	1	North 3 Sc 20	South 3 Ta 20
Sep	1	North 0 Sc 23	South 0 Ta 23
Oct	1	North 29 Li 18	South 29 Ar 18
Oct	12	*Solar Eclipse*	20:40 18 Li 37
Oct	28	*Lunar Eclipse*	6:36 3 Ta 54
Nov	1	North 29 Li 17	South 29 Ar 17
Dec	1	North 28 Li 36	South 28 Ar 36

1940

Jan	1	North 26 Li 13	South 26 Ar 13
Feb	1	North 23 Li 05	South 23 Ar 05
Mar	1	North 20 Li 50	South 20 Ar 50
Mar	23	*Lunar Eclipse*	19:48 3 Li 10
Apr	1	North 20 Li 04	South 20 Ar 04
Apr	7	*Solar Eclipse*	20:21 17 Ar 52
Apr	22	*Lunar Eclipse*	4:26 1 Sc 47
May	1	North 19 Li 53	South 19 Ar 53
Jun	1	North 18 Li 54	South 18 Ar 54
Jul	1	North 16 Li 26	South 16 Ar 26
Aug	1	North 13 Li 21	South 13 Ar 21
Sep	1	North 11 Li 22	South 11 Ar 22
Oct	1	North 11 Li 02	South 11 Ar 02
Oct	1	*Solar Eclipse*	12:44 8 Li 11
Oct	16	*Lunar Eclipse*	8:01 22 Ar 42
Nov	1	North 10 Li 51	South 10 Ar 51
Dec	1	North 9 Li 11	South 9 Ar 11

1941

Jan	1	North 5 Li 45	South 5 Ar 45
Feb	1	North 2 Li 54	South 2 Ar 54
Mar	1	North 1 Li 50	South 1 Ar 50
Mar	13	*Lunar Eclipse*	11:55 22 Vi 36
Mar	27	*Solar Eclipse*	20:08 6 Ar 46
Apr	1	North 1 Li 47	South 1 Ar 47
May	1	North 1 Li 04	South 1 Ar 04
Jun	1	North 28 Vi 47	South 28 Pi 47
Jul	1	North 25 Vi 54	South 25 Pi 54
Aug	1	North 23 Vi 43	South 23 Pi 43
Sep	1	North 22 Vi 49	South 22 Pi 49
Sep	5	*Lunar Eclipse*	17:47 12 Pi 50
Sep	21	*Solar Eclipse*	4:34 27 Vi 48
Oct	1	North 22 Vi 45	South 22 Pi 45
Nov	1	North 22 Vi 02	South 22 Pi 02
Dec	1	North 19 Vi 29	South 19 Pi 29

1942

Jan	1	North 15 Vi 49	South 15 Pi 49
Feb	1	North 13 Vi 39	South 13 Pi 39
Mar	1	North 13 Vi 25	South 13 Pi 25
Mar	3	*Lunar Eclipse*	0:21 11 Vi 48
Mar	16	*Solar Eclipse*	23:37 25 Pi 45
Apr	1	North 13 Vi 17	South 13 Pi 17
May	1	North 11 Vi 46	South 11 Pi 46
Jun	1	North 8 Vi 35	South 8 Pi 35
Jul	1	North 5 Vi 46	South 5 Pi 46
Aug	1	North 4 Vi 27	South 4 Pi 27
Aug	12	*Solar Eclipse*	2:45 18 Le 46
Aug	26	*Lunar Eclipse*	3:48 2 Pi 18
Sep	1	North 4 Vi 13	South 4 Pi 13
Sep	10	*Solar Eclipse*	15:39 17 Vi 17
Oct	1	North 3 Vi 42	South 3 Pi 42
Nov	1	North 1 Vi 45	South 1 Pi 45
Dec	1	North 28 Le 39	South 28 Aq 39

1943

Jan	1	North 26 Le 04	South 26 Aq 04
Feb	1	North 25 Le 02	South 25 Aq 02
Feb	4	*Solar Eclipse*	23:38 15 Aq 18
Feb	20	*Lunar Eclipse*	5:38 0 Vi 39
Mar	1	North 24 Le 54	South 24 Aq 54
Apr	1	North 24 Le 08	South 24 Aq 08
May	1	North 21 Le 50	South 21 Aq 50
Jun	1	North 18 Le 34	South 18 Aq 34
Jul	1	North 16 Le 26	South 16 Aq 26
Aug	1	North 15 Le 54	South 15 Aq 54
Aug	1	*Solar Eclipse*	4:16 8 Le 03
Aug	15	*Lunar Eclipse*	19:28 22 Aq 01
Sep	1	North 15 Le 53	South 15 Aq 53
Oct	1	North 14 Le 39	South 14 Aq 39
Nov	1	North 11 Le 32	South 11 Aq 32
Dec	1	North 8 Le 31	South 8 Aq 31

1944

Jan	1	North 7 Le 02	South 7 Aq 02
Jan	25	*Solar Eclipse*	15:26 4 Aq 33
Feb	1	North 6 Le 46	South 6 Aq 46
Feb	9	*Lunar Eclipse*	5:14 19 Le 13
Mar	1	North 6 Le 16	South 6 Aq 16
Apr	1	North 4 Le 23	South 4 Aq 23
May	1	North 1 Le 27	South 1 Aq 27
Jun	1	North 28 Ca 55	South 28 Cp 55
Jul	1	North 27 Ca 49	South 27 Cp 49
Jul	6	*Lunar Eclipse*	4:40 14 Cp 05
Jul	20	*Solar Eclipse*	5:43 27 Ca 22
Aug	1	North 27 Ca 40	South 27 Cp 40
Aug	4	*Lunar Eclipse*	12:26 11 Aq 51
Sep	1	North 27 Ca 05	South 27 Cp 05
Oct	1	North 24 Ca 50	South 24 Cp 50
Nov	1	North 21 Ca 18	South 21 Cp 18
Dec	1	North 18 Ca 56	South 18 Cp 56
Dec	29	*Lunar Eclipse*	14:49 7 Ca 53

1945

Jan	1	North 18 Ca 23	South 18 Cp 23
Jan	14	*Solar Eclipse*	5:01 23 Cp 41
Feb	1	North 18 Ca 13	South 18 Cp 13
Mar	1	North 17 Ca 00	South 17 Cp 00
Apr	1	North 13 Ca 46	South 13 Cp 46
May	1	North 10 Ca 47	South 10 Cp 47
Jun	1	North 9 Ca 23	South 9 Cp 23
Jun	25	*Lunar Eclipse*	15:14 3 Cp 43
Jul	1	North 9 Ca 10	South 9 Cp 10
Jul	9	*Solar Eclipse*	13:27 16 Ca 57
Aug	1	North 8 Ca 50	South 8 Cp 50
Sep	1	North 7 Ca 24	South 7 Cp 24
Oct	1	North 4 Ca 36	South 4 Cp 36
Nov	1	North 1 Ca 33	South 1 Cp 33
Dec	1	North 0 Ca 06	South 0 Cp 06
Dec	19	*Lunar Eclipse*	2:20 26 Ge 51

1946

Jan	1	North 29 Ge 59	South 29 Sa 59
Jan	3	*Solar Eclipse*	12:16 12 Cp 32
Feb	1	North 29 Ge 23	South 29 Sa 23
Mar	1	North 27 Ge 15	South 27 Sa 15
Apr	1	North 23 Ge 46	South 23 Sa 46
May	1	North 21 Ge 25	South 21 Sa 25
May	30	*Solar Eclipse*	21:00 8 Ge 49
Jun	1	North 20 Ge 46	South 20 Sa 46
Jun	14	*Lunar Eclipse*	18:39 23 Sa 03
Jun	29	*Solar Eclipse*	3:51 6 Ca 48
Jul	1	North 20 Ge 44	South 20 Sa 44
Aug	1	North 19 Ge 38	South 19 Sa 38
Sep	1	North 16 Ge 57	South 16 Sa 57
Oct	1	North 13 Ge 59	South 13 Sa 59
Nov	1	North 12 Ge 12	South 12 Sa 12
Nov	23	*Solar Eclipse*	17:37 0 Sa 50
Dec	1	North 11 Ge 45	South 11 Sa 45
Dec	8	*Lunar Eclipse*	17:48 16 Ge 00

1947

Jan	1	North 11 Ge 23	South 11 Sa 23
Feb	1	North 9 Ge 47	South 9 Sa 47
Mar	1	North 6 Ge 51	South 6 Sa 51
Apr	1	North 4 Ge 04	South 4 Sa 04
May	1	North 2 Ge 43	South 2 Sa 43
May	20	*Solar Eclipse*	13:47 28 Ta 42
Jun	1	North 2 Ge 34	South 2 Sa 34
Jun	3	*Lunar Eclipse*	19:15 12 Sa 16
Jul	1	North 2 Ge 15	South 2 Sa 15
Aug	1	North 0 Ge 17	South 0 Sa 17
Sep	1	North 26 Ta 50	South 26 Sc 50
Oct	1	North 24 Ta 15	South 24 Sc 15
Nov	1	North 23 Ta 25	South 23 Sc 25
Nov	12	*Solar Eclipse*	20:05 19 Sc 36
Nov	28	*Lunar Eclipse*	8:34 5 Ge 09
Dec	1	North 23 Ta 24	South 23 Sc 24

1948

Jan	1	North 22 Ta 18	South 22 Sc 18
Feb	1	North 19 Ta 33	South 19 Sc 33
Mar	1	North 16 Ta 27	South 16 Sc 27
Apr	1	North 14 Ta 35	South 14 Sc 35
Apr	23	*Lunar Eclipse*	13:39 3 Sc 23
May	1	North 14 Ta 05	South 14 Sc 05
May	9	*Solar Eclipse*	2:26 18 Ta 22
Jun	1	North 13 Ta 47	South 13 Sc 47
Jul	1	North 12 Ta 26	South 12 Sc 26
Aug	1	North 9 Ta 45	South 9 Sc 45
Sep	1	North 6 Ta 44	South 6 Sc 44
Oct	1	North 5 Ta 08	South 5 Sc 08
Oct	18	*Lunar Eclipse*	2:35 24 Ar 43
Nov	1	North 4 Ta 56	South 4 Sc 56
Nov	1	*Solar Eclipse*	5:59 8 Sc 44
Dec	1	North 4 Ta 38	South 4 Sc 38

1949

Jan	1	North 2 Ta 22	South 2 Sc 22
Feb	1	North 28 Ar 43	South 28 Li 43
Mar	1	North 26 Ar 24	South 26 Li 24
Apr	1	North 25 Ar 36	South 25 Li 36
Apr	13	*Lunar Eclipse*	4:11 22 Li 56
Apr	28	*Solar Eclipse*	7:48 7 Ta 41
May	1	North 25 Ar 38	South 25 Li 38
Jun	1	North 24 Ar 38	South 24 Li 38
Jul	1	North 22 Ar 16	South 22 Li 16
Aug	1	North 19 Ar 25	South 19 Li 25
Sep	1	North 17 Ar 25	South 17 Li 25
Oct	1	North 16 Ar 43	South 16 Li 43
Oct	7	*Lunar Eclipse*	2:56 13 Ar 32
Oct	21	*Solar Eclipse*	21:13 28 Li 08
Nov	1	North 16 Ar 36	South 16 Li 36
Dec	1	North 15 Ar 30	South 15 Li 30

1950

Jan	1	North 12 Ar 34	South 12 Li 34
Feb	1	North 9 Ar 10	South 9 Li 10
Mar	1	North 7 Ar 44	South 7 Li 44
Mar	18	*Solar Eclipse*	15:32 27 Pi 28
Apr	1	North 7 Ar 27	South 7 Li 27
Apr	2	*Lunar Eclipse*	20:44 12 Li 29
May	1	North 7 Ar 09	South 7 Li 09
Jun	1	North 5 Ar 15	South 5 Li 15
Jul	1	North 2 Ar 09	South 2 Li 09
Aug	1	North 29 Pi 26	South 29 Vi 26
Sep	1	North 28 Pi 26	South 28 Vi 26
Sep	12	*Solar Eclipse*	3:38 18 Vi 49
Sep	26	*Lunar Eclipse*	4:17 2 Ar 28
Oct	1	North 28 Pi 20	South 28 Vi 20
Nov	1	North 27 Pi 29	South 27 Vi 29
Dec	1	North 25 Pi 05	South 25 Vi 05

1951

Jan	1	North 21 Pi 53	South 21 Vi 53
Feb	1	North 19 Pi 41	South 19 Vi 41
Mar	1	North 19 Pi 03	South 19 Vi 03
Mar	7	*Solar Eclipse*	20:53 16 Pi 29
Mar	23	*Lunar Eclipse*	10:37 1 Li 52
Apr	1	North 18 Pi 54	South 18 Vi 54
May	1	North 17 Pi 52	South 17 Vi 52
Jun	1	North 15 Pi 17	South 15 Vi 17
Jul	1	North 12 Pi 12	South 12 Vi 12
Aug	1	North 10 Pi 10	South 10 Vi 10
Aug	17	*Lunar Eclipse*	3:14 23 Aq 33
Sep	1	North 9 Pi 51	South 9 Vi 51
Sep	1	*Solar Eclipse*	12:51 8 Vi 17
Sep	15	*Lunar Eclipse*	12:27 21 Pi 45
Oct	1	North 9 Pi 45	South 9 Vi 45
Nov	1	North 8 Pi 01	South 8 Vi 01
Dec	1	North 4 Pi 48	South 4 Vi 48

1952

Jan	1	North 1 Pi 50	South 1 Vi 50
Feb	1	North 0 Pi 43	South 0 Vi 43
Feb	11	*Lunar Eclipse*	0:39 21 Le 19
Feb	25	*Solar Eclipse*	9:11 5 Pi 43
Mar	1	North 0 Pi 32	South 0 Vi 32
Apr	1	North 29 Aq 43	South 29 Le 43
May	1	North 27 Aq 29	South 27 Le 29
Jun	1	North 24 Aq 34	South 24 Le 34
Jul	1	North 22 Aq 25	South 22 Le 25
Aug	1	North 21 Aq 36	South 21 Le 36
Aug	5	*Lunar Eclipse*	19:47 13 Aq 22
Aug	20	*Solar Eclipse*	15:13 27 Le 31
Sep	1	North 21 Aq 30	South 21 Le 30
Oct	1	North 20 Aq 41	South 20 Le 41
Nov	1	North 18 Aq 01	South 18 Le 01
Dec	1	North 14 Aq 40	South 14 Le 40

1953

Jan	1	North 12 Aq 34	South 12 Le 34	
Jan	29	*Lunar Eclipse*	23:47	9 Le 49
Feb	1	North 12 Aq 22	South 12 Le 22	
Feb	14	*Solar Eclipse*	0:59	25 Aq 03
Mar	1	North 12 Aq 16	South 12 Le 16	
Apr	1	North 10 Aq 27	South 10 Le 27	
May	1	North 7 Aq 18	South 7 Le 18	
Jun	1	North 4 Aq 30	South 4 Le 30	
Jul	1	North 3 Aq 24	South 3 Le 24	
Jul	11	*Solar Eclipse*	2:44	18 Ca 30
Jul	26	*Lunar Eclipse*	12:21	3 Aq 12
Aug	1	North 3 Aq 16	South 3 Le 16	
Aug	9	*Solar Eclipse*	15:55	16 Le 45
Sep	1	North 2 Aq 47	South 2 Le 47	
Oct	1	North 0 Aq 59	South 0 Le 59	
Nov	1	North 27 Cp 55	South 27 Ca 55	
Dec	1	North 25 Cp 13	South 25 Ca 13	

1954

Jan	1	North 24 Cp 05	South 24 Ca 05	
Jan	5	*Solar Eclipse*	2:31	14 Cp 14
Jan	19	*Lunar Eclipse*	2:32	28 Ca 27
Feb	1	North 24 Cp 00	South 24 Ca 00	
Mar	1	North 23 Cp 03	South 23 Ca 03	
Apr	1	North 20 Cp 28	South 20 Ca 28	
May	1	North 17 Cp 15	South 17 Ca 15	
Jun	1	North 15 Cp 07	South 15 Ca 07	
Jun	30	*Solar Eclipse*	12:32	8 Ca 10
Jul	1	North 14 Cp 44	South 14 Ca 44	
Jul	16	*Lunar Eclipse*	0:20	22 Cp 52
Aug	1	North 14 Cp 39	South 14 Ca 39	
Sep	1	North 13 Cp 09	South 13 Ca 09	
Oct	1	North 10 Cp 11	South 10 Ca 11	
Nov	1	North 7 Cp 09	South 7 Ca 09	
Dec	1	North 5 Cp 44	South 5 Ca 44	
Dec	25	*Solar Eclipse*	7:36	2 Cp 59

1955

Jan	1	North 5 Cp 31	South 5 Ca 31	
Jan	8	*Lunar Eclipse*	12:33	17 Ca 21
Feb	1	North 5 Cp 00	South 5 Ca 00	
Mar	1	North 3 Cp 05	South 3 Ca 05	
Apr	1	North 0 Cp 07	South 0 Ca 07	
May	1	North 27 Sa 37	South 27 Ge 37	
Jun	1	North 26 Sa 30	South 26 Ge 30	
Jun	5	*Lunar Eclipse*	14:23	14 Sa 15
Jun	20	*Solar Eclipse*	4:10	28 Ge 05
Jul	1	North 26 Sa 24	South 26 Ge 24	
Aug	1	North 25 Sa 52	South 25 Ge 52	
Sep	1	North 23 Sa 34	South 23 Ge 34	
Oct	1	North 20 Sa 18	South 20 Ge 18	
Nov	1	North 17 Sa 52	South 17 Ge 52	
Nov	29	*Lunar Eclipse*	16:59	6 Ge 47
Dec	1	North 17 Sa 19	South 17 Ge 19	
Dec	14	*Solar Eclipse*	7:02	21 Sa 31

1956

Jan	1	North 17 Sa 12	South 17 Ge 12
Feb	1	North 15 Sa 39	South 15 Ge 39
Mar	1	North 12 Sa 45	South 12 Ge 45
Apr	1	North 9 Sa 48	South 9 Ge 48
May	1	North 8 Sa 24	South 8 Ge 24
May	24	*Lunar Eclipse*	15:31 3 Sa 27
Jun	1	North 8 Sa 08	South 8 Ge 08
Jun	8	*Solar Eclipse*	21:20 18 Ge 01
Jul	1	North 7 Sa 41	South 7 Ge 41
Aug	1	North 6 Sa 03	South 6 Ge 03
Sep	1	North 3 Sa 12	South 3 Ge 12
Oct	1	North 0 Sa 27	South 0 Ge 27
Nov	1	North 29 Sc 05	South 29 Ta 05
Nov	18	*Lunar Eclipse*	6:48 25 Ta 56
Dec	1	North 29 Sc 04	South 29 Ta 04
Dec	2	*Solar Eclipse*	8:00 10 Sa 08

1957

Jan	1	North 28 Sc 27	South 28 Ta 27
Feb	1	North 25 Sc 38	South 25 Ta 38
Mar	1	North 22 Sc 35	South 22 Ta 35
Apr	1	North 20 Sc 06	South 20 Ta 06
Apr	30	*Solar Eclipse*	0:05 9 Ta 23
May	1	North 19 Sc 38	South 19 Ta 38
May	13	*Lunar Eclipse*	22:31 22 Sc 50
Jun	1	North 19 Sc 35	South 19 Ta 35
Jul	1	North 18 Sc 25	South 18 Ta 25
Aug	1	North 15 Sc 46	South 15 Ta 46
Sep	1	North 12 Sc 55	South 12 Ta 55
Oct	1	North 11 Sc 06	South 11 Ta 06
Oct	23	*Solar Eclipse*	4:53 29 Li 31
Nov	1	North 10 Sc 34	South 10 Ta 34
Nov	7	*Lunar Eclipse*	14:27 14 Ta 53
Dec	1	North 10 Sc 15	South 10 Ta 15

1958

Jan	1	North 8 Sc 41	South 8 Ta 41
Feb	1	North 5 Sc 29	South 5 Ta 29
Mar	1	North 2 Sc 46	South 2 Ta 46
Apr	1	North 1 Sc 24	South 1 Ta 24
Apr	4	*Lunar Eclipse*	3:60 14 Li 02
Apr	19	*Solar Eclipse*	3:27 28 Ar 34
May	1	North 1 Sc 17	South 1 Ta 17
May	3	*Lunar Eclipse*	12:13 12 Sc 27
Jun	1	North 0 Sc 48	South 0 Ta 48
Jul	1	North 28 Li 46	South 28 Ar 46
Aug	1	North 25 Li 25	South 25 Ar 25
Sep	1	North 22 Li 57	South 22 Ar 57
Oct	1	North 22 Li 16	South 22 Ar 16
Oct	12	*Solar Eclipse*	20:55 19 Li 01
Oct	27	*Lunar Eclipse*	15:27 3 Ta 36
Nov	1	North 22 Li 13	South 22 Ar 13
Dec	1	North 21 Li 07	South 21 Ar 07

1959

Jan	1	North 18 Li 20	South 18 Ar 20
Feb	1	North 15 Li 19	South 15 Ar 19
Mar	1	North 13 Li 31	South 13 Ar 31
Mar	24	*Lunar Eclipse*	20:11 3 Li 31
Apr	1	North 13 Li 06	South 13 Ar 06
Apr	8	*Solar Eclipse*	3:24 17 Ar 33
May	1	North 12 Li 50	South 12 Ar 50
Jun	1	North 11 Li 32	South 11 Ar 32
Jul	1	North 8 Li 50	South 8 Ar 50
Aug	1	North 5 Li 50	South 5 Ar 50
Sep	1	North 4 Li 11	South 4 Ar 11
Sep	17	*Lunar Eclipse*	1:03 23 Pi 29
Oct	1	North 4 Li 02	South 4 Ar 02
Oct	2	*Solar Eclipse*	12:26 8 Li 34
Nov	1	North 3 Li 40	South 3 Ar 40
Dec	1	North 1 Li 37	South 1 Ar 37

1960

Jan	1	North 28 Vi 01	South 28 Pi 01
Feb	1	North 25 Vi 26	South 25 Pi 26
Mar	1	North 24 Vi 39	South 24 Pi 39
Mar	13	*Lunar Eclipse*	8:28 22 Vi 47
Mar	27	*Solar Eclipse*	7:25 6 Ar 38
Apr	1	North 24 Vi 32	South 24 Pi 32
May	1	North 23 Vi 27	South 23 Pi 27
Jun	1	North 20 Vi 50	South 20 Pi 50
Jul	1	North 17 Vi 57	South 17 Pi 57
Aug	1	North 16 Vi 06	South 16 Pi 06
Sep	1	North 15 Vi 31	South 15 Pi 31
Sep	5	*Lunar Eclipse*	11:21 12 Pi 54
Sep	20	*Solar Eclipse*	22:59 27 Vi 58
Oct	1	North 15 Vi 25	South 15 Pi 25
Nov	1	North 14 Vi 18	South 14 Pi 18
Dec	1	North 11 Vi 23	South 11 Pi 23

1961

Jan	1	North 7 Vi 53	South 7 Pi 53
Feb	1	North 6 Vi 15	South 6 Pi 15
Feb	15	*Solar Eclipse*	8:19 26 Aq 26
Mar	1	North 6 Vi 15	South 6 Pi 15
Mar	2	*Lunar Eclipse*	13:28 11 Vi 41
Apr	1	North 5 Vi 55	South 5 Pi 55
May	1	North 3 Vi 57	South 3 Pi 57
Jun	1	North 0 Vi 38	South 0 Pi 38
Jul	1	North 28 Le 11	South 28 Aq 11
Aug	1	North 27 Le 17	South 27 Aq 17
Aug	11	*Solar Eclipse*	10:46 18 Le 31
Aug	26	*Lunar Eclipse*	3:08 2 Pi 35
Sep	1	North 27 Le 09	South 27 Aq 09
Oct	1	North 26 Le 24	South 26 Aq 24
Nov	1	North 24 Le 11	South 24 Aq 11
Dec	1	North 21 Le 04	South 21 Aq 04

1962

Jan	1	North 18 Le 46	South 18 Aq 46	
Feb	1	North 18 Le 03	South 18 Aq 03	
Feb	5	*Solar Eclipse*	0:12	15 Aq 43
Feb	19	*Lunar Eclipse*	13:03	0 Vi 18
Mar	1	North 17 Le 51	South 17 Aq 51	
Apr	1	North 16 Le 39	South 16 Aq 39	
May	1	North 13 Le 58	South 13 Aq 58	
Jun	1	North 10 Le 50	South 10 Aq 50	
Jul	1	North 9 Le 09	South 9 Aq 09	
Jul	17	*Lunar Eclipse*	11:54	24 Cp 32
Jul	31	*Solar Eclipse*	12:25	7 Le 49
Aug	1	North 8 Le 56	South 8 Aq 56	
Aug	15	*Lunar Eclipse*	19:57	22 Aq 22
Sep	1	North 8 Le 43	South 8 Aq 43	
Oct	1	North 6 Le 57	South 6 Aq 57	
Nov	1	North 3 Le 33	South 3 Aq 33	
Dec	1	North 0 Le 46	South 0 Aq 46	

1963

Jan	1	North 29 Ca 44	South 29 Cp 44	
Jan	9	*Lunar Eclipse*	23:19	19 Ca 04
Jan	25	*Solar Eclipse*	13:37	4 Aq 52
Feb	1	North 29 Ca 36	South 29 Cp 36	
Mar	1	North 28 Ca 52	South 28 Cp 52	
Apr	1	North 26 Ca 36	South 26 Cp 36	
May	1	North 23 Ca 36	South 23 Cp 36	
Jun	1	North 21 Ca 20	South 21 Cp 20	
Jul	1	North 20 Ca 30	South 20 Cp 30	
Jul	6	*Lunar Eclipse*	22:02	14 Cp 09
Jul	20	*Solar Eclipse*	20:36	27 Ca 24
Aug	1	North 20 Ca 23	South 20 Cp 23	
Sep	1	North 19 Ca 31	South 19 Cp 31	
Oct	1	North 16 Ca 59	South 16 Cp 59	
Nov	1	North 13 Ca 32	South 13 Cp 32	
Dec	1	North 11 Ca 31	South 11 Cp 31	
Dec	30	*Lunar Eclipse*	11:07	8 Ca 03

1964

Jan	1	North 11 Ca 11	South 11 Cp 11	
Jan	14	*Solar Eclipse*	20:30	23 Cp 43
Feb	1	North 10 Ca 52	South 10 Cp 52	
Mar	1	North 9 Ca 09	South 9 Cp 09	
Apr	1	North 5 Ca 48	South 5 Cp 48	
May	1	North 3 Ca 10	South 3 Cp 10	
Jun	1	North 2 Ca 10	South 2 Cp 10	
Jun	10	*Solar Eclipse*	4:34	19 Ge 19
Jun	25	*Lunar Eclipse*	1:06	3 Cp 29
Jul	1	North 2 Ca 02	South 2 Cp 02	
Jul	9	*Solar Eclipse*	11:17	17 Ca 15
Aug	1	North 1 Ca 26	South 1 Cp 26	
Sep	1	North 29 Ge 36	South 29 Sa 36	
Oct	1	North 26 Ge 41	South 26 Sa 41	
Nov	1	North 24 Ge 00	South 24 Sa 00	
Dec	1	North 23 Ge 02	South 23 Sa 02	
Dec	4	*Solar Eclipse*	1:31	11 Sa 56
Dec	19	*Lunar Eclipse*	2:37	27 Ge 11

1965

Jan	1	North 23 Ge 03	South 23 Sa 03
Feb	1	North 22 Ge 01	South 22 Sa 01
Mar	1	North 19 Ge 32	South 19 Sa 32
Apr	1	North 16 Ge 01	South 16 Sa 01
May	1	North 14 Ge 07	South 14 Sa 07
May	30	*Solar Eclipse*	21:17 9 Ge 13
Jun	1	North 13 Ge 48	South 13 Sa 48
Jun	14	*Lunar Eclipse*	1:49 22 Sa 43
Jul	1	North 13 Ge 40	South 13 Sa 40
Aug	1	North 12 Ge 08	South 12 Sa 08
Sep	1	North 9 Ge 16	South 9 Sa 16
Oct	1	North 6 Ge 28	South 6 Sa 28
Nov	1	North 4 Ge 59	South 4 Sa 59
Nov	23	*Solar Eclipse*	4:14 0 Sa 40
Dec	1	North 4 Ge 39	South 4 Sa 39
Dec	8	*Lunar Eclipse*	17:10 16 Ge 18

1966

Jan	1	North 4 Ge 04	South 4 Sa 04
Feb	1	North 1 Ge 59	South 1 Sa 59
Mar	1	North 28 Ta 51	South 28 Sc 51
Apr	1	North 26 Ta 20	South 26 Sc 20
May	1	North 25 Ta 23	South 25 Sc 23
May	4	*Lunar Eclipse*	21:11 14 Sc 02
May	20	*Solar Eclipse*	9:38 28 Ta 55
Jun	1	North 25 Ta 20	South 25 Sc 20
Jul	1	North 24 Ta 42	South 24 Sc 42
Aug	1	North 22 Ta 14	South 22 Sc 14
Sep	1	North 18 Ta 45	South 18 Sc 45
Oct	1	North 16 Ta 36	South 16 Sc 36
Oct	29	*Lunar Eclipse*	10:12 5 Ta 38
Nov	1	North 16 Ta 09	South 16 Sc 09
Nov	12	*Solar Eclipse*	14:23 19 Sc 45
Dec	1	North 16 Ta 04	South 16 Sc 04

1967

Jan	1	North 14 Ta 32	South 14 Sc 32
Feb	1	North 11 Ta 33	South 11 Sc 33
Mar	1	North 8 Ta 40	South 8 Sc 40
Apr	1	North 7 Ta 13	South 7 Sc 13
Apr	24	*Lunar Eclipse*	12:06 3 Sc 39
May	1	North 6 Ta 54	South 6 Sc 54
May	9	*Solar Eclipse*	14:42 18 Ta 17
Jun	1	North 6 Ta 29	South 6 Sc 29
Jul	1	North 4 Ta 51	South 4 Sc 51
Aug	1	North 2 Ta 02	South 2 Sc 02
Sep	1	North 29 Ar 17	South 29 Li 17
Oct	1	North 28 Ar 03	South 28 Li 03
Oct	18	*Lunar Eclipse*	10:15 24 Ar 22
Nov	1	North 27 Ar 57	South 27 Li 57
Nov	2	*Solar Eclipse*	5:38 9 Sc 07
Dec	1	North 27 Ar 22	South 27 Li 22

1968

Jan	1	North 24 Ar 46	South 24 Li 46
Feb	1	North 21 Ar 10	South 21 Li 10
Mar	1	North 19 Ar 06	South 19 Li 06
Mar	28	*Solar Eclipse*	23:00 8 Ar 19
Apr	1	North 18 Ar 41	South 18 Li 41
Apr	13	*Lunar Eclipse*	4:47 23 Li 17
May	1	North 18 Ar 34	South 18 Li 34
Jun	1	North 17 Ar 07	South 17 Li 07
Jul	1	North 14 Ar 23	South 14 Li 23
Aug	1	North 11 Ar 38	South 11 Li 38
Sep	1	North 10 Ar 02	South 10 Li 02
Sep	22	*Solar Eclipse*	11:18 29 Vi 30
Oct	1	North 9 Ar 38	South 9 Li 38
Oct	6	*Lunar Eclipse*	11:42 13 Ar 14
Nov	1	North 9 Ar 27	South 9 Li 27
Dec	1	North 7 Ar 57	South 7 Li 57

1969

Jan	1	North 4 Ar 37	South 4 Li 37
Feb	1	North 1 Ar 23	South 1 Li 23
Mar	1	North 0 Ar 23	South 0 Li 23
Mar	18	*Solar Eclipse*	4:54 27 Pi 25
Apr	1	North 0 Ar 18	South 0 Li 18
Apr	2	*Lunar Eclipse*	18:32 12 Li 43
May	1	North 29 Pi 43	South 29 Vi 43
Jun	1	North 27 Pi 21	South 27 Vi 21
Jul	1	North 24 Pi 10	South 24 Vi 10
Aug	1	North 21 Pi 50	South 21 Vi 50
Aug	27	*Lunar Eclipse*	10:48 4 Pi 07
Sep	1	North 21 Pi 09	South 21 Vi 09
Sep	11	*Solar Eclipse*	19:58 18 Vi 53
Sep	25	*Lunar Eclipse*	20:10 2 Ar 28
Oct	1	North 20 Pi 59	South 20 Vi 59
Nov	1	North 19 Pi 50	South 19 Vi 50
Dec	1	North 17 Pi 09	South 17 Vi 09

1970

Jan	1	North 14 Pi 04	South 14 Vi 04
Feb	1	North 12 Pi 14	South 12 Vi 14
Feb	21	*Lunar Eclipse*	8:30 2 Vi 23
Mar	1	North 11 Pi 50	South 11 Vi 50
Mar	7	*Solar Eclipse*	17:38 16 Pi 44
Apr	1	North 11 Pi 32	South 11 Vi 32
May	1	North 10 Pi 07	South 10 Vi 07
Jun	1	North 7 Pi 16	South 7 Vi 16
Jul	1	North 4 Pi 25	South 4 Vi 25
Aug	1	North 2 Pi 54	South 2 Vi 54
Aug	17	*Lunar Eclipse*	3:23 23 Aq 53
Aug	31	*Solar Eclipse*	21:55 8 Vi 04
Sep	1	North 2 Pi 50	South 2 Vi 50
Oct	1	North 2 Pi 30	South 2 Vi 30
Nov	1	North 0 Pi 15	South 0 Vi 15
Dec	1	North 26 Aq 54	South 26 Le 54

1971

Jan	1	North 24 Aq 23	South 24 Le 23
Feb	1	North 23 Aq 41	South 23 Le 41
Feb	10	*Lunar Eclipse*	7:45 20 Le 56
Feb	25	*Solar Eclipse*	9:37 6 Pi 08
Mar	1	North 23 Aq 33	South 23 Le 33
Apr	1	North 22 Aq 27	South 22 Le 27
May	1	North 19 Aq 56	South 19 Le 56
Jun	1	North 17 Aq 02	South 17 Le 02
Jul	1	North 15 Aq 10	South 15 Le 10
Jul	22	*Solar Eclipse*	9:31 28 Ca 56
Aug	1	North 14 Aq 35	South 14 Le 35
Aug	6	*Lunar Eclipse*	19:43 13 Aq 41
Aug	20	*Solar Eclipse*	22:39 27 Le 15
Sep	1	North 14 Aq 24	South 14 Le 24
Oct	1	North 13 Aq 11	South 13 Le 11
Nov	1	North 10 Aq 15	South 10 Le 15
Dec	1	North 7 Aq 02	South 7 Le 02

1972

Jan	1	North 5 Aq 20	South 5 Le 20
Jan	16	*Solar Eclipse*	11:03 25 Cp 25
Jan	30	*Lunar Eclipse*	10:53 9 Le 36
Feb	1	North 5 Aq 15	South 5 Le 15
Mar	1	North 4 Aq 52	South 4 Le 52
Apr	1	North 2 Aq 31	South 2 Le 31
May	1	North 29 Cp 13	South 29 Ca 13
Jun	1	North 26 Cp 46	South 26 Ca 46
Jul	1	North 26 Cp 03	South 26 Ca 03
Jul	10	*Solar Eclipse*	19:46 18 Ca 37
Jul	26	*Lunar Eclipse*	7:16 3 Aq 19
Aug	1	North 25 Cp 58	South 25 Ca 58
Sep	1	North 25 Cp 12	South 25 Ca 12
Oct	1	North 23 Cp 04	South 23 Ca 04
Nov	1	North 19 Cp 56	South 19 Ca 56
Dec	1	North 17 Cp 33	South 17 Ca 33

1973

Jan	1	North 16 Cp 48	South 16 Ca 48
Jan	4	*Solar Eclipse*	15:46 14 Cp 10
Jan	18	*Lunar Eclipse*	21:17 28 Ca 33
Feb	1	North 16 Cp 44	South 16 Ca 44
Mar	1	North 15 Cp 29	South 15 Ca 29
Apr	1	North 12 Cp 32	South 12 Ca 32
May	1	North 9 Cp 28	South 9 Ca 28
Jun	1	North 7 Cp 49	South 7 Ca 49
Jun	15	*Lunar Eclipse*	20:50 24 Sa 42
Jun	30	*Solar Eclipse*	11:38 8 Ca 32
Jul	1	North 7 Cp 40	South 7 Ca 40
Jul	15	*Lunar Eclipse*	11:39 22 Cp 42
Aug	1	North 7 Cp 21	South 7 Ca 21
Sep	1	North 5 Cp 27	South 5 Ca 27
Oct	1	North 2 Cp 25	South 2 Ca 25
Nov	1	North 29 Sa 46	South 29 Ge 46
Dec	1	North 28 Sa 42	South 28 Ge 42
Dec	10	*Lunar Eclipse*	1:44 17 Ge 57
Dec	24	*Solar Eclipse*	15:02 2 Cp 40

1974

Jan	1	North 28 Sa 31	South 28 Ge 31
Feb	1	North 27 Sa 38	South 27 Ge 38
Mar	1	North 25 Sa 16	South 25 Ge 16
Apr	1	North 22 Sa 16	South 22 Ge 16
May	1	North 20 Sa 09	South 20 Ge 09
Jun	1	North 19 Sa 26	South 19 Ge 26
Jun	4	*Lunar Eclipse*	22:16 13 Sa 57
Jun	20	*Solar Eclipse*	4:47 28 Ge 30
Jul	1	North 19 Sa 25	South 19 Ge 25
Aug	1	North 18 Sa 31	South 18 Ge 31
Sep	1	North 15 Sa 42	South 15 Ge 42
Oct	1	North 12 Sa 27	South 12 Ge 27
Nov	1	North 10 Sa 29	South 10 Ge 29
Nov	29	*Lunar Eclipse*	15:13 7 Ge 03
Dec	1	North 10 Sa 16	South 10 Ge 16
Dec	13	*Solar Eclipse*	16:12 21 Sa 16

1975

Jan	1	North 9 Sa 57	South 9 Ge 57
Feb	1	North 7 Sa 58	South 7 Ge 58
Mar	1	North 4 Sa 57	South 4 Ge 57
Apr	1	North 2 Sa 10	South 2 Ge 10
May	1	North 1 Sa 04	South 1 Ge 04
May	11	*Solar Eclipse*	7:17 20 Ta 00
May	25	*Lunar Eclipse*	5:48 3 Sa 23
Jun	1	North 0 Sa 52	South 0 Ge 52
Jul	1	North 0 Sa 12	South 0 Ge 12
Aug	1	North 28 Sc 13	South 28 Ta 13
Sep	1	North 25 Sc 16	South 25 Ta 16
Oct	1	North 22 Sc 49	South 22 Ta 49
Nov	1	North 21 Sc 49	South 21 Ta 49
Nov	3	*Solar Eclipse*	13:15 10 Sc 30
Nov	18	*Lunar Eclipse*	22:23 25 Ta 55
Dec	1	North 21 Sc 48	South 21 Ta 48

1976

Jan	1	North 20 Sc 52	South 20 Ta 52
Feb	1	North 17 Sc 47	South 17 Ta 47
Mar	1	North 14 Sc 37	South 14 Ta 37
Apr	1	North 12 Sc 42	South 12 Ta 42
Apr	29	*Solar Eclipse*	10:24 9 Ta 13
May	1	North 12 Sc 31	South 12 Ta 31
May	13	*Lunar Eclipse*	19:54 23 Sc 03
Jun	1	North 12 Sc 17	South 12 Ta 17
Jul	1	North 10 Sc 42	South 10 Ta 42
Aug	1	North 7 Sc 49	South 7 Ta 49
Sep	1	North 5 Sc 14	South 5 Ta 14
Oct	1	North 3 Sc 51	South 3 Ta 51
Oct	23	*Solar Eclipse*	5:13 29 Li 56
Nov	1	North 3 Sc 33	South 3 Ta 33
Nov	6	*Lunar Eclipse*	23:01 14 Ta 34
Dec	1	North 3 Sc 08	South 3 Ta 08

1977

Jan	1	North 1 Sc 10	South 1 Ta 10
Feb	1	North 27 Li 44	South 27 Ar 44
Mar	1	North 25 Li 23	South 25 Ar 23
Apr	1	North 24 Li 23	South 24 Ar 23
Apr	4	*Lunar Eclipse*	4:18 14 Li 22
Apr	18	*Solar Eclipse*	10:31 28 Ar 16
May	1	North 24 Li 19	South 24 Ar 19
Jun	1	North 23 Li 27	South 23 Ar 27
Jul	1	North 20 Li 58	South 20 Ar 58
Aug	1	North 17 Li 40	South 17 Ar 40
Sep	1	North 15 Li 40	South 15 Ar 40
Sep	27	*Lunar Eclipse*	8:29 4 Ar 13
Oct	1	North 15 Li 14	South 15 Ar 14
Oct	12	*Solar Eclipse*	20:27 19 Li 24
Nov	1	North 15 Li 01	South 15 Ar 01
Dec	1	North 13 Li 28	South 13 Ar 28

1978

Jan	1	North 10 Li 21	South 10 Ar 21
Feb	1	North 7 Li 29	South 7 Ar 29
Mar	1	North 6 Li 06	South 6 Ar 06
Mar	24	*Lunar Eclipse*	16:22 3 Li 41
Apr	1	North 5 Li 53	South 5 Ar 53
Apr	7	*Solar Eclipse*	15:03 17 Ar 26
May	1	North 5 Li 27	South 5 Ar 27
Jun	1	North 3 Li 46	South 3 Ar 46
Jul	1	North 0 Li 51	South 0 Ar 51
Aug	1	North 28 Vi 00	South 28 Pi 00
Sep	1	North 26 Vi 47	South 26 Pi 47
Sep	16	*Lunar Eclipse*	19:04 23 Pi 35
Oct	1	North 26 Vi 48	South 26 Pi 48
Oct	2	*Solar Eclipse*	6:28 8 Li 43
Nov	1	North 26 Vi 08	South 26 Pi 08
Dec	1	North 23 Vi 38	South 23 Pi 38

1979

Jan	1	North 20 Vi 04	South 20 Pi 04
Feb	1	North 17 Vi 57	South 17 Pi 57
Feb	26	*Solar Eclipse*	16:54 7 Pi 30
Mar	1	North 17 Vi 28	South 17 Pi 28
Mar	13	*Lunar Eclipse*	21:08 22 Vi 38
Apr	1	North 17 Vi 17	South 17 Pi 17
May	1	North 15 Vi 53	South 15 Pi 53
Jun	1	North 13 Vi 05	South 13 Pi 05
Jul	1	North 10 Vi 21	South 10 Pi 21
Aug	1	North 8 Vi 50	South 8 Pi 50
Aug	22	*Solar Eclipse*	17:22 29 Le 01
Sep	1	North 8 Vi 28	South 8 Pi 28
Sep	6	*Lunar Eclipse*	10:54 13 Pi 12
Oct	1	North 8 Vi 10	South 8 Pi 10
Nov	1	North 6 Vi 40	South 6 Pi 40
Dec	1	North 3 Vi 37	South 3 Pi 37

1980

Jan	1	North 0 Vi 28	South 0 Pi 28
Feb	1	North 29 Le 15	South 29 Aq 15
Feb	16	*Solar Eclipse*	8:53 26 Aq 50
Mar	1	North 29 Le 20	South 29 Aq 20
Mar	1	*Lunar Eclipse*	20:45 11 Vi 19
Apr	1	North 28 Le 38	South 28 Aq 38
May	1	North 26 Le 11	South 26 Aq 11
Jun	1	North 22 Le 47	South 22 Aq 47
Jul	1	North 20 Le 45	South 20 Aq 45
Jul	27	*Lunar Eclipse*	19:08 5 Aq 00
Aug	1	North 20 Le 13	South 20 Aq 13
Aug	10	*Solar Eclipse*	19:12 18 Le 17
Aug	26	*Lunar Eclipse*	3:30 2 Pi 56
Sep	1	North 20 Le 05	South 20 Aq 05
Oct	1	North 19 Le 03	South 19 Aq 03
Nov	1	North 16 Le 32	South 16 Aq 32
Dec	1	North 13 Le 24	South 13 Aq 24

1981

Jan	1	North 11 Le 21	South 11 Aq 21
Jan	20	*Lunar Eclipse*	7:50 0 Le 16
Feb	1	North 10 Le 54	South 10 Aq 54
Feb	4	*Solar Eclipse*	22:09 16 Aq 01
Mar	1	North 10 Le 34	South 10 Aq 34
Apr	1	North 8 Le 56	South 8 Aq 56
May	1	North 5 Le 57	South 5 Aq 57
Jun	1	North 3 Le 01	South 3 Aq 01
Jul	1	North 1 Le 46	South 1 Aq 46
Jul	17	*Lunar Eclipse*	4:47 24 Cp 35
Jul	31	*Solar Eclipse*	3:46 7 Le 51
Aug	1	North 1 Le 42	South 1 Aq 42
Sep	1	North 1 Le 09	South 1 Aq 09
Oct	1	North 28 Ca 58	South 28 Cp 58
Nov	1	North 25 Ca 31	South 25 Cp 31
Dec	1	North 23 Ca 08	South 23 Cp 08

1982

Jan	1	North 22 Ca 28	South 22 Cp 28
Jan	9	*Lunar Eclipse*	19:56 19 Ca 16
Jan	25	*Solar Eclipse*	4:42 4 Aq 53
Feb	1	North 22 Ca 17	South 22 Cp 17
Mar	1	North 21 Ca 12	South 21 Cp 12
Apr	1	North 18 Ca 37	South 18 Cp 37
May	1	North 15 Ca 45	South 15 Cp 45
Jun	1	North 13 Ca 52	South 13 Cp 52
Jun	21	*Solar Eclipse*	12:04 29 Ge 47
Jul	1	North 13 Ca 22	South 13 Cp 22
Jul	6	*Lunar Eclipse*	7:31 13 Cp 54
Jul	20	*Solar Eclipse*	18:44 27 Ca 43
Aug	1	North 13 Ca 15	South 13 Cp 15
Sep	1	North 12 Ca 02	South 12 Cp 02
Oct	1	North 9 Ca 09	South 9 Cp 09
Nov	1	North 5 Ca 52	South 5 Cp 52
Dec	1	North 4 Ca 22	South 4 Cp 22
Dec	15	*Solar Eclipse*	9:31 23 Sa 05
Dec	30	Lunar Eclipse	11:29 8 Ca 24

1983

Jan	1	North 4 Ca 16	South 4 Cp 16
Feb	1	North 3 Ca 38	South 3 Cp 38
Mar	1	North 1 Ca 39	South 1 Cp 39
Apr	1	North 28 Ge 13	South 28 Sa 13
May	1	North 25 Ge 51	South 25 Sa 51
Jun	1	North 25 Ge 07	South 25 Sa 07
Jun	11	*Solar Eclipse*	4:43 19 Ge 43
Jun	25	*Lunar Eclipse*	8:22 3 Cp 09
Jul	1	North 25 Ge 00	South 25 Sa 00
Aug	1	North 24 Ge 04	South 24 Sa 04
Sep	1	North 21 Ge 46	South 21 Sa 46
Oct	1	North 18 Ge 49	South 18 Sa 49
Nov	1	North 16 Ge 35	South 16 Sa 35
Dec	1	North 15 Ge 56	South 15 Sa 56
Dec	4	*Solar Eclipse*	12:30 11 Sa 47
Dec	20	*Lunar Eclipse*	1:49 27 Ge 29

1984

Jan	1	North 15 Ge 53	South 15 Sa 53
Feb	1	North 14 Ge 29	South 14 Sa 29
Mar	1	North 11 Ge 31	South 11 Sa 31
Apr	1	North 8 Ge 06	South 8 Sa 06
May	1	North 6 Ge 40	South 6 Sa 40
May	15	*Lunar Eclipse*	4:40 24 Sc 38
May	30	*Solar Eclipse*	16:45 9 Ge 26
Jun	1	North 6 Ge 36	South 6 Sa 36
Jun	13	*Lunar Eclipse*	14:26 22 Sa 35
Jul	1	North 6 Ge 14	South 6 Sa 14
Aug	1	North 4 Ge 17	South 4 Sa 17
Sep	1	North 1 Ge 18	South 1 Sa 18
Oct	1	North 28 Ta 46	South 28 Sc 46
Nov	1	North 27 Ta 37	South 27 Sc 37
Nov	8	*Lunar Eclipse*	17:55 16 Ta 36
Nov	22	*Solar Eclipse*	22:53 0 Sa 50
Dec	1	North 27 Ta 22	South 27 Sc 22

1985

Jan	1	North 26 Ta 35	South 26 Sc 35
Feb	1	North 24 Ta 09	South 24 Sc 09
Mar	1	North 21 Ta 02	South 21 Sc 02
Apr	1	North 18 Ta 50	South 18 Sc 50
May	1	North 18 Ta 13	South 18 Sc 13
May	4	*Lunar Eclipse*	19:56 14 Sc 19
May	19	*Solar Eclipse*	21:29 28 Ta 50
Jun	1	North 18 Ta 08	South 18 Sc 08
Jul	1	North 17 Ta 05	South 17 Sc 05
Aug	1	North 14 Ta 16	South 14 Sc 16
Sep	1	North 11 Ta 01	South 11 Sc 01
Oct	1	North 9 Ta 21	South 9 Sc 21
Oct	28	*Lunar Eclipse*	17:42 5 Ta 17
Nov	1	North 9 Ta 11	South 9 Sc 11
Nov	12	*Solar Eclipse*	14:11 20 Sc 08
Dec	1	North 8 Ta 52	South 8 Sc 52

1986

Jan	1	North 6 Ta 49	South 6 Sc 49
Feb	1	North 3 Ta 38	South 3 Sc 38
Mar	1	North 1 Ta 06	South 1 Sc 06
Apr	1	North 0 Ta 06	South 0 Sc 06
Apr	9	*Solar Eclipse*	6:20 19 Ar 07
Apr	24	*Lunar Eclipse*	12:43 4 Sc 00
May	1	North 29 Ar 56	South 29 Li 56
Jun	1	North 29 Ar 19	South 29 Li 19
Jul	1	North 27 Ar 21	South 27 Li 21
Aug	1	North 24 Ar 20	South 24 Li 20
Sep	1	North 21 Ar 46	South 21 Li 46
Oct	1	North 20 Ar 55	South 20 Li 55
Oct	3	*Solar Eclipse*	19:05 10 Li 16
Oct	17	*Lunar Eclipse*	19:18 24 Ar 05
Nov	1	North 20 Ar 53	South 20 Li 53
Dec	1	North 19 Ar 54	South 19 Li 54

1987

Jan	1	North 16 Ar 50	South 16 Li 50
Feb	1	North 13 Ar 23	South 13 Li 23
Mar	1	North 11 Ar 45	South 11 Li 45
Mar	29	*Solar Eclipse*	12:49 8 Ar 18
Apr	1	North 11 Ar 30	South 11 Li 30
Apr	14	*Lunar Eclipse*	2:19 23 Li 30
May	1	North 11 Ar 14	South 11 Li 14
Jun	1	North 9 Ar 24	South 9 Li 24
Jul	1	North 6 Ar 26	South 6 Li 26
Aug	1	North 3 Ar 48	South 3 Li 48
Sep	1	North 2 Ar 35	South 2 Li 35
Sep	23	*Solar Eclipse*	3:11 29 Vi 34
Oct	1	North 2 Ar 21	South 2 Li 21
Oct	7	*Lunar Eclipse*	4:01 13 Ar 15
Nov	1	North 1 Ar 56	South 1 Li 56
Dec	1	North 0 Ar 05	South 0 Li 05

1988

Jan	1	North 26 Pi 42	South 26 Vi 42
Feb	1	North 23 Pi 51	South 23 Vi 51
Mar	1	North 23 Pi 06	South 23 Vi 06
Mar	3	*Lunar Eclipse*	16:13 13 Vi 23
Mar	18	*Solar Eclipse*	1:58 27 Pi 42
Apr	1	North 23 Pi 07	South 23 Vi 07
May	1	North 22 Pi 12	South 22 Vi 12
Jun	1	North 19 Pi 25	South 19 Vi 25
Jul	1	North 16 Pi 20	South 16 Vi 20
Aug	1	North 14 Pi 29	South 14 Vi 29
Aug	27	*Lunar Eclipse*	11:05 4 Pi 28
Sep	1	North 14 Pi 06	South 14 Vi 06
Sep	11	*Solar Eclipse*	4:44 18 Vi 40
Oct	1	North 13 Pi 51	South 13 Vi 51
Nov	1	North 12 Pi 24	South 12 Vi 24
Dec	1	North 9 Pi 32	South 9 Vi 32

1989

Jan	1	North 6 Pi 37	South 6 Vi 37
Feb	1	North 5 Pi 07	South 5 Vi 07
Feb	20	*Lunar Eclipse*	15:35 2 Vi 00
Mar	1	North 4 Pi 51	South 4 Vi 51
Mar	7	*Solar Eclipse*	18:08 17 Pi 09
Apr	1	North 4 Pi 18	South 4 Vi 18
May	1	North 2 Pi 25	South 2 Vi 25
Jun	1	North 29 Aq 22	South 29 Le 22
Jul	1	North 26 Aq 50	South 26 Le 50
Aug	1	North 25 Aq 48	South 25 Le 48
Aug	17	*Lunar Eclipse*	3:08 24 Aq 12
Aug	31	*Solar Eclipse*	5:31 7 Vi 48
Sep	1	North 25 Aq 50	South 25 Le 50
Oct	1	North 25 Aq 07	South 25 Le 07
Nov	1	North 22 Aq 20	South 22 Le 20
Dec	1	North 18 Aq 56	South 18 Le 56

1990

Jan	1	North 16 Aq 52	South 16 Le 52
Jan	26	*Solar Eclipse*	19:30 6 Aq 35
Feb	1	North 16 Aq 29	South 16 Le 29
Feb	9	*Lunar Eclipse*	19:11 20 Le 44
Mar	1	North 16 Aq 18	South 16 Le 18
Apr	1	North 14 Aq 48	South 14 Le 48
May	1	North 12 Aq 02	South 12 Le 02
Jun	1	North 9 Aq 16	South 9 Le 16
Jul	1	North 7 Aq 41	South 7 Le 41
Jul	22	*Solar Eclipse*	3:02 29 Ca 04
Aug	1	North 7 Aq 18	South 7 Le 18
Aug	6	*Lunar Eclipse*	14:12 13 Aq 48
Sep	1	North 7 Aq 02	South 7 Le 02
Oct	1	North 5 Aq 26	South 5 Le 26
Nov	1	North 2 Aq 13	South 2 Le 13
Dec	1	North 29 Cp 16	South 29 Ca 16

1991

Jan	1	North 28 Cp 03	South 28 Ca 03
Jan	15	*Solar Eclipse*	23:53 25 Cp 20
Jan	30	*Lunar Eclipse*	5:59 9 Le 43
Feb	1	North 28 Cp 02	South 28 Ca 02
Mar	1	North 27 Cp 24	South 27 Ca 24
Apr	1	North 24 Cp 44	South 24 Ca 44
May	1	North 21 Cp 28	South 21 Ca 28
Jun	1	North 19 Cp 22	South 19 Ca 22
Jun	27	*Lunar Eclipse*	3:15 5 Cp 07
Jul	1	North 18 Cp 55	South 18 Ca 55
Jul	11	*Solar Eclipse*	19:06 18 Ca 59
Jul	26	*Lunar Eclipse*	18:08 3 Aq 08
Aug	1	North 18 Cp 48	South 18 Ca 48
Sep	1	North 17 Cp 38	South 17 Ca 38
Oct	1	North 15 Cp 09	South 15 Ca 09
Nov	1	North 12 Cp 13	South 12 Ca 13
Dec	1	North 10 Cp 19	South 10 Ca 19
Dec	21	*Lunar Eclipse*	10:33 29 Ge 08

1992

Jan	1	North 9 Cp 52	South 9 Ca 52
Jan	4	*Solar Eclipse*	23:05 13 Cp 51
Feb	1	North 9 Cp 41	South 9 Ca 41
Mar	1	North 8 Cp 03	South 8 Ca 03
Apr	1	North 4 Cp 44	South 4 Ca 44
May	1	North 1 Cp 54	South 1 Ca 54
Jun	1	North 0 Cp 43	South 0 Ca 43
Jun	15	*Lunar Eclipse*	4:57 24 Sa 23
Jun	30	*Solar Eclipse*	12:10 8 Ca 56
Jul	1	North 0 Cp 42	South 0 Ca 42
Aug	1	North 0 Cp 05	South 0 Ca 05
Sep	1	North 27 Sa 48	South 27 Ge 48
Oct	1	North 24 Sa 42	South 24 Ge 42
Nov	1	North 22 Sa 23	South 22 Ge 23
Dec	1	North 21 Sa 35	South 21 Ge 35
Dec	9	*Lunar Eclipse*	23:44 18 Ge 12
Dec	24	*Solar Eclipse*	0:31 2 Cp 27

1993

Jan	1	North 21 Sa 19	South 21 Ge 19
Feb	1	North 20 Sa 05	South 20 Ge 05
Mar	1	North 17 Sa 20	South 17 Ge 20
Apr	1	North 14 Sa 21	South 14 Ge 21
May	1	North 12 Sa 36	South 12 Ge 36
May	21	*Solar Eclipse*	14:19 0 Ge 32
Jun	1	North 12 Sa 11	South 12 Ge 11
Jun	4	*Lunar Eclipse*	13:00 13 Sa 53
Jul	1	North 12 Sa 04	South 12 Ge 04
Aug	1	North 10 Sa 44	South 10 Ge 44
Sep	1	North 7 Sa 34	South 7 Ge 34
Oct	1	North 4 Sa 30	South 4 Ge 30
Nov	1	North 3 Sa 04	South 3 Ge 04
Nov	13	*Solar Eclipse*	21:45 21 Sc 32
Nov	29	*Lunar Eclipse*	6:26 7 Ge 00
Dec	1	North 3 Sa 03	South 3 Ge 03

1994

Jan	1	North 2 Sa 26	South 2 Ge 26
Feb	1	North 0 Sa 02	South 0 Ge 02
Mar	1	North 26 Sc 59	South 26 Ta 59
Apr	1	North 24 Sc 38	South 24 Ta 38
May	1	North 23 Sc 52	South 23 Ta 52
May	10	*Solar Eclipse*	17:11 19 Ta 49
May	25	*Lunar Eclipse*	3:30 3 Sa 37
Jun	1	North 23 Sc 42	South 23 Ta 42
Jul	1	North 22 Sc 48	South 22 Ta 48
Aug	1	North 20 Sc 34	South 20 Ta 34
Sep	1	North 17 Sc 35	South 17 Ta 35
Oct	1	North 15 Sc 28	South 15 Ta 28
Nov	1	North 14 Sc 49	South 14 Ta 49
Nov	3	*Solar Eclipse*	13:39 10 Sc 54
Nov	18	*Lunar Eclipse*	6:44 25 Ta 35
Dec	1	North 14 Sc 43	South 14 Ta 43

1995

Jan	1	North 13 Sc 17	South 13 Ta 17
Feb	1	North 9 Sc 55	South 9 Ta 55
Mar	1	North 7 Sc 09	South 7 Ta 09
Apr	1	North 5 Sc 38	South 5 Ta 38
Apr	15	*Lunar Eclipse*	12:18 25 Li 09
Apr	29	*Solar Eclipse*	17:32 8 Ta 56
May	1	North 5 Sc 36	South 5 Ta 36
Jun	1	North 5 Sc 09	South 5 Ta 09
Jul	1	North 3 Sc 08	South 3 Ta 08
Aug	1	North 29 Li 58	South 29 Ar 58
Sep	1	North 27 Li 35	South 27 Ar 35
Oct	1	North 26 Li 38	South 26 Ar 38
Oct	8	*Lunar Eclipse*	16:04 15 Ar 00
Oct	24	*Solar Eclipse*	4:33 0 Sc 17
Nov	1	North 26 Li 28	South 26 Ar 28
Dec	1	North 25 Li 47	South 25 Ar 47

1996

Jan	1	North 23 Li 29	South 23 Ar 29
Feb	1	North 19 Li 59	South 19 Ar 59
Mar	1	North 17 Li 48	South 17 Ar 48
Apr	1	North 17 Li 09	South 17 Ar 09
Apr	4	*Lunar Eclipse*	0:10 14 Li 32
Apr	17	*Solar Eclipse*	22:37 28 Ar 11
May	1	North 17 Li 04	South 17 Ar 04
Jun	1	North 15 Li 48	South 15 Ar 48
Jul	1	North 12 Li 57	South 12 Ar 57
Aug	1	North 9 Li 48	South 9 Ar 48
Sep	1	North 8 Li 15	South 8 Ar 15
Sep	27	*Lunar Eclipse*	2:54 4 Ar 18
Oct	1	North 8 Li 00	South 8 Ar 00
Oct	12	*Solar Eclipse*	14:02 19 Li 31
Nov	1	North 7 Li 33	South 7 Ar 33
Dec	1	North 5 Li 38	South 5 Ar 38

1997

Jan	1	North 2 Li 26	South 2 Ar 26
Feb	1	North 29 Vi 51	South 29 Pi 51
Mar	1	North 28 Vi 49	South 28 Pi 49
Mar	9	*Solar Eclipse*	1:24 18 Pi 31
Mar	24	*Lunar Eclipse*	4:39 3 Li 32
Apr	1	North 28 Vi 40	South 28 Pi 40
May	1	North 27 Vi 56	South 27 Pi 56
Jun	1	North 25 Vi 52	South 25 Pi 52
Jul	1	North 22 Vi 55	South 22 Pi 55
Aug	1	North 20 Vi 28	South 20 Pi 28
Sep	1	North 19 Vi 43	South 19 Pi 43
Sep	2	*Solar Eclipse*	0:04 9 Vi 34
Sep	16	*Lunar Eclipse*	18:47 23 Pi 53
Oct	1	North 19 Vi 46	South 19 Pi 46
Nov	1	North 18 Vi 41	South 18 Pi 41
Dec	1	North 15 Vi 45	South 15 Pi 45

1998

Jan	1	North 12 Vi 20	South 12 Pi 20
Feb	1	North 10 Vi 45	South 10 Pi 45
Feb	26	*Solar Eclipse*	17:28 7 Pi 55
Mar	1	North 10 Vi 32	South 10 Pi 32
Mar	13	*Lunar Eclipse*	4:20 22 Vi 16
Apr	1	North 10 Vi 09	South 10 Pi 09
May	1	North 8 Vi 23	South 8 Pi 23
Jun	1	North 5 Vi 28	South 5 Pi 28
Jul	1	North 2 Vi 56	South 2 Pi 56
Aug	1	North 1 Vi 42	South 1 Pi 42
Aug	8	*Lunar Eclipse*	2:25 15 Aq 29
Aug	22	*Solar Eclipse*	2:06 28 Le 48
Sep	1	North 1 Vi 27	South 1 Pi 27
Sep	6	*Lunar Eclipse*	11:10 13 Pi 33
Oct	1	North 0 Vi 55	South 0 Pi 55
Nov	1	North 28 Le 55	South 28 Aq 55
Dec	1	North 25 Le 38	South 25 Aq 38

1999

Jan	1	North 22 Le 51	South 22 Aq 51
Jan	31	*Lunar Eclipse*	16:18 11 Le 25
Feb	1	North 22 Le 06	South 22 Aq 06
Feb	16	*Solar Eclipse*	6:34 27 Aq 08
Mar	1	North 22 Le 09	South 22 Aq 09
Apr	1	North 21 Le 08	South 21 Aq 08
May	1	North 18 Le 20	South 18 Aq 20
Jun	1	North 14 Le 56	South 14 Aq 56
Jul	1	North 13 Le 12	South 13 Aq 12
Jul	28	*Lunar Eclipse*	11:34 5 Aq 02
Aug	1	North 12 Le 56	South 12 Aq 56
Aug	11	*Solar Eclipse*	11:03 18 Le 21
Sep	1	North 12 Le 43	South 12 Aq 43
Oct	1	North 11 Le 18	South 11 Aq 18
Nov	1	North 8 Le 32	South 8 Aq 32
Dec	1	North 5 Le 37	South 5 Aq 37

2000

Jan	1	North 3 Le 59	South 3 Aq 59
Jan	21	*Lunar Eclipse*	4:44 0 Le 27
Feb	1	North 3 Le 42	South 3 Aq 42
Feb	5	*Solar Eclipse*	12:49 16 Aq 01
Mar	1	North 3 Le 13	South 3 Aq 13
Apr	1	North 1 Le 12	South 1 Aq 12
May	1	North 28 Ca 04	South 28 Cp 04
Jun	1	North 25 Ca 27	South 25 Cp 27
Jul	1	North 24 Ca 37	South 24 Cp 37
Jul	1	*Solar Eclipse*	19:33 10 Ca 15
Jul	16	*Lunar Eclipse*	13:56 24 Cp 19
Jul	31	*Solar Eclipse*	2:13 8 Le 11
Aug	1	North 24 Ca 37	South 24 Cp 37
Sep	1	North 23 Ca 41	South 23 Cp 41
Oct	1	North 21 Ca 10	South 21 Cp 10
Nov	1	North 17 Ca 54	South 17 Cp 54
Dec	1	North 15 Ca 56	South 15 Cp 56
Dec	25	*Solar Eclipse*	17:35 4 Cp 15

2001

Jan	1	North 15 Ca 31	South 15 Cp 31
Jan	9	*Lunar Eclipse*	20:21 19 Ca 36
Feb	1	North 15 Ca 09	South 15 Cp 09
Mar	1	North 13 Ca 38	South 13 Cp 38
Apr	1	North 10 Ca 44	South 10 Cp 44
May	1	North 8 Ca 03	South 8 Cp 03
Jun	1	North 6 Ca 37	South 6 Cp 37
Jun	21	*Solar Eclipse*	12:04 0 Ca 11
Jul	1	North 6 Ca 22	South 6 Cp 22
Jul	5	*Lunar Eclipse*	14:55 13 Cp 34
Aug	1	North 6 Ca 08	South 6 Cp 08
Sep	1	North 4 Ca 25	South 4 Cp 25
Oct	1	North 1 Ca 14	South 1 Cp 14
Nov	1	North 28 Ge 10	South 28 Sa 10
Dec	1	North 27 Ge 09	South 27 Sa 09
Dec	14	*Solar Eclipse*	20:52 22 Sa 56
Dec	30	*Lunar Eclipse*	10:29 8 Ca 41

2002

Jan	1	North 27 Ge 10	South 27 Sa 10
Feb	1	North 26 Ge 09	South 26 Sa 09
Mar	1	North 23 Ge 45	South 23 Sa 45
Apr	1	North 20 Ge 21	South 20 Sa 21
May	1	North 18 Ge 22	South 18 Sa 22
May	26	*Lunar Eclipse*	12:03 5 Sa 10
Jun	1	North 17 Ge 52	South 17 Sa 52
Jun	10	*Solar Eclipse*	23:44 19 Ge 54
Jun	24	*Lunar Eclipse*	21:27 3 Cp 02
Jul	1	North 17 Ge 38	South 17 Sa 38
Aug	1	North 16 Ge 24	South 16 Sa 24
Sep	1	North 13 Ge 50	South 13 Sa 50
Oct	1	North 10 Ge 55	South 10 Sa 55
Nov	1	North 9 Ge 04	South 9 Sa 04
Nov	20	*Lunar Eclipse*	1:47 27 Ta 39
Dec	1	North 8 Ge 41	South 8 Sa 41
Dec	4	*Solar Eclipse*	7:31 11 Sa 58

2003

Jan	1	North 8 Ge 29	South 8 Sa 29
Feb	1	North 6 Ge 34	South 6 Sa 34
Mar	1	North 3 Ge 38	South 3 Sa 38
Apr	1	North 0 Ge 32	South 0 Sa 32
May	1	North 29 Ta 28	South 29 Sc 28
May	16	*Lunar Eclipse*	3:40 24 Sc 55
May	31	*Solar Eclipse*	4:08 9 Ge 19
Jun	1	North 29 Ta 30	South 29 Sc 30
Jul	1	North 28 Ta 55	South 28 Sc 55
Aug	1	North 26 Ta 33	South 26 Sc 33
Sep	1	North 23 Ta 26	South 23 Sc 26
Oct	1	North 21 Ta 17	South 21 Sc 17
Nov	1	North 20 Ta 32	South 20 Sc 32
Nov	9	*Lunar Eclipse*	1:19 16 Ta 15
Nov	23	*Solar Eclipse*	22:49 1 Sa 14
Dec	1	North 20 Ta 20	South 20 Sc 20

187

2004

Jan	1	North 19 Ta 17	South 19 Sc 17
Feb	1	North 16 Ta 35	South 16 Sc 35
Mar	1	North 13 Ta 31	South 13 Sc 31
Apr	1	North 11 Ta 37	South 11 Sc 37
Apr	19	*Solar Eclipse*	13:34 29 Ar 50
May	1	North 11 Ta 15	South 11 Sc 15
May	4	*Lunar Eclipse*	20:30 14 Sc 39
Jun	1	North 11 Ta 02	South 11 Sc 02
Jul	1	North 9 Ta 31	South 9 Sc 31
Aug	1	North 6 Ta 23	South 6 Sc 23
Sep	1	North 3 Ta 25	South 3 Sc 25
Oct	1	North 2 Ta 12	South 2 Sc 12
Oct	14	*Solar Eclipse*	2:59 21 Li 06
Oct	28	*Lunar Eclipse*	3:04 5 Ta 00
Nov	1	North 2 Ta 07	South 2 Sc 07
Dec	1	North 1 Ta 27	South 1 Sc 27

2005

Jan	1	North 28 Ar 55	South 28 Li 55
Feb	1	North 25 Ar 39	South 25 Li 39
Mar	1	North 23 Ar 26	South 23 Li 26
Apr	1	North 22 Ar 48	South 22 Li 48
Apr	8	*Solar Eclipse*	20:36 19 Ar 06
Apr	24	*Lunar Eclipse*	9:55 4 Sc 12
May	1	North 22 Ar 39	South 22 Li 39
Jun	1	North 21 Ar 44	South 21 Li 44
Jul	1	North 19 Ar 27	South 19 Li 27
Aug	1	North 16 Ar 21	South 16 Li 21
Sep	1	North 14 Ar 07	South 14 Li 07
Oct	1	North 13 Ar 38	South 13 Li 38
Oct	3	*Solar Eclipse*	10:32 10 Li 19
Oct	17	*Lunar Eclipse*	12:03 24 Ar 07
Nov	1	North 13 Ar 35	South 13 Li 35
Dec	1	North 12 Ar 10	South 12 Li 10

2006

Jan	1	North 8 Ar 47	South 8 Li 47
Feb	1	North 5 Ar 39	South 5 Li 39
Mar	1	North 4 Ar 26	South 4 Li 26
Mar	14	*Lunar Eclipse*	23:48 24 Vi 20
Mar	29	*Solar Eclipse*	10:11 8 Ar 35
Apr	1	North 4 Ar 21	South 4 Li 21
May	1	North 3 Ar 47	South 3 Li 47
Jun	1	North 1 Ar 37	South 1 Li 37
Jul	1	North 28 Pi 40	South 28 Vi 40
Aug	1	North 26 Pi 22	South 26 Vi 22
Sep	1	North 25 Pi 28	South 25 Vi 28
Sep	7	*Lunar Eclipse*	18:51 15 Pi 05
Sep	22	*Solar Eclipse*	11:40 29 Vi 20
Oct	1	North 25 Pi 17	South 25 Vi 17
Nov	1	North 24 Pi 32	South 24 Vi 32
Dec	1	North 22 Pi 13	South 22 Vi 13

2007

Jan	1	North 18 Pi 51	South 18 Vi 51
Feb	1	North 16 Pi 30	South 16 Vi 30
Mar	1	North 16 Pi 09	South 16 Vi 09
Mar	3	*Lunar Eclipse*	23:21 13 Vi 01
Mar	19	*Solar Eclipse*	2:32 28 Pi 07
Apr	1	North 16 Pi 07	South 16 Vi 07
May	1	North 14 Pi 51	South 14 Vi 51
Jun	1	North 11 Pi 44	South 11 Vi 44
Jul	1	North 8 Pi 44	South 8 Vi 44
Aug	1	North 7 Pi 13	South 7 Vi 13
Aug	28	*Lunar Eclipse*	10:37 4 Pi 46
Sep	1	North 7 Pi 04	South 7 Vi 04
Sep	11	*Solar Eclipse*	12:31 18 Vi 24
Oct	1	North 6 Pi 42	South 6 Vi 42
Nov	1	North 4 Pi 52	South 4 Vi 52
Dec	1	North 1 Pi 49	South 1 Vi 49

2008

Jan	1	North 29 Aq 04	South 29 Le 04
Feb	1	North 27 Aq 52	South 27 Le 52
Feb	7	*Solar Eclipse*	3:55 17 Aq 45
Feb	21	*Lunar Eclipse*	3:26 1 Vi 50
Mar	1	North 27 Aq 39	South 27 Le 39
Apr	1	North 26 Aq 50	South 26 Le 50
May	1	North 24 Aq 31	South 24 Le 31
Jun	1	North 21 Aq 22	South 21 Le 22
Jul	1	North 19 Aq 11	South 19 Le 11
Aug	1	North 18 Aq 32	South 18 Le 32
Aug	1	*Solar Eclipse*	10:21 9 Le 32
Aug	16	*Lunar Eclipse*	21:10 24 Aq 17
Sep	1	North 18 Aq 31	South 18 Le 31
Oct	1	North 17 Aq 21	South 17 Le 21
Nov	1	North 14 Aq 14	South 14 Le 14
Dec	1	North 11 Aq 02	South 11 Le 02

2009

Jan	1	North 9 Aq 27	South 9 Le 27
Jan	26	*Solar Eclipse*	7:59 6 Aq 30
Feb	1	North 9 Aq 16	South 9 Le 16
Feb	9	*Lunar Eclipse*	14:38 20 Le 52
Mar	1	North 8 Aq 53	South 8 Le 53
Apr	1	North 6 Aq 57	South 6 Le 57
May	1	North 4 Aq 04	South 4 Le 04
Jun	1	North 1 Aq 36	South 1 Le 36
Jul	1	North 0 Aq 25	South 0 Le 25
Jul	7	*Lunar Eclipse*	9:39 15 Cp 32
Jul	22	*Solar Eclipse*	2:35 29 Ca 27
Aug	1	North 0 Aq 13	South 0 Le 13
Aug	6	*Lunar Eclipse*	0:39 13 Aq 35
Sep	1	North 29 Cp 48	South 29 Ca 48
Oct	1	North 27 Cp 49	South 27 Ca 49
Nov	1	North 24 Cp 24	South 24 Ca 24
Dec	1	North 21 Cp 51	South 21 Ca 51
Dec	31	*Lunar Eclipse*	19:23 10 Ca 20

2010

Jan	1	North 21 Cp 05	South 21 Ca 05
Jan	15	*Solar Eclipse*	7:07 25 Cp 01
Feb	1	North 21 Cp 01	South 21 Ca 01
Mar	1	North 19 Cp 58	South 19 Ca 58
Apr	1	North 16 Cp 56	South 16 Ca 56
May	1	North 13 Cp 50	South 13 Ca 50
Jun	1	North 12 Cp 12	South 12 Ca 12
Jun	26	*Lunar Eclipse*	11:39 4 Cp 50
Jul	1	North 11 Cp 57	South 11 Ca 57
Jul	11	*Solar Eclipse*	19:34 19 Ca 24
Aug	1	North 11 Cp 37	South 11 Ca 37
Sep	1	North 10 Cp 01	South 10 Ca 01
Oct	1	North 7 Cp 13	South 7 Ca 13
Nov	1	North 4 Cp 25	South 4 Ca 25
Dec	1	North 2 Cp 58	South 2 Ca 58
Dec	21	*Lunar Eclipse*	8:17 29 Ge 22

2011

Jan	1	North 2 Cp 46	South 2 Ca 46
Jan	4	*Solar Eclipse*	8:51 13 Cp 38
Feb	1	North 2 Cp 20	South 2 Ca 20
Mar	1	North 0 Cp 21	South 0 Ca 21
Apr	1	North 26 Sa 54	South 26 Ge 54
May	1	North 24 Sa 18	South 24 Ge 18
Jun	1	North 23 Sa 26	South 23 Ge 26
Jun	1	*Solar Eclipse*	21:16 11 Ge 02
Jun	15	*Lunar Eclipse*	20:13 24 Sa 22
Jul	1	North 23 Sa 28	South 23 Ge 28
Jul	1	*Solar Eclipse*	8:39 9 Ca 12
Aug	1	North 22 Sa 35	South 22 Ge 35
Sep	1	North 19 Sa 55	South 19 Ge 55
Oct	1	North 16 Sa 50	South 16 Ge 50
Nov	1	North 14 Sa 51	South 14 Ge 51
Nov	25	*Solar Eclipse*	6:20 2 Sa 37
Dec	1	North 14 Sa 18	South 14 Ge 18
Dec	10	*Lunar Eclipse*	14:32 18 Ge 08

2012

Jan	1	North 13 Sa 59	South 13 Ge 59
Feb	1	North 12 Sa 26	South 12 Ge 26
Mar	1	North 9 Sa 29	South 9 Ge 29
Apr	1	North 6 Sa 41	South 6 Ge 41
May	1	North 5 Sa 18	South 5 Ge 18
May	20	*Solar Eclipse*	23:53 0 Ge 21
Jun	1	North 5 Sa 05	South 5 Ge 05
Jun	4	*Lunar Eclipse*	11:03 14 Sa 08
Jul	1	North 4 Sa 44	South 4 Ge 44
Aug	1	North 2 Sa 56	South 2 Ge 56
Sep	1	North 29 Sc 37	South 29 Ta 37
Oct	1	North 26 Sc 58	South 26 Ta 58
Nov	1	North 26 Sc 02	South 26 Ta 02
Nov	13	*Solar Eclipse*	22:12 21 Sc 57
Nov	28	*Lunar Eclipse*	14:33 6 Ge 40
Dec	1	North 26 Sc 04	South 26 Ta 04

2013

Jan	1	North 25 Sc 01	South 25 Ta 01
Feb	1	North 22 Sc 09	South 22 Ta 09
Mar	1	North 19 Sc 10	South 19 Ta 10
Apr	1	North 17 Sc 18	South 17 Ta 18
Apr	25	*Lunar Eclipse*	20:08 5 Sc 51
May	1	North 16 Sc 53	South 16 Ta 53
May	10	*Solar Eclipse*	0:25 19 Ta 31
May	25	*Lunar Eclipse*	4:10 3 Sa 58
Jun	1	North 16 Sc 39	South 16 Ta 39
Jul	1	North 15 Sc 28	South 15 Ta 28
Aug	1	North 12 Sc 56	South 12 Ta 56
Sep	1	North 9 Sc 54	South 9 Ta 54
Oct	1	North 8 Sc 08	South 8 Ta 08
Oct	18	*Lunar Eclipse*	23:50 25 Ar 51
Nov	1	North 7 Sc 46	South 7 Ta 46
Nov	3	*Solar Eclipse*	12:47 11 Sc 16
Dec	1	North 7 Sc 31	South 7 Ta 31

2014

Jan	1	North 5 Sc 33	South 5 Ta 33
Feb	1	North 1 Sc 57	South 1 Ta 57
Mar	1	North 29 Li 26	South 29 Ar 26
Apr	1	North 28 Li 23	South 28 Ar 23
Apr	15	*Lunar Eclipse*	7:46 25 Li 17
Apr	29	*Solar Eclipse*	6:04 8 Ta 51
May	1	North 28 Li 23	South 28 Ar 23
Jun	1	North 27 Li 32	South 27 Ar 32
Jul	1	North 25 Li 08	South 25 Ar 08
Aug	1	North 21 Li 58	South 21 Ar 58
Sep	1	North 19 Li 56	South 19 Ar 56
Oct	1	North 19 Li 18	South 19 Ar 18
Oct	8	*Lunar Eclipse*	10:55 15 Ar 07
Oct	23	*Solar Eclipse*	21:45 0 Sc 24
Nov	1	North 19 Li 08	South 19 Ar 08
Dec	1	North 18 Li 06	South 18 Ar 06

2015

Jan	1	North 15 Li 26	South 15 Ar 26
Feb	1	North 12 Li 03	South 12 Ar 03
Mar	1	North 10 Li 24	South 10 Ar 24
Mar	20	*Solar Eclipse*	9:46 29 Pi 28
Apr	1	North 10 Li 00	South 10 Ar 00
Apr	4	*Lunar Eclipse*	12:00 14 Li 21
May	1	North 9 Li 49	South 9 Ar 49
Jun	1	North 8 Li 13	South 8 Ar 13
Jul	1	North 5 Li 13	South 5 Ar 13
Aug	1	North 2 Li 16	South 2 Ar 16
Sep	1	North 1 Li 05	South 1 Ar 05
Sep	13	*Solar Eclipse*	6:54 20 Vi 11
Sep	28	*Lunar Eclipse*	2:47 4 Ar 38
Oct	1	North 1 Li 00	South 1 Ar 00
Nov	1	North 0 Li 20	South 0 Ar 20
Dec	1	North 28 Vi 06	South 28 Pi 06

2016

Jan	1	North 24 Vi 53	South 24 Pi 53	
Feb	1	North 22 Vi 35	South 22 Pi 35	
Mar	1	North 21 Vi 50	South 21 Pi 50	
Mar	9	*Solar Eclipse*	1:57	18 Pi 56
Mar	23	*Lunar Eclipse*	11:47	3 Li 10
Apr	1	North 21 Vi 37	South 21 Pi 37	
May	1	North 20 Vi 30	South 20 Pi 30	
Jun	1	North 18 Vi 01	South 18 Pi 01	
Jul	1	North 15 Vi 06	South 15 Pi 06	
Aug	1	North 13 Vi 06	South 13 Pi 06	
Sep	1	North 12 Vi 43	South 12 Pi 43	
Sep	1	*Solar Eclipse*	9:07	9 Vi 21
Sep	16	*Lunar Eclipse*	18:54	24 Pi 13
Oct	1	North 12 Vi 40	South 12 Pi 40	
Nov	1	North 11 Vi 01	South 11 Pi 01	
Dec	1	North 7 Vi 43	South 7 Pi 43	

2017

Jan	1	North 4 Vi 32	South 4 Pi 32	
Feb	1	North 3 Vi 26	South 3 Pi 26	
Feb	11	*Lunar Eclipse*	0:44	22 Le 34
Feb	26	*Solar Eclipse*	14:54	8 Pi 12
Mar	1	North 3 Vi 23	South 3 Pi 23	
Apr	1	North 2 Vi 42	South 2 Pi 42	
May	1	North 0 Vi 33	South 0 Pi 33	
Jun	1	North 27 Le 35	South 27 Aq 35	
Jul	1	North 25 Le 18	South 25 Aq 18	
Aug	1	North 24 Le 20	South 24 Aq 20	
Aug	7	*Lunar Eclipse*	18:21	15 Aq 30
Aug	21	*Solar Eclipse*	18:26	28 Le 53
Sep	1	North 24 Le 10	South 24 Aq 10	
Oct	1	North 23 Le 25	South 23 Aq 25	
Nov	1	North 21 Le 00	South 21 Aq 00	
Dec	1	North 17 Le 41	South 17 Aq 41	

2018

Jan	1	North 15 Le 21	South 15 Aq 21	
Jan	31	*Lunar Eclipse*	13:30	11 Le 38
Feb	1	North 14 Le 56	South 14 Aq 56	
Feb	15	*Solar Eclipse*	20:52	27 Aq 07
Mar	1	North 14 Le 52	South 14 Aq 52	
Apr	1	North 13 Le 21	South 13 Aq 21	
May	1	North 10 Le 18	South 10 Aq 18	
Jun	1	North 7 Le 14	South 7 Aq 14	
Jul	1	North 5 Le 58	South 5 Aq 58	
Jul	13	*Solar Eclipse*	3:01	20 Ca 42
Jul	27	*Lunar Eclipse*	20:22	4 Aq 45
Aug	1	North 5 Le 53	South 5 Aq 53	
Aug	11	*Solar Eclipse*	9:46	18 Le 41
Sep	1	North 5 Le 23	South 5 Aq 23	
Oct	1	North 3 Le 33	South 3 Aq 33	
Nov	1	North 0 Le 37	South 0 Aq 37	
Dec	1	North 28 Ca 03	South 28 Cp 03	

2019

Jan	1	North 26 Ca 52	South 26 Cp 52
Jan	6	*Solar Eclipse*	1:42 15 Cp 26
Jan	21	*Lunar Eclipse*	5:12 0 Le 49
Feb	1	North 26 Ca 47	South 26 Cp 47
Mar	1	North 26 Ca 01	South 26 Cp 01
Apr	1	North 23 Ca 40	South 23 Cp 40
May	1	North 20 Ca 30	South 20 Cp 30
Jun	1	North 18 Ca 11	South 18 Cp 11
Jul	1	North 17 Ca 37	South 17 Cp 37
Jul	2	*Solar Eclipse*	19:23 10 Ca 38
Jul	16	*Lunar Eclipse*	21:31 24 Cp 00
Aug	1	North 17 Ca 35	South 17 Cp 35
Sep	1	North 16 Ca 20	South 16 Cp 20
Oct	1	North 13 Ca 30	South 13 Cp 30
Nov	1	North 10 Ca 19	South 10 Cp 19
Dec	1	North 8 Ca 40	South 8 Cp 40
Dec	26	*Solar Eclipse*	5:18 4 Cp 07

2020

Jan	1	North 8 Ca 23	South 8 Cp 23
Jan	10	*Lunar Eclipse*	19:10 19 Ca 53
Feb	1	North 7 Ca 49	South 7 Cp 49
Mar	1	North 5 Ca 49	South 5 Cp 49
Apr	1	North 2 Ca 44	South 2 Cp 44
May	1	North 0 Ca 16	South 0 Cp 16
Jun	1	North 29 Ge 13	South 29 Sa 13
Jun	5	*Lunar Eclipse*	19:25 15 Sa 41
Jun	21	*Solar Eclipse*	6:40 0 Ca 21
Jul	1	North 29 Ge 06	South 29 Sa 06
Jul	5	*Lunar Eclipse*	4:30 13 Cp 29
Aug	1	North 28 Ge 37	South 28 Sa 37
Sep	1	North 26 Ge 26	South 26 Sa 26
Oct	1	North 23 Ge 07	South 23 Sa 07
Nov	1	North 20 Ge 29	South 20 Sa 29
Nov	30	*Lunar Eclipse*	9:43 8 Ge 44
Dec	1	North 19 Ge 53	South 19 Sa 53
Dec	14	*Solar Eclipse*	16:14 23 Sa 08

2021

Jan	1	North 19 Ge 53	South 19 Sa 53
Feb	1	North 18 Ge 25	South 18 Sa 25
Mar	1	North 15 Ge 44	South 15 Sa 44
Apr	1	North 12 Ge 33	South 12 Sa 33
May	1	North 11 Ge 01	South 11 Sa 01
May	26	*Lunar Eclipse*	11:19 5 Sa 28
Jun	1	North 10 Ge 44	South 10 Sa 44
Jun	10	*Solar Eclipse*	10:42 19 Ge 47
Jul	1	North 10 Ge 23	South 10 Sa 23
Aug	1	North 8 Ge 53	South 8 Sa 53
Sep	1	North 6 Ge 08	South 6 Sa 08
Oct	1	North 3 Ge 23	South 3 Sa 23
Nov	1	North 1 Ge 55	South 1 Sa 55
Nov	19	*Lunar Eclipse*	9:03 27 Ta 17
Dec	1	North 1 Ge 43	South 1 Sa 43
Dec	4	*Solar Eclipse*	7:34 12 Sa 22

2022

Jan	1	North 1 Ge 12	South 1 Sa 12
Feb	1	North 28 Ta 47	South 28 Sc 47
Mar	1	North 25 Ta 45	South 25 Sc 45
Apr	1	North 23 Ta 06	South 23 Sc 06
Apr	30	*Solar Eclipse*	20:42 10 Ta 29
May	1	North 22 Ta 28	South 22 Sc 28
May	16	*Lunar Eclipse*	4:12 25 Sc 16
Jun	1	North 22 Ta 30	South 22 Sc 30
Jul	1	North 21 Ta 29	South 21 Sc 29
Aug	1	North 18 Ta 40	South 18 Sc 40
Sep	1	North 15 Ta 35	South 15 Sc 35
Oct	1	North 13 Ta 50	South 13 Sc 50
Oct	25	*Solar Eclipse*	11:00 2 Sc 01
Nov	1	North 13 Ta 24	South 13 Sc 24
Nov	8	*Lunar Eclipse*	10:59 15 Ta 59
Dec	1	North 13 Ta 09	South 13 Sc 09

2023

Jan	1	North 11 Ta 45	South 11 Sc 45
Feb	1	North 8 Ta 42	South 8 Sc 42
Mar	1	North 5 Ta 50	South 5 Sc 50
Apr	1	North 4 Ta 16	South 4 Sc 16
Apr	20	*Solar Eclipse*	4:17 29 Ar 50
May	1	North 4 Ta 02	South 4 Sc 02
May	5	*Lunar Eclipse*	17:23 14 Sc 51
Jun	1	North 3 Ta 37	South 3 Sc 37
Jul	1	North 1 Ta 46	South 1 Sc 46
Aug	1	North 28 Ar 32	South 28 Li 32
Sep	1	North 25 Ar 48	South 25 Li 48
Oct	1	North 24 Ar 54	South 24 Li 54
Oct	14	*Solar Eclipse*	18:00 21 Li 08
Oct	28	*Lunar Eclipse*	20:14 5 Ta 03
Nov	1	North 24 Ar 51	South 24 Li 51
Dec	1	North 23 Ar 54	South 23 Li 54

2024

Jan	1	North 21 Ar 05	South 21 Li 05
Feb	1	North 17 Ar 51	South 17 Li 51
Mar	1	North 16 Ar 00	South 16 Li 00
Mar	25	*Lunar Eclipse*	7:13 5 Li 13
Apr	1	North 15 Ar 37	South 15 Li 37
Apr	8	*Solar Eclipse*	18:17 19 Ar 24
May	1	North 15 Ar 21	South 15 Li 21
Jun	1	North 14 Ar 02	South 14 Li 02
Jul	1	North 11 Ar 29	South 11 Li 29
Aug	1	North 8 Ar 34	South 8 Li 34
Sep	1	North 6 Ar 50	South 6 Li 50
Sep	18	*Lunar Eclipse*	2:44 25 Pi 46
Oct	1	North 6 Ar 39	South 6 Li 39
Oct	2	*Solar Eclipse*	18:45 10 Li 04
Nov	1	North 6 Ar 26	South 6 Li 26
Dec	1	North 4 Ar 31	South 4 Li 31

2025

Jan	1	North 0 Ar 53	South 0 Li 53
Feb	1	North 28 Pi 10	South 28 Vi 10
Mar	1	North 27 Pi 24	South 27 Vi 24
Mar	14	*Lunar Eclipse*	6:59 23 Vi 58
Mar	29	*Solar Eclipse*	10:48 9 Ar 00
Apr	1	North 27 Pi 22	South 27 Vi 22
May	1	North 26 Pi 29	South 26 Vi 29
Jun	1	North 23 Pi 59	South 23 Vi 59
Jul	1	North 21 Pi 04	South 21 Vi 04
Aug	1	North 19 Pi 04	South 19 Vi 04
Sep	1	North 18 Pi 24	South 18 Vi 24
Sep	7	*Lunar Eclipse*	18:12 15 Pi 24
Sep	21	*Solar Eclipse*	19:42 29 Vi 05
Oct	1	North 18 Pi 10	South 18 Vi 10
Nov	1	North 17 Pi 03	South 17 Vi 03
Dec	1	North 14 Pi 18	South 14 Vi 18

2026

Jan	1	North 10 Pi 58	South 10 Vi 58
Feb	1	North 9 Pi 07	South 9 Vi 07
Feb	17	*Solar Eclipse*	12:12 28 Aq 50
Mar	1	North 8 Pi 59	South 8 Vi 59
Mar	3	*Lunar Eclipse*	11:34 12 Vi 51
Apr	1	North 8 Pi 46	South 8 Vi 46
May	1	North 7 Pi 01	South 7 Vi 01
Jun	1	North 3 Pi 36	South 3 Vi 36
Jul	1	North 0 Pi 53	South 0 Vi 53
Aug	1	North 29 Aq 50	South 29 Le 50
Aug	12	*Solar Eclipse*	17:46 20 Le 02
Aug	28	*Lunar Eclipse*	4:13 4 Pi 51
Sep	1	North 29 Aq 48	South 29 Le 48
Oct	1	North 29 Aq 09	South 29 Le 09
Nov	1	North 26 Aq 56	South 26 Le 56
Dec	1	North 23 Aq 52	South 23 Le 52

2027

Jan	1	North 21 Aq 28	South 21 Le 28
Feb	1	North 20 Aq 36	South 20 Le 36
Feb	6	*Solar Eclipse*	16:00 17 Aq 38
Feb	20	*Lunar Eclipse*	23:13 1 Vi 58
Mar	1	North 20 Aq 24	South 20 Le 24
Apr	1	North 19 Aq 19	South 19 Le 19
May	1	North 16 Aq 45	South 16 Le 45
Jun	1	North 13 Aq 44	South 13 Le 44
Jul	1	North 11 Aq 55	South 11 Le 55
Jul	18	*Lunar Eclipse*	16:03 25 Cp 57
Aug	1	North 11 Aq 30	South 11 Le 30
Aug	2	*Solar Eclipse*	10:07 9 Le 55
Aug	17	*Lunar Eclipse*	7:14 24 Aq 04
Sep	1	North 11 Aq 21	South 11 Le 21
Oct	1	North 9 Aq 52	South 9 Le 52
Nov	1	North 6 Aq 35	South 6 Le 35
Dec	1	North 3 Aq 37	South 3 Le 37

2028

Jan	1	North 2 Aq 25	South 2 Le 25
Jan	12	*Lunar Eclipse*	4:13 21 Ca 33
Jan	26	*Solar Eclipse*	15:08 6 Aq 11
Feb	1	North 2 Aq 18	South 2 Le 18
Mar	1	North 1 Aq 35	South 1 Le 35
Apr	1	North 29 Cp 10	South 29 Ca 10
May	1	North 26 Cp 12	South 26 Ca 12
Jun	1	North 24 Cp 05	South 24 Ca 05
Jul	1	North 23 Cp 18	South 23 Ca 18
Jul	6	*Lunar Eclipse*	18:20 15 Cp 15
Jul	22	*Solar Eclipse*	2:56 29 Ca 50
Aug	1	North 23 Cp 13	South 23 Ca 13
Sep	1	North 22 Cp 29	South 22 Ca 29
Oct	1	North 20 Cp 03	South 20 Ca 03
Nov	1	North 16 Cp 30	South 16 Ca 30
Dec	1	North 14 Cp 21	South 14 Ca 21
Dec	31	*Lunar Eclipse*	16:52 10 Ca 34

2029

Jan	1	North 13 Cp 59	South 13 Ca 59
Jan	14	*Solar Eclipse*	17:13 24 Cp 50
Feb	1	North 13 Cp 46	South 13 Ca 46
Mar	1	North 12 Cp 17	South 12 Ca 17
Apr	1	North 8 Cp 57	South 8 Ca 57
May	1	North 6 Cp 05	South 6 Ca 05
Jun	1	North 4 Cp 52	South 4 Ca 52
Jun	12	*Solar Eclipse*	4:05 21 Ge 30
Jun	26	*Lunar Eclipse*	3:22 4 Cp 49
Jul	1	North 4 Cp 41	South 4 Ca 41
Jul	11	*Solar Eclipse*	15:36 19 Ca 37
Aug	1	North 4 Cp 07	South 4 Ca 07
Sep	1	North 2 Cp 12	South 2 Ca 12
Oct	1	North 29 Sa 15	South 29 Ge 15
Nov	1	North 26 Sa 42	South 26 Ge 42
Dec	1	North 25 Sa 37	South 25 Ge 37
Dec	5	*Solar Eclipse*	15:03 13 Sa 46
Dec	20	*Lunar Eclipse*	22:42 29 Ge 18

2030

Jan	1	North 25 Sa 31	South 25 Ge 31
Feb	1	North 24 Sa 42	South 24 Ge 42
Mar	1	North 22 Sa 21	South 22 Ge 21
Apr	1	North 18 Sa 55	South 18 Ge 55
May	1	North 16 Sa 47	South 16 Ge 47
Jun	1	North 16 Sa 19	South 16 Ge 19
Jun	1	*Solar Eclipse*	6:28 10 Ge 50
Jun	15	*Lunar Eclipse*	18:33 24 Sa 38
Jul	1	North 16 Sa 19	South 16 Ge 19
Aug	1	North 14 Sa 59	South 14 Ge 59
Sep	1	North 11 Sa 59	South 11 Ge 59
Oct	1	North 9 Sa 07	South 9 Ge 07
Nov	1	North 7 Sa 37	South 7 Ge 37
Nov	25	*Solar Eclipse*	6:51 3 Sa 02
Dec	1	North 7 Sa 19	South 7 Ge 19
Dec	9	*Lunar Eclipse*	22:28 17 Ge 47

2031

Jan	1	North 6 Sa 51	South 6 Ge 51
Feb	1	North 5 Sa 00	South 5 Ge 00
Mar	1	North 1 Sa 55	South 1 Ge 55
Apr	1	North 29 Sc 20	South 29 Ta 20
May	1	North 28 Sc 16	South 28 Ta 16
May	7	*Lunar Eclipse*	3:51 16 Sc 31
May	21	*Solar Eclipse*	7:15 0 Ge 04
Jun	1	North 28 Sc 05	South 28 Ta 05
Jun	5	*Lunar Eclipse*	11:44 14 Sa 30
Jul	1	North 27 Sc 26	South 27 Ta 26
Aug	1	North 25 Sc 17	South 25 Ta 17
Sep	1	North 21 Sc 57	South 21 Ta 57
Oct	1	North 19 Sc 36	South 19 Ta 36
Oct	30	*Lunar Eclipse*	7:46 6 Ta 47
Nov	1	North 18 Sc 57	South 18 Ta 57
Nov	14	*Solar Eclipse*	21:06 22 Sc 17
Dec	1	North 18 Sc 56	South 18 Ta 56

2032

Jan	1	North 17 Sc 30	South 17 Ta 30
Feb	1	North 14 Sc 14	South 14 Ta 14
Mar	1	North 11 Sc 16	South 11 Ta 16
Apr	1	North 9 Sc 50	South 9 Ta 50
Apr	25	*Lunar Eclipse*	15:14 6 Sc 00
May	1	North 9 Sc 38	South 9 Ta 38
May	9	*Solar Eclipse*	13:26 19 Ta 29
Jun	1	North 9 Sc 15	South 9 Ta 15
Jul	1	North 7 Sc 43	South 7 Ta 43
Aug	1	North 4 Sc 57	South 4 Ta 57
Sep	1	North 2 Sc 03	South 2 Ta 03
Oct	1	North 0 Sc 40	South 0 Ta 40
Oct	18	*Lunar Eclipse*	19:03 25 Ar 59
Nov	1	North 0 Sc 33	South 0 Ta 33
Nov	3	*Solar Eclipse*	5:33 11 Sc 21
Dec	1	North 0 Sc 04	South 0 Ta 04

2033

Jan	1	North 27 Li 37	South 27 Ar 37
Feb	1	North 23 Li 59	South 23 Ar 59
Mar	1	North 21 Li 52	South 21 Ar 52
Mar	30	*Solar Eclipse*	18:02 10 Ar 21
Apr	1	North 21 Li 14	South 21 Ar 14
Apr	14	*Lunar Eclipse*	19:13 25 Li 06
May	1	North 21 Li 11	South 21 Ar 11
Jun	1	North 19 Li 56	South 19 Ar 56
Jul	1	North 17 Li 17	South 17 Ar 17
Aug	1	North 14 Li 22	South 14 Ar 22
Sep	1	North 12 Li 42	South 12 Ar 42
Sep	23	*Solar Eclipse*	13:53 0 Li 51
Oct	1	North 12 Li 17	South 12 Ar 17
Oct	8	*Lunar Eclipse*	10:55 15 Ar 26
Nov	1	North 11 Li 58	South 11 Ar 58
Dec	1	North 10 Li 29	South 10 Ar 29

2034

Jan	1	North 7 Li 31	South 7 Ar 31
Feb	1	North 4 Li 24	South 4 Ar 24
Mar	1	North 3 Li 13	South 3 Ar 13
Mar	20	*Solar Eclipse*	10:18 29 Pi 53
Apr	1	North 3 Li 05	South 3 Ar 05
Apr	3	*Lunar Eclipse*	19:06 13 Li 59
May	1	North 2 Li 41	South 2 Ar 41
Jun	1	North 0 Li 33	South 0 Ar 33
Jul	1	North 27 Vi 21	South 27 Pi 21
Aug	1	North 24 Vi 44	South 24 Pi 44
Sep	1	North 23 Vi 59	South 23 Pi 59
Sep	12	*Solar Eclipse*	16:18 19 Vi 59
Sep	28	*Lunar Eclipse*	2:47 4 Ar 57
Oct	1	North 23 Vi 57	South 23 Pi 57
Nov	1	North 22 Vi 57	South 22 Pi 57
Dec	1	North 20 Vi 22	South 20 Pi 22

2035

Jan	1	North 17 Vi 11	South 17 Pi 11
Feb	1	North 15 Vi 10	South 15 Pi 10
Feb	22	*Lunar Eclipse*	9:05 3 Vi 39
Mar	1	North 14 Vi 38	South 14 Pi 38
Mar	9	*Solar Eclipse*	23:05 19 Pi 12
Apr	1	North 14 Vi 17	South 14 Pi 17
May	1	North 12 Vi 48	South 12 Pi 48
Jun	1	North 10 Vi 04	South 10 Pi 04
Jul	1	North 7 Vi 18	South 7 Pi 18
Aug	1	North 5 Vi 42	South 5 Pi 42
Aug	19	*Lunar Eclipse*	1:11 26 Aq 00
Sep	1	North 5 Vi 29	South 5 Pi 29
Sep	2	*Solar Eclipse*	1:56 9 Vi 28
Oct	1	North 5 Vi 15	South 5 Pi 15
Nov	1	North 3 Vi 15	South 3 Pi 15
Dec	1	North 29 Le 50	South 29 Aq 50

2036

Jan	1	North 26 Le 57	South 26 Aq 57
Feb	1	North 26 Le 10	South 26 Aq 10
Feb	11	*Lunar Eclipse*	22:12 22 Le 47
Feb	27	*Solar Eclipse*	4:46 8 Pi 10
Mar	1	North 26 Le 10	South 26 Aq 10
Apr	1	North 25 Le 06	South 25 Aq 06
May	1	North 22 Le 36	South 22 Aq 36
Jun	1	North 19 Le 44	South 19 Aq 44
Jul	1	North 17 Le 50	South 17 Aq 50
Jul	23	*Solar Eclipse*	10:31 1 Le 10
Aug	1	North 17 Le 12	South 17 Aq 12
Aug	7	*Lunar Eclipse*	2:52 15 Aq 13
Aug	21	*Solar Eclipse*	17:25 29 Le 14
Sep	1	North 17 Le 05	South 17 Aq 05
Oct	1	North 16 Le 03	South 16 Aq 03
Nov	1	North 13 Le 15	South 13 Aq 15
Dec	1	North 10 Le 02	South 10 Aq 02

2037

Jan	1	North 8 Le 11	South 8 Aq 11
Jan	16	*Solar Eclipse*	9:48 26 Cp 36
Jan	31	*Lunar Eclipse*	14:01 11 Le 59
Feb	1	North 8 Le 02	South 8 Aq 02
Mar	1	North 7 Le 44	South 7 Aq 44
Apr	1	North 5 Le 41	South 5 Aq 41
May	1	North 2 Le 28	South 2 Aq 28
Jun	1	North 29 Ca 48	South 29 Cp 48
Jul	1	North 28 Ca 55	South 28 Cp 55
Jul	13	*Solar Eclipse*	2:40 21 Ca 04
Jul	27	*Lunar Eclipse*	4:09 4 Aq 26
Aug	1	North 28 Ca 50	South 28 Cp 50
Sep	1	North 28 Ca 01	South 28 Cp 01
Oct	1	North 25 Ca 44	South 25 Cp 44
Nov	1	North 22 Ca 41	South 22 Cp 41
Dec	1	North 20 Ca 26	South 20 Cp 26

2038

Jan	1	North 19 Ca 40	South 19 Cp 40
Jan	5	*Solar Eclipse*	13:46 15 Cp 19
Jan	21	*Lunar Eclipse*	3:49 1 Le 05
Feb	1	North 19 Ca 36	South 19 Cp 36
Mar	1	North 18 Ca 30	South 18 Cp 30
Apr	1	North 15 Ca 44	South 15 Cp 44
May	1	North 12 Ca 34	South 12 Cp 34
Jun	1	North 10 Ca 38	South 10 Cp 38
Jun	17	*Lunar Eclipse*	2:44 26 Sa 10
Jul	1	North 10 Ca 23	South 10 Cp 23
Jul	2	*Solar Eclipse*	13:32 10 Ca 47
Jul	16	*Lunar Eclipse*	11:35 23 Cp 56
Aug	1	North 10 Ca 14	South 10 Cp 14
Sep	1	North 8 Ca 31	South 8 Cp 31
Oct	1	North 5 Ca 27	South 5 Cp 27
Nov	1	North 2 Ca 34	South 2 Cp 34
Dec	1	North 1 Ca 20	South 1 Cp 20
Dec	11	*Lunar Eclipse*	17:44 19 Ge 52
Dec	26	*Solar Eclipse*	0:59 4 Cp 20

2039

Jan	1	North 1 Ca 08	South 1 Cp 08
Feb	1	North 0 Ca 20	South 0 Cp 20
Mar	1	North 28 Ge 04	South 28 Sa 04
Apr	1	North 24 Ge 57	South 24 Sa 57
May	1	North 22 Ge 48	South 22 Sa 48
Jun	1	North 22 Ge 04	South 22 Sa 04
Jun	6	*Lunar Eclipse*	18:53 15 Sa 59
Jun	21	*Solar Eclipse*	17:12 0 Ca 12
Jul	1	North 21 Ge 56	South 21 Sa 56
Aug	1	North 21 Ge 07	South 21 Sa 07
Sep	1	North 18 Ge 40	South 18 Sa 40
Oct	1	North 15 Ge 29	South 15 Sa 29
Nov	1	North 13 Ge 16	South 13 Sa 16
Nov	30	*Lunar Eclipse*	16:55 8 Ge 22
Dec	1	North 12 Ge 57	South 12 Sa 57
Dec	15	*Solar Eclipse*	16:23 23 Sa 32

2040

Jan	1	North 12 Ge 49	South 12 Sa 49	
Feb	1	North 10 Ge 54	South 10 Sa 54	
Mar	1	North 7 Ge 49	South 7 Sa 49	
Apr	1	North 4 Ge 57	South 4 Sa 57	
May	1	North 3 Ge 53	South 3 Sa 53	
May	11	*Solar Eclipse*	3:42	21 Ta 04
May	26	*Lunar Eclipse*	11:45	5 Sa 49
Jun	1	North 3 Ge 45	South 3 Sa 45	
Jul	1	North 3 Ge 12	South 3 Sa 12	
Aug	1	North 1 Ge 23	South 1 Sa 23	
Sep	1	North 28 Ta 26	South 28 Sc 26	
Oct	1	North 25 Ta 51	South 25 Sc 51	
Nov	1	North 24 Ta 43	South 24 Sc 43	
Nov	4	*Solar Eclipse*	19:08	12 Sc 59
Nov	18	*Lunar Eclipse*	19:04	27 Ta 01
Dec	1	North 24 Ta 37	South 24 Sc 37	

2041

Jan	1	North 23 Ta 45	South 23 Sc 45	
Feb	1	North 20 Ta 49	South 20 Sc 49	
Mar	1	North 17 Ta 47	South 17 Sc 47	
Apr	1	North 15 Ta 36	South 15 Sc 36	
Apr	30	*Solar Eclipse*	11:51	10 Ta 31
May	1	North 15 Ta 16	South 15 Sc 16	
May	16	*Lunar Eclipse*	0:42	25 Sc 26
Jun	1	North 15 Ta 08	South 15 Sc 08	
Jul	1	North 13 Ta 40	South 13 Sc 40	
Aug	1	North 10 Ta 35	South 10 Sc 35	
Sep	1	North 7 Ta 44	South 7 Sc 44	
Oct	1	North 6 Ta 22	South 6 Sc 22	
Oct	25	*Solar Eclipse*	1:35	2 Sc 01
Nov	1	North 6 Ta 08	South 6 Sc 08	
Nov	8	*Lunar Eclipse*	4:34	16 Ta 03
Dec	1	North 5 Ta 41	South 5 Sc 41	

2042

Jan	1	North 3 Ta 52	South 3 Sc 52	
Feb	1	North 0 Ta 39	South 0 Sc 39	
Mar	1	North 28 Ar 08	South 28 Li 08	
Apr	1	North 26 Ar 59	South 26 Li 59	
Apr	5	*Lunar Eclipse*	14:29	16 Li 02
Apr	20	*Solar Eclipse*	2:16	0 Ta 09
May	1	North 26 Ar 53	South 26 Li 53	
Jun	1	North 26 Ar 14	South 26 Li 14	
Jul	1	North 24 Ar 00	South 24 Li 00	
Aug	1	North 20 Ar 41	South 20 Li 41	
Sep	1	North 18 Ar 25	South 18 Li 25	
Sep	29	*Lunar Eclipse*	10:45	6 Ar 31
Oct	1	North 17 Ar 53	South 17 Li 53	
Oct	14	*Solar Eclipse*	2:00	20 Li 52
Nov	1	North 17 Ar 46	South 17 Li 46	
Dec	1	North 16 Ar 26	South 16 Li 26	

2043

Jan	1	North 13 Ar 24	South 13 Li 24
Feb	1	North 10 Ar 25	South 10 Li 25
Mar	1	North 8 Ar 53	South 8 Li 53
Mar	25	*Lunar Eclipse*	14:31 4 Li 52
Apr	1	North 8 Ar 39	South 8 Li 39
Apr	9	*Solar Eclipse*	18:57 19 Ar 49
May	1	North 8 Ar 09	South 8 Li 09
Jun	1	North 6 Ar 23	South 6 Li 23
Jul	1	North 3 Ar 36	South 3 Li 36
Aug	1	North 1 Ar 00	South 1 Li 00
Sep	1	North 29 Pi 42	South 29 Vi 42
Sep	19	*Lunar Eclipse*	1:51 26 Pi 04
Oct	1	North 29 Pi 38	South 29 Vi 38
Oct	3	*Solar Eclipse*	3:01 9 Li 48
Nov	1	North 29 Pi 10	South 29 Vi 10
Dec	1	North 26 Pi 51	South 26 Vi 51

2044

Jan	1	North 23 Pi 04	South 23 Vi 04
Feb	1	North 20 Pi 37	South 20 Vi 37
Feb	28	*Solar Eclipse*	20:24 9 Pi 54
Mar	1	North 20 Pi 11	South 20 Vi 11
Mar	13	*Lunar Eclipse*	19:37 23 Vi 50
Apr	1	North 20 Pi 07	South 20 Vi 07
May	1	North 18 Pi 49	South 18 Vi 49
Jun	1	North 16 Pi 03	South 16 Vi 03
Jul	1	North 13 Pi 15	South 13 Vi 15
Aug	1	North 11 Pi 34	South 11 Vi 34
Aug	23	*Solar Eclipse*	1:16 0 Vi 35
Sep	1	North 11 Pi 06	South 11 Vi 06
Sep	7	*Lunar Eclipse*	11:20 15 Pi 26
Oct	1	North 10 Pi 49	South 10 Vi 49
Nov	1	North 9 Pi 21	South 9 Vi 21
Dec	1	North 6 Pi 20	South 6 Vi 20

2045

Jan	1	North 3 Pi 12	South 3 Vi 12
Feb	1	North 1 Pi 50	South 1 Vi 50
Feb	16	*Solar Eclipse*	23:55 28 Aq 43
Mar	1	North 1 Pi 49	South 1 Vi 49
Mar	3	*Lunar Eclipse*	7:42 13 Vi 01
Apr	1	North 1 Pi 17	South 1 Vi 17
May	1	North 29 Aq 05	South 29 Le 05
Jun	1	North 25 Aq 40	South 25 Le 40
Jul	1	North 23 Aq 22	South 23 Le 22
Aug	1	North 22 Aq 45	South 22 Le 45
Aug	12	*Solar Eclipse*	17:42 20 Le 25
Aug	27	*Lunar Eclipse*	13:54 4 Pi 36
Sep	1	North 22 Aq 41	South 22 Le 41
Oct	1	North 21 Aq 39	South 21 Le 39
Nov	1	North 19 Aq 03	South 19 Le 03
Dec	1	North 16 Aq 04	South 16 Le 04

2046

Jan	1	North 14 Aq 08	South 14 Le 08
Jan	22	*Lunar Eclipse*	13:02 2 Le 45
Feb	1	North 13 Aq 38	South 13 Le 38
Feb	5	*Solar Eclipse*	23:05 17 Aq 18
Mar	1	North 13 Aq 22	South 13 Le 22
Apr	1	North 11 Aq 58	South 11 Le 58
May	1	North 9 Aq 07	South 9 Le 07
Jun	1	North 6 Aq 08	South 6 Le 08
Jul	1	North 4 Aq 42	South 4 Le 42
Jul	18	*Lunar Eclipse*	1:05 25 Cp 42
Aug	1	North 4 Aq 31	South 4 Le 31
Aug	2	*Solar Eclipse*	10:20 10 Le 19
Sep	1	North 4 Aq 08	South 4 Le 08
Oct	1	North 2 Aq 10	South 2 Le 10
Nov	1	North 28 Cp 44	South 28 Ca 44
Dec	1	North 26 Cp 07	South 26 Ca 07

2047

Jan	1	North 25 Cp 16	South 25 Ca 16
Jan	12	*Lunar Eclipse*	1:25 21 Ca 46
Jan	26	*Solar Eclipse*	1:32 6 Aq 00
Feb	1	North 25 Cp 05	South 25 Ca 05
Mar	1	North 24 Cp 05	South 24 Ca 05
Apr	1	North 21 Cp 16	South 21 Ca 16
May	1	North 18 Cp 15	South 18 Ca 15
Jun	1	North 16 Cp 29	South 16 Ca 29
Jun	23	*Solar Eclipse*	10:51 1 Ca 56
Jul	1	North 16 Cp 00	South 16 Ca 00
Jul	7	*Lunar Eclipse*	10:35 15 Cp 17
Jul	22	*Solar Eclipse*	22:35 0 Le 04
Aug	1	North 15 Cp 51	South 15 Ca 51
Sep	1	North 14 Cp 48	South 14 Ca 48
Oct	1	North 12 Cp 07	South 12 Ca 07
Nov	1	North 8 Cp 43	South 8 Ca 43
Dec	1	North 6 Cp 57	South 6 Ca 57
Dec	16	*Solar Eclipse*	23:49 24 Sa 56

2048

Jan	1	North 6 Cp 48	South 6 Ca 48
Jan	1	*Lunar Eclipse*	6:53 10 Ca 28
Feb	1	North 6 Cp 24	South 6 Ca 24
Mar	1	North 4 Cp 27	South 4 Ca 27
Apr	1	North 0 Cp 58	South 0 Ca 58
May	1	North 28 Sa 31	South 28 Ge 31
Jun	1	North 27 Sa 41	South 27 Ge 41
Jun	11	*Solar Eclipse*	12:58 21 Ge 17
Jun	26	*Lunar Eclipse*	2:01 5 Cp 06
Jul	1	North 27 Sa 34	South 27 Ge 34
Aug	1	North 26 Sa 46	South 26 Ge 46
Sep	1	North 24 Sa 36	South 24 Ge 36
Oct	1	North 21 Sa 38	South 21 Ge 38
Nov	1	North 19 Sa 22	South 19 Ge 22
Dec	1	North 18 Sa 37	South 18 Ge 37
Dec	5	*Solar Eclipse*	15:34 14 Sa 11
Dec	20	*Lunar Eclipse*	6:27 28 Ge 56

2049

Jan	1	North 18 Sa 28	South 18 Ge 28
Feb	1	North 17 Sa 11	South 17 Ge 11
Mar	1	North 14 Sa 28	South 14 Ge 28
Apr	1	North 11 Sa 11	South 11 Ge 11
May	1	North 9 Sa 33	South 9 Ge 33
May	17	*Lunar Eclipse*	11:26 27 Sc 06
May	31	*Solar Eclipse*	13:59 10 Ge 34
Jun	1	North 9 Sa 23	South 9 Ge 23
Jun	15	*Lunar Eclipse*	19:13 24 Sa 59
Jul	1	North 9 Sa 11	South 9 Ge 11
Aug	1	North 7 Sa 18	South 7 Ge 18
Sep	1	North 4 Sa 02	South 4 Ge 02
Oct	1	North 1 Sa 24	South 1 Ge 24
Nov	1	North 0 Sa 21	South 0 Ge 21
Nov	9	*Lunar Eclipse*	15:51 17 Ta 47
Nov	25	*Solar Eclipse*	5:33 3 Sa 23
Dec	1	North 0 Sa 12	South 0 Ge 12

2050

Jan	1	North 29 Sc 30	South 29 Ta 30
Feb	1	North 27 Sc 16	South 27 Ta 16
Mar	1	North 24 Sc 07	South 24 Ta 07
Apr	1	North 21 Sc 45	South 21 Ta 45
May	1	North 20 Sc 58	South 20 Ta 58
May	6	*Lunar Eclipse*	22:31 16 Sc 37
May	20	*Solar Eclipse*	20:42 0 Ge 02
Jun	1	North 20 Sc 49	South 20 Ta 49
Jul	1	North 19 Sc 52	South 19 Ta 52
Aug	1	North 17 Sc 18	South 17 Ta 18
Sep	1	North 14 Sc 00	South 14 Ta 00
Oct	1	North 12 Sc 05	South 12 Ta 05
Oct	30	*Lunar Eclipse*	3:21 6 Ta 56
Nov	1	North 11 Sc 45	South 11 Ta 45
Nov	14	*Solar Eclipse*	13:30 22 Sc 22
Dec	1	North 11 Sc 32	South 11 Ta 32

ABOUT THE AUTOR

Agneta Borstein is a professional astrologer with an international clientele. With over 30 years experience, she has appeared on TV and radio, been interviewed by numerous publications, and has spoken at several astrology organizations throughout the world. Born in Sweden, Agneta incorporated her BA in business with metaphysics and operated an alternative bookstore for twenty-one years. After many years as a professional astrologer, Agneta merged her education in Advanced Shamanism and Advanced Healing into her private practice, workshops, and lectures with her AstroShamanic approach. Agneta maintains a private practice in West Hartford, CT. She is a past president of the Astrological Society of Connecticut and an ongoing member of the National Council for Geocosmic Research (NCGR). Her website is *www.agnetaborstein.com.*